STATION LIFE IN AUSTRALIA

Some other books by the same author

Pastoral Properties of Australia
Thoroughbred Studs of Australia and New Zealand
Australia—The First Twelve Years
An End to Silence—The Building of the Overland Telegraph Line
An Australian Country Life
Springfield: The Story of a Sheep Station
Food From Far Away
A Taste of Australia in Food and in Pictures
A Celebration of Shore

For children

How People Lived
How People with Cattle Settled the Outback
Keeping in Touch with Each Other
On the Sheep's Back
The Bush Pioneers
The Bushrangers
The Convict Settlement
The Goldrush Era

STATION LIFE IN AUSTRALIA

Pioneers and Pastoralists

PETER TAYLOR

Allen & Unwin
Sydney Wellington London Boston

First published in 1988
Second impression 1988
Allen & Unwin Australia Pty Ltd
An Unwin Hyman company
8 Napier Street, North Sydney, NSW 2060 Australia

Allen & Unwin New Zealand Limited
60 Cambridge Terrace, Wellington, New Zealand

Unwin Hyman Limited
15–17 Broadwick Street, London W1V 1FP England

Unwin Hyman Inc.
8 Winchester Place, Winchester, Mass 01890 USA

National Library of Australia
Cataloguing-in-Publication entry:

Taylor, Peter
  Station Life in Australia.

  Bibliography.
  Includes index.
  ISBN 0 04 332135 6.

  1. Country life — Australia — History.   2. Ranch life —
  Australia — History.   3. Australia — Rural conditions.
  I. Title.

994

Library of Congress Catalog Card Number: 88-70313

Set in 11/13pt Caledonia by Best-set Typesetters, Hong Kong
Printed by Australian Print Group

Contents

Acknowledgements

I would like to thank Jim Maple-Brown, a descendant of William Pitt Faithfull and now owner of Springfield, for reading the manuscript and for allowing me to reproduce photographs and other material from the Faithfull family papers.

I am also grateful to the following for permission to quote from published works: Lansdowne-Rigby for *My Bush Book—K. Langloh Parker's Story of Outback Station Life*, edited by Marcie Muir and *Beyond the Bitumen* by W. A. Winter-Irving; Angus & Robertson for *On the Wool Track* by C. E. W. Bean, *The Territory* by Ernestine Hill and *The Letters of Rachel Henning*, edited by David Adams; Constable Publishers for *Kings in Grass Castles* by Mary Durack; Darling Downs I. A. E. for *Katie Hume on the Darling Downs*; Century Hutchinson for *The Governesses* by Patricia Clarke; Thomas Nelson for *The Shearers* by Patsy Adam-Smith; Pacific Publishers for *Life in the Australian Backblocks* by Sorenson; and Ruth Lockwood for *Alice on the Line* by Douglas Lockwood.

I would also like to thank the Mitchell Library in Sydney and the National Library of Australia in Canberra for permission to reproduce illustrations in their collections.

Preface

OUT on the Barkly Tableland in Northern Australia the horizon is so flat that it cuts across the setting sun like a ruler. The landscape seems huge. In the distance a line of trees marks a waterhole, a few kilometres away a bore stands out against the sky and wispy clouds are streaked high across the sky. It is a lonely place.

During these quiet moments of a dying day I often wondered what life was like for those who pioneered land such as this. Much of it is still remote, but what was it like when the only way of reaching it was on two legs or four? What was it like when there were no comforts, no help, no machines and when the future was determined by your own capacity to survive?

I have tried to answer some of these questions in this book.

The people who settled inland Australia were remarkable, but their achievements are rarely recognised. They lived and worked a long way from the cities that even then were the homes of most Australians, and their achievements, great though they were, were not very visible to the rest of the country, and sometimes not even to their neighbours. Nor was that a matter of concern. The need to survive, physically and financially, was paramount. Recognition for what they were doing had no bearing on that.

These people took an alien landscape and settled it, and in the process they established two industries, beef and wool, which became the source of much of Australia's prosperity. They did it with their bare hands, they did it for a lifetime, and their children in many cases give it theirs as well. When they started, districts that later became closely settled were still remote and isolated. The outback started beyond the Blue Mountains and it took longer to travel to Bathurst from Sydney than it now takes to fly to Alice Springs.

Some became rich and influential, others failed. Some founded dynasties that still exist, others faded into obscurity. But they were all part of the bush before the comforts came.

This book is about them, the stations they ran or worked on, and the life they knew. And it is about their achievements, which were considerable.

Peter Taylor
Sydney
1988

Note: The change to metric measurements causes problems with a book such as this. In the end I decided to use metric measurement where this seemed appropriate and to retain imperial measurements in quoted material. For those who are confused by this, 1 acre is the equivalent of 0.4 hectares.

Money is more difficult. Multiplying pounds by two and calling the result dollars is meaningless as the figure gives no idea of worth in the nineteenth century. Pounds, shillings and pence have therefore been left alone. As a very rough guide, £10 in 1860 was worth about $600.

For Jonathan Taylor
who left Sydney as a school leaver in 1986 to start work as a
jackaroo in the far north of Queensland. With no experience
of the land, and alone for the first time, he showed many of
the qualities described in this book. I happily dedicate it to
him.

1

The squatters—
who were they?

NY collection of early Australian photographs has at least one picture of a squatter. In his best clothes and with his full beard freshly combed, he stood there in his old age and confronted the camera for the first time. He was self-possessed, wealthy and influential and was determined not to be overawed by his first contact with this new technology. He did as the photographer asked because this was a skill he did not understand, but he did so with the air of a man more used to giving orders than taking them. When the photograph had been taken the squatter relaxed and the photographer, emerging from under his black cloth, knew he was no longer in control.

When we look at the picture a hundred years later we see most of the qualities that made the squatter important. His clothes and discreet tie pin indicate his wealth and his face shows the authority of a leader. He looks determined and aloof, as if he has known nothing but success and affluence all his life, except for one detail: his hands. They are the hands of a worker.

As a contrast to this image of Victorian solidity and respectability there is another view of the squatter. It was written by Edward Curr in his book *Recollections of Squatting in Victoria* and describes the squatter as he was in the days of his youth:

> The prevailing notion [in town] seemed to be that the squatters'
> habitat in all cases was some fearfully remote and lonely locality
> which it would be quite impossible for ordinary people to reach;
> that without his horse the squatter could not exist; that he wore
> habitually Hessian boots and spurs, of which it was uncertain
> whether he ever divested himself; that he was much given to emu
> and kangaroo hunting; had constant encounters with hordes of

1

blacks; rode as a rule fifty miles a day, chiefly at a gallop . . . and at night slept anywhere, with his saddle for a pillow. It was also surmised that some sense, peculiar to the young squatter, enabled him to find his way in the most unerring manner through trackless forests and waterless wastes; that (when out of town) he lived solely on tea, mutton and damper, and enjoyed, when in the saddle, a perfect immunity from fatigue . . .

Not only are these different images accurate, but they could both be of the same man. The photograph of the squatter in his old age is enduring and, because of its familiarity, suggests that squatters were always like that. But they were not. The photograph shows the same man when he was 40 or 50 years older. Nor did all the younger squatters arrive at the stage of having their photographs taken. Some died and some failed. Only the successful had their photographs taken, and even some of those were to discover that wealth that came from the land could be impermanent.

These were the people who pioneered the land, who stocked it with sheep and cattle and who were not deterred by isolation or hardship. If they were to succeed, even in the short term, it would be better if they were still young. And it would be even better if they had money.

Although officers, government officials and ex-convicts had been granted land earlier, it was not until the middle of the 1820s that land became available to a wide range of people. Then, the prospect of taking up land was greeted so enthusiastically that it became almost a mania. One writer, J. D. Lang, seems to have found it all rather boring, as no doubt others did. In his *Historical and Statistical Account of New South Wales* he describes the situation as it was in 1826:

> It was impossible to live in New South Wales . . . without acquiring much more knowledge of this kind than was at all desirable . . . If an advice was given in company, it was by all means to get into a good stock, for there was nothing like it . . . In short, the whole community seemed for a considerable period to have only one idea; and this exclusive and universally-predominant idea was that of rapidly acquiring an independent fortune by the rearing of sheep and cattle.

The government, meanwhile, had recognised two dangers. One was that land would be taken up so far from Sydney as to make civil administration impossible, and the other was that land might be taken up by those who did not have the means to use it. On 9 September 1826 the *Sydney Gazette* published a notice from the government which said that applications could be made for land within a clearly defined area and that it would be granted at the rate of 1 square mile (2.6 square kilometres) for every £500 of capital that the applicant commanded. The maximum grant of 4 square miles (10.4 square kilometres) would be made to those who proved capital worth £2000. Although that capital could include 'stock of every description, implements of husbandry, and other articles which may be applicable to agricultural purposes', the amount meant that only the rich need apply.

William Pitt Faithfull successfully applied for land under this order and was eventually granted 2 square miles (5.2 square kilometres) of land, which surprised and annoyed him because he had proved £2232 in capital and this should have brought him twice that area. He took up his land near Goulburn in New South Wales in 1828 and established a property called Springfield which is still in the hands of his descendants 160 years later.

Although William Pitt Faithfull might seem to be a typical squatter, he would probably have taken his horse whip to anybody at that time who called him one. He was a settler, which was respectable, rather than a squatter, which was not.

This English word, squatter, had come to Australia via America, where it was used to describe somebody who settled on Crown land without permission and thus had no legal title to it. In Australia, however, it took on a different meaning, signifying somebody who was not only on land without permission but who stocked it by stealing from neighbours. At that time squatters were described as bushrangers with a base and they were a serious problem in the bush. On 28 April 1835 the *Sydney Gazette* said:

> The system of squatting has lately increased to an alarming extent; and cattle-stealing and every other crime that not only tends to demoralize the moral population, but to increase the general insecurity of property, continues to keep pace, in a remarkable manner, with an evil against which the Governor has hitherto strangely neglected to apply any radical or alleviating remedy.

Andrew Gibson, who was a neighbour of William Pitt Faithfull at Terranna near Goulburn, was equally vocal:

> Almost all the people who obtain their freedom in the district locate themselves in it as squatters. Although these persons are without any visible means of support, except a few who pretend to be dealers in slops and other stores, yet their services can never be obtained for hire by the neighbouring landowners or settlers. I have no doubt that more than half of them gain a livelihood by bartering spirits for stolen goods and cattle.

By the middle of the 1830s it was obvious that the government's attempt to confine the area of settlement had failed. Most land within that area was now occupied and new migrants had no alter-

3

native but to go further out and occupy land without permission. They often referred to themselves jokingly as squatters, although they did not indulge in cattle-stealing any more than Andrew Gibson. They were also known as 'gentlemen squatters', which previously would have been an obvious contradiction.

Unable to control this outward movement any longer, Governor Bourke realised that it was time to give it a degree of legality. In 1836 the Squatting Act gave every person the right to take up unoccupied land in return for an annual fee of £10 plus a halfpenny for every animal pastured on it. There was no limit provided the fees were paid and sufficient stock grazed on the land. This meant that people who had already taken up land 'further out' could now legalise their holding by paying the licence fee, and those who had not could now go in search of land knowing that payment of the fee would secure it.

The result was a massive outward movement as people left in search of land. And this in turn brought the term squatter closer to its present meaning of someone legitimately occupying Crown land by permission of the government and, subsequently, someone who grazed livestock on land that they either owned or had licence to occupy. The change was so swift that in 1840 the Governor said:

> Among the Squatters of New South Wales are the wealthiest of the land, occupying, with the permission of the Government, thousands and tens of thousands of acres. Young men of good families and connections in England, officers of the army and navy, graduates of Oxford and Cambridge, are also in no small number amongst them.

Young men of good families, officers from the forces and graduates from the leading universities in England. These were the squatters.

In spite of the modest licence fees, would-be squatters still had to be wealthy. They had to stock the land they occupied and they had to survive a cash-flow problem that would terrify most modern accountants. Not only was the price of stock at a premium as a result of this new demand but they also had to support themselves and their labourers for anything up to twelve months before they had wool to sell. They could bridge this gap to some extent by growing cash crops or selling sheep and cattle for meat, but if they had no capital they were unlikely to last very long. A flock of 1000 sheep might cost £3000 and running expenses for the year would be at least another £1000 after selling meat or crops. In 1864 Biddulph Henning, who was a successful pioneer squatter in Queensland, thought that there was not much hope for anyone who did not have £8000 or £10 000 with which to begin. It was often easy enough to raise this amount of money but, then as now, it was important to raise it before it was desperately needed.

The original squatters, then, were mostly wealthy middle-class migrants from the United Kingdom, with those from Scotland making a significant number, especially in what is now the western district of Victoria. They included the Learmonths, who settled on the Barwon, the Robertsons of Coleraine, Angus Macmillan, who discovered Gippsland, and even a Highland chief called Macdonnell of Glengarry, who unfortunately did not do very well.

This migrant origin could also be seen in Queensland. Patrick Leslie, pioneer of the Darling Downs, was born in Aberdeen and sent out to Australia by his uncle to run a property in the upper Hunter district of New South Wales. David McConnel was born in Manchester of Scottish extraction and trained as a chemist before arriving in Australia in 1840. He travelled north and on 15 July 1841, barely twelve months after arriving in Sydney, marked his trees on Cressbrook Creek, a tributary of the Upper Brisbane River, 'as the country appeared to offer all the advantages he had sought for, and he never had occasion to subsequently alter his opinion'. And William Harvey Holt, who had been educated at Eton, found himself at the age of eighteen getting experience on a

William Pitt Faithfull, a successful squatter who took up land near Goulburn in New South Wales in 1828 when he was 22 years old. Faithfull was one of the few squatters at that time to have been born in Australia.

Queensland station before going into partnership to start Kolonga station on the Kolan River.

Most of the migrants who became squatters had something else in common besides money: they knew very little about sheep or cattle. In *Australia, Visited and Revisited*, published in London in 1853, Mossman and Banister said:

> Nine out of ten of these squatters are therefore merely amateur woolgrowers and graziers men who never bred a ewe or an ox in their lives before they set foot in Australia. No doubt they have gleaned sufficient knowledge of cattlebreeding and sheep farming from books and other sources, to pursue either occupation in these colonies, but very few of them have been regularly bred to the business. The fact is, that a knowledge of the management of live stock in Australia is so easily acquired, that any educated man possessed of common shrewdness may be qualified in the course of twelve months to superintend a sheep or cattle station. So that if you are desirous of establishing yourself as a squatter on the waste lands of Australia, it is of greater importance that you should go into the market with a heavy purse than with skill and experience.

Although intended as encouragement to those in Britain thinking that they might achieve more in Australia, the point was not exaggerated and was often made by others. It was true that while most migrants who took up land were educated, they rarely came from the farms of Britain. Running a sheep or cattle property in Australia was certainly not as technical a business as it is today, but it was hard work and usually quite different from what the migrant had been doing in Britain. It was the ability to adapt which led to success.

One example was Alfred Joyce, who was born in London and became an apprentice engineer before settling in Australia. It is true that his mechanical experience proved invaluable to him as a squatter, but the fact remains that he came from an urban and industrialised environment. Edward Curr, although born in Tasmania, was only thirteen and at school in England when the Hentys settled at Portland to pioneer Port Phillip. He finished school in 1838 when he was seventeen and in 1841, when only twenty, he started to manage his father's stations in central and northern Victoria.

This is not to imply that everybody with a similiar lack of experience was successful. Edward Bell, who arrived in Sydney in 1839, was hardly successful as a squatter and was probably more suited to the position he held later as private secretary to Governor La Trobe, but at least he tried.

> I had read the treatises on sheep and cattle in the "Library of Useful Knowledge", and had endeavoured to gain some information respecting colonial life from Major Mitchell's "Travels in Australia",

Mr Waugh's "Three Years' Experience", and Dr Lang's "New South Wales", all which works I had industriously perused on the voyage. Beyond this, my general information regarding live stock was limited to a confused knowledge of sheep by their distinctive titles of rams, wethers, and ewes; and a vague idea of cattle as heifers, cows, bulls, and oxen, and as beasts that had horns, and made a great bellowing; but I am not sure that I could have distinguished any of either description of animal on view.

In spite of this, Bell decided to 'go into stock' and while travelling south to Victoria he bought about a thousand head of cattle at a property near Tumut and held them there until he was ready to continue south.

> I was very much afraid of losing my cattle, and therefore tried to keep them within sight, counting them regularly every day, which, considering that more than half were broken into the run, was an absurdity which nothing but experience convinced me of; for when we wished to remove them, about six weeks later, it was found to be impossible, with our insufficient help, to drive them off the run.

He therefore gave up all idea of settling in Victoria for the time being and sensibly founded a station nearby where he kept his cattle, presumably to their entire satisfaction, for twelve months. He then took up sheep on the northern part of the Broken River in Victoria and lost many of them in the first winter because of catarrh. He tried to cross the ranges to reach the newly opened land in Gippsland, and when that failed he sold his sheep to the butchers and went to live in Glenelg.

While Edward Bell was clearly aware of his shortcomings as a squatter, others seemed totally ignorant of theirs. Alexander Harris, in his book *Settlers and Convicts*, described the arrival of a new settler who was to be his neighbour. This newcomer had been an army officer for more than 30 years and now that his family was growing up he had sold his commission in order to become a squatter.

> [He] was a perfectly well-bred man, in short a gentleman in every sense of the word, in manners, feelings, and opinions; but he was entirely lacking in independence of character. Whatever you proposed to him he did directly. Directly he was invited to come in, he dismounted, left his horse standing at the door, and entered. When the only chair was placed for him he sat down in it; and when the rum-bottle and a tin pot were set on the table beside him, he poured out and drank; and just what he did this first ten minutes he did all the next ten months. If a brother settler advised him to do this thing or that in the morning, he did it; and if a government man advised him in the afternoon to undo it, he undid it.

This man had ten men and an overseer who was determined to make no enemies among those he was supposed to control. As soon

7

as they had erected their tent they all crowded into it, and it was only on the suggestion of Harris that they thought of unloading and protecting their stores. In the following days the squatter amused himelf by going shooting and on his return each day he rarely asked how the work had been going.

Eventually he sent two of his men to Bathurst to bring a flock of 1000 sheep that he had bought there. By the time they returned they had lost 150 sheep and those that remained included some old ewes that were unlikely to see out the winter.

At the end of the first ten months the men had erected one side of a paddock fence, the squatter had a reasonable hut, all but one of the bullocks had been lost, the squatter had lost £400 on his sheep and had bought and paid £1500 for a herd of cattle which he had not seen mustered and which were so wild that their owner had not been able to yard them for the last seven years. Finally, having lost more than £2000 in a very short time, the new squatter gave up the land and turned his attention to other things.

People such as this were dismissed as fools, and English fools at that. Indeed, their origin was of no importance until they revealed their foolishness. When two men arrived at a homestead while searching for land it did not take long for this attitude to surface. One was an Englishman with money, the other was Australian-born and a true bushman. He clearly had had enough of the Englishman:

> [He] is the biggest chuckle-headed ass God ever created. He is going back to England—a good job too; we don't want fools in this country. I can't say what England is like; if it is the same as Australia, except he has a brand put on him, and fastens a bell round his neck, he'll lose himself as sure as God made little apples.

Adaptation and a willingness to learn were what migrants needed, and if they displayed those qualities and acquired a level of practical skills, then their origin was of little concern to anybody.

What, then, of those who were already in Australia when squatting became possible? The native-born and time-expired convicts did not need to adapt to the country and so had less to learn than the migrants. Surely with these advantages they were prominent as early squatters? Surprisingly, they were not. There were, of course, some exceptions. William Pitt Faithfull had been born in Australia and he thought that might have been the reason he was granted less land than he was entitled to. But on the whole the native-born were not to the fore as new squatters.

One reason is that there were not many of them. For example, the 1828 census showed that of the 1546 whites living in the counties of Argyle and St Vincent in New South Wales, only 72 adults had been born in Australia. In the early days they were prominent, and when the first free settlers headed off for Bathurst in 1818 all ten were either native-born or ex-convicts. But of the ex-convicts who went on to make a fortune in New South Wales or Tasmania, nearly all were established by 1821 and few managed to achieve that later. Most of the native-born who did succeed as squatters were children of people who were already prominent in the colony. William Pitt Faithfull, for example, was the son of a member of the New South Wales Corps who had become a pioneer of the Hawkesbury district and who was a wealthy man by the time William Pitt started Springfield.

It was the need for capital that was the restriction. Migrants brought it with them, while most native-born or ex-convicts had little access to it. In the end, the number of migrants swamped the rest anyway and those in the colony who did succeed were a very small minority.

It is misleading, then, to suppose that people in the colonies were able to take advantage of the opportunities that opened up in the thirties. On the contrary, they were swept aside by the migrants and the best most could hope for was to find steady work on the new stations. By 1840 nearly two-thirds of all workers in the bush were either serving convicts, ex-convicts or native-born Australians.

Even some of the exceptions were not highly regarded. Captain Foster Fyans, who was commissioner of Crown lands in the Port-land district of Victoria, spoke disparagingly of shepherds and others who had risen above themselves. His lack of sympathy is evident in this description he wrote in 1853:

> For seasons the hut would be just the same—on one side of the door you will see an aged tobacco plant; there is no garden—no vegetables, but bones, rotten sheep skins, and filth in plenty. . . As for beds, this gentry are not particular. I lay on one for hours in great torment, tired and wishing for sleep; I envied five or six who were snoring close about me. Sleep I could not, from something hard and long under my loins. I took my knife, cut the sacking, when I pulled out the leg of a sheep with a long piece of hide as crisp as toast.

Perhaps the most notable exception was Sidney Kidman, but it is important to recognise that he was an exception. He was born near Adelaide in 1856 and after leaving school at the age of thirteen he went to the Barrier Ranges in search of work. He received an inheritance of £400 and in 1880 he bought his first station, Owen Springs. Within ten years he owned or had an interest in 21 stations in four colonies and later had a controlling interest in more land than any other living man in the British Empire. Kidman was knighted in 1921 and by the time he died in 1935 he owned or had an interest in 68 stations. Even so, he remained a genuine bushman all his life and the story of his rise from rags to riches became legendary. But it was also exceptional.

There were other battlers, of course, but they were as likely to be migrants as not. One, William Hayes, was born in Liverpool in England and arrived in Australia in the early 1850s at the age of 21. In 1884 he was given a contract by Sir Thomas Elder to build fences and dams on two stations in central Australia. He subsequently leased a property of his own, and when Elder became discouraged by his own lack of success there in the 1890s, Hayes bought the leases from him. By 1907 Hayes owned a vast area of grazing land which was 250 kilometres wide and whose southern boundary was 300 kilometres from his home station near Alice Springs.

It is noticeable that both Kidman and Hayes were of a later period, when a succession of booms and busts had to some extent rewritten the rules in pastoral Australia. It is impossible to tell whether their qualities would have achieved similar success in the middle of the century, but Sir Thomas Elder was probably a more typical squatter. Born in Scotland in 1818, he came to Australia in 1854 and his firm of Elder, Smith & Co. eventually controlled pastoral holdings that were greater in area than the Scotland he had left.

The squatters of the thirties and forties were certainly recognisable in colonial society at that time. In 1839 Curr described them as he saw them in Melbourne:

> As a variety of *genus homo* they were distinguishable by their hirsute appearance; whiskers, beards and moustaches being decidedly ascendant among them. Many of them, I noticed, indulged also in the blue serge suits in lieu of coats, cabbage-tree hats, belts supporting leather tobacco-pouches, and in some cases a pistol, which, with breeches, boots and spurs, completed the costume . . . One young squatter, I remember, was particularly noticeable, as it was his custom to have a black boy in livery mounted on his horse's croup. Nor did such eccentricities seem to surprise the residents or attract much notice, the accepted idea seeming to be, that bushmen were not by any means amenable to the slow ways of the town dwellers, and that many things were proper enough in them which might have been esteemed strange, or even objectionable, in others.

It was this difference, and the isolation they endured, that had already made them romantic figures in towns, and it is not surprising if women were especially aware of this romance. 'The squatters of those times, the 1840s, were a brave, reckless band. Quick to love and quick to hate, full of pluck and endurance, dauntless before danger, iron in physique and nerve, and ready for any difficulty or dare-devil feat...'

It is difficult to recognise this in the face of the old man in the photograph, but a great deal had happened by the time it was taken.

2

Finding land

IT seems incredible now that in the first half of the nineteenth century, and indeed in some areas until much later, a resource as valuable as land could be obtained by almost anybody simply by occupying it and taking out a government licence. But at that time land was of no great value unless it contained gold, and then it was subject to a different set of rules. Pastoral land might be almost as productive, but it did not have any great intrinsic value. The value lay in what, if anything, the land could produce.

As land became available for occupation, there started one of the most fascinating aspects of Australian history. While much credit is given to the explorers of inland Australia (even though some were hardly worthy of credit of any kind), much of the detailed knowledge of Australia came not from them but from the early squatters who, with little experience of stock, almost no knowledge of Australia and alone or in small parties, set out to find themselves land.

What is even more remarkable is that they did so without help from the government. It is true that the government had made it possible, but beyond that it contributed nothing. While government often supported exploring expeditions, it offered no help to the squatter other than granting a licence to occupy the land the squatter found.

The squatters were motivated by thoughts of profit, as indeed were some explorers. It was the prospect of wealth that drew them towards the horizon and that was enough for the time being. Collectively, they were developing an industry that was to be of great importance to Australia, and hence its governments, but they had to finance themselves and endure the hazards and uncertainties in the hope of owning a part of that industry. That was what success meant. Failure meant financial ruin or, more immediately, death by violence or thirst in a vast and lonely landscape. There was no compromise between the two. Success and failure were both absolute.

The timid stayed in the cities, just as those even more timid remained in Britain. But the adventurous or foolhardy set out with barely an anxious thought. They made their way past the fringes of settlement and disappeared into the land beyond, leaving nothing but the marks of their horse or dray in the dust.

At first the settlement of land was quite patchy and was contained within the Hawkesbury and the Hunter Rivers of New South Wales, with the Blue Mountains forming a barrier to the west. When the Blue Mountains were crossed in 1813 this relieved the pressure and settlers could now move out from the Cumberland Plains. In 1825 Hume and Hovell succeeded in reaching Port Phillip Bay after an overland journey from Lake George near Goulburn and although the government discouraged settlement in the district, the Hentys moved to Portland from Tasmania because of the pressure of settlement that had developed there.

Although districts were settled almost as soon as they were discovered, the settlement was often patchy. People travelling overland saw only as far as the horizon. If they simply trecked on they remained within a corridor that was only a few kilometres wide and some very good land and even rivers remained undiscovered until much later. For example, the land between the Darling and the lower Condamine in Queensland remained unoccupied long after the Darling Downs had been settled.

There were three ways new squatters could obtain land. They could find it, they could buy it, or they could try wedging, which was slotting between established properties on land which had not been taken up. Of the three, finding land offered the most reward, was the most hazardous and, because it took longer to produce income, the most expensive.

Some people took livestock with them when searching for land, but Harris advised that it was much better to put on a knapsack and go on a tour of inspection first. Having reached the edge of the settled country, potential squatters were then to travel inconspicuously and spend as much time as possible in labourers' huts so that they might learn about the price of stock and the level of wages from those who would have nothing to gain by deceiving. Harris admitted that such contact might be unpleasant, but he pointed out that the traveller could learn more in three months this way 'than in seven years spent in the usual routine of life among those of his own station'.

As for finding land, Harris's description of his own journey in the company of a friend who was to run cattle with him might be taken

13

as typical. It is certainly one of the best accounts as it was written not long afterwards whereas most recollections of successful squatters were recorded many years later.

On the first day Harris and his friend, without their stock, rode out of Bathurst and headed south. They spent the night on a station but although they received much kindness the owner said he did not know of any available land. The next day they continued across the plains but found the country to be poorly watered. Eleven days later they were at Yarralla Creek, not far from William Pitt Faithfull at Springfield, which was already occupied. The next day, at Lake Bathurst on the Goulburn Plain, they found 'a fine plot of water of several miles in circumference and a flat forest around it; but it seemed to be pretty well fed off by one kind of stock and another in all directions'.

On the sixteenth day they arrived at Jambecombene, south of present-day Braidwood, and again found the best country occupied. They rested for a few days, partly because the weather had turned against them and partly because the landowner was glad of their company. They mended gear, wandered in the bush and spent the rest of the time talking and smoking. 'Who has not felt how agreeable it is sometimes to be thoughtless?'

They left on the nineteenth day and spent the next week travelling across Limestone Plains and back across the Goulburn Plain but found 'the ground all occupied'. Then on the twenty-seventh day, when about to leave Bong Bong, a man told them of a run two days' ride away which he had located for his master. Harris and his friend rode out and spent a night at the station nearest to the run which was, he said, 'in one of the most solitary parts of the extreme verge of colonization' even though it was not far from Goulburn.

The next day they became lost as a result of following the directions they had been given but eventually found the run they were seeking. It was well-grassed flat country, lightly timbered and with a kilometre of creek frontage. Beyond the flats the ground rose to stony ridges and thick forest. Satisfied that they had at last found a good run that was unoccupied, they spent a couple of nights at a nearby station. They found the owner to be most hospitable but understandably reluctant to have them as neighbours, especially as he had managed to increase his herd four-fold by 'gully raking'. Realising that they were not to be put off, however, he accepted the situation on the basis of 'live and let live'.

That journey, which took nearly a month, was at least successful. Some people were not so lucky and others found that discovering a good run was not the end of the matter. In Queensland the government tried to discourage those who looked for a run in order

to sell it by insisting that the run be stocked before a licence was issued unless it was clearly incapable of carrying stock at that time. Runs had no value without a licence, and in many cases the finders did not have stock with them. It became usual for squatters to describe their run as unwatered and few, even in the Lands Office, took these lies very seriously. Nehemiah Bartley in his book *Australian Pioneers and Reminiscences* describes how two men on a run-hunting expedition tracked through endless dry country before finding a long lagoon surrounded by Mitchell grass. They subsequently took it up as 'unwatered' but when their agent offered it for sale it was more accurately described as 'unstocked, but well watered by numerous permanent creeks and lagoons'.

What, then, did people look for when searching for unoccupied land? The first requirement was water, and perferably water that was permanent. A permanent creek or waterhole would take care of both stock and people provided it really was permanent and reasonably accessible. At that time there was no way of moving

People set out alone or in small groups to find land. These journeys often lasted for several weeks and frequently went into areas that had not been explored by Europeans.

15

water in large quantities and a creek or waterhole was simply a large trough. The difficulty was knowing whether it was permanent, especially if it was a good season, as only a dry spell would prove it one way or the other. Apart from that, a waterhole might be fed by an underground spring and although seemingly permanent at first, the arrival of large numbers of stock might create a demand that the spring was incapable of supplying.

Land beyond the edge of settlement had certain advantages. Fencing could be delayed until it became necessary and adjacent land that was unoccupied could be used until somebody took it up.

The squatter looked for land that was fairly clear of timber, as this saved much time and expense, but a stand of usable timber on the land was an advantage as it could be used for building. Timber on adjacent land could be used until the land was occupied, but timber more than 4 or 5 kilometres away required much carting and was thought to be too far away to be convenient.

An informed observer could tell much about the land by studying the trees growing on it. The presence of certain trees, yellow box for instance, was an indication of good land, but in any case the squatter looked for trees that were mature and thriving. Spindly and stunted trees were a sign that the soil was probably deficient.

The most reliable guide to the quality of untried land was the squatter's stock. The squatter could see immediately whether the stock were grazing with enthusiasm or not, and that was really all the squatter needed to know. Over a longer period, the squatter could see whether the stock were losing condition or doing well—both would be obvious within two weeks. Assuming there was water, timber and nicely varied land, the stock told the squatter the rest.

There is no doubt that many early settlers knew how to evaluate land when all they had was their own observation. They could identify the best areas and leave untouched the poorer land a few kilometres away, and modern usage has rarely challenged their judgment.

But there were traps, especially for those who judged Australian land by the standards they would have applied in England. Edward Curr described in 1840 how land on one side of the Sydney road at Tallarook in Victoria was quite different from that on the other side. To the east was mountainous country with green grass and running streams, while on the other side of the road the land was flat and looked dry and burnt-up. Not surprisingly, most people thought the land to the east was much better than that to the west and those who settled on the mountains had little doubt that they were on the better land.

Of course we all know now that the estimate formed on this subject
was quite an erroneous one, and, as a fact, that those overlanders
who took up country to the eastward of the Sydney-road, amidst
abundance of water and green grass, met with but scant success as
sheep-farmers; those whose fortune led them westward, or down the
rivers, as a rule doing exceedingly well. Indeed, now-a-days, green-
grass country and bad country are pretty generally synonymous
terms.

The reason for this was stock disease. In high rainfall areas standing
water led to a high incidence of disease so that although the
country might look attractive to European eyes, the reality was
that wethers barely had enough time to fatten before they died of
disease. When water was contained in large and confined areas the
surrounding land might look dry and unattractive but it was far
more productive. So not only is Curr's description accurate, but
it also indicates that it did not take people long to realise the
significance of what was going on around them.

The other problem new squatters faced when looking at land for
the first time was that they did not know whether they were seeing
it at its best or its worst. In 1841 a traveller to the Wimmera in
Victoria found it did not match the earlier description of Thomas
Mitchell: 'A series of dry seasons had altered the face of the
country, and the fertile country which had presented itself to his
delighted view had been converted into an arid waste, destitute of
either grass or water.'

With no local knowledge to draw on, squatters had to rely again
on their own observation. High water marks around waterholes or
along creeks gave an indication of whether the present season,
judged by the curent level of the water, was good or bad. Gullies
that were dry might have signs that they carried water at other
times, and observation of the pasture also provided a guide. But
only time proved how good or bad the season was, and many
squatters found that the land that had seemed so promising when
they took it up was not capable of maintaining their stock.

Most successful squatters remembered for the rest of their life
the beauty of the country when they first saw it. Charles Browning
Hall, who settled in the Wimmera, wrote:

> The creeks were then all fringed with reeds and rushes, undevoured
> by hungry cows and gaunt working bullocks. These reeds and rushes
> formed a beautiful edging to the dark solemn pools overhung by the
> water-loving gum-trees, where wild fowls abounded, as the plains
> did with quail and turkey.

And John Robertson, who settled Wando Vale near Casterton in
Victoria, wrote: 'When I arrived through the thick forest-land from
Portland, I cannot express the joy I felt at seeing such a splendid

country before me where my little all that I was driving before me was to feed... I could neither think nor sleep for admiring this new world...'

Robertson was able to identify 37 different grasses in the pasture, but he also recorded the changes that took place during the next few years. The herbaceous plants began to disappear and silk grass took over. The deep-rooted grass that held a clay hill together died out and the exposed ground cracked and slipped in all directions. 'Ruts, seven, eight, and ten feet deep, and as wide, are found for miles, where two years ago it was covered with tussocky grass like a land marsh.'

At that time there was a view that stocking land would actually improve it. In 1858 the Royal Geographical Society of London published a report by Peter Warburton who, in describing land north-west of Port Augusta, said that it would be greatly improved by being stocked: '...the surface would become firmer, and the thin coating of small stones would be just sufficient to prevent rapid evaporation, but not to interfere with the growing of grass, which would soon spring up under sheep.' He thought the carrying capacity would be three times greater in the third year than in the first.

If the land proved disappointing, squatters simply moved on, provided they had not gone broke first. There was little to hold them to the land they had first settled and if it turned out to be useless they simply left it and looked elsewhere.

Squatters who did not have the time, skill or the capital to look for land bought it from those who had. In most cases they were simply buying the stock that was on the run, and the land itself was thrown in as part of the deal. The price of the stock might reflect the fact that the land was to be included, so that when Alfred Joyce and his brother bought their run in 1844, sheep alone cost about 2 shillings a head, whereas they cost 4 or 5 shillings if the run was included.

They paid £50 for 10 000 acres of unstocked land on the Loddon River in Victoria, while their neighbour who settled three months earlier had paid £250, not for the run but for the 1000 ewes that were on it. As Joyce says, £50 might seem insignificant for 10 000 acres, but there was not an acre of freehold among them and runs were available for nothing to those who chose to go far enough for them. They already had a flock of sheep ready to move onto the run, but they had to spend a further £150 on a dray, bullocks and stores within the first few months.

In the rush to 'get into stock' some people bought a run without even seeing it. One of the first things Edward Curr did as a squatter was to inspect a run that his father had bought unseen. Curr, who said he was quite ignorant of sheep and their management and who had never seen a station or counted a flock before, took a friend with him who was experienced in such things. But when they arrived even Edward could see that their run was not one of the best.

The run had two slab huts, one used by the hands and the other by the overseer. On the flats were three flocks of sheep while beyond them was a tumble-down structure of bark and poles lashed together which was the woolshed. When Curr entered the overseer's hut he began to realise what squatting was really like:

> Against the walls, around which were hung a pair or two of horse-hobbles, a gun, stock-whip, some tin dishes, pannikins, a rickety looking-glass, and other odds and ends appertaining to the gentle craft of squatting, were set three rough stools; and on the mantlepiece were disposed, evidently with some regard to effect, a couple of Hall's powder canisters, of a flaming red colour; a horse's hoof. . .[and] a large glass-stoppered druggist's bottle as a centrepiece, containing some three pints of a sherry-coloured liquid, and labelled butyr of antimony.

At the other end of the scale was a successful pastoralist in Victoria and Tasmania, William Clarke, who in 1850 surprised government officials in Melbourne by paying cash for 31 375 acres at £1 an acre under the Waste Land Act. Clarke took up his land near Sunbury in Victoria and when he later obtained a further 31 000 acres his holding reached from Sunbury to the Sydney road. When he died he left £2.5 million.

The third alternative was to acquire land by wedging. This meant locating land, perhaps between two holdings, which looked as if it was part of one of them but which had never been subject to a licence. Alternatively, the land might have been licensed but not stocked to the extent that the licence required.

Those looking for land in this way had nothing to lose. If successful, they acquired occupancy of land that was usually far better and more accessible than land in the back country, and if they failed they simply tried elsewhere. It was not a widely used technique, however, because of the uncertainty of success. Squatters travelling in search of land further out would be aware of the possibility of wedging as they travelled through settled country, but it is doubtful that many set out with that intention in mind.

Although most of the land in south-eastern Australia was taken up fairly quickly, the search for new land went on elsewhere for most of the century. The land around the Barcoo in Queensland was not settled until 1861, when three men applied for licences to

'Bachelors Hall.' When searching for land, people had no local knowledge to draw on and instead had to rely on their own observations.

occupy an area which later became Lansdowne station, and it was not until 1863 that Patrick Durack took his family on an expedition to find land in Queensland.

Their journey was longer and more trying than that taken by Harris. The Duracks took two and a half months to reach Bourke and from there made their way to the Paroo, south of the Queensland border. Durack and three others went on from there with the cattle, but the mob died when they rushed the water of the Bulloo River. The men carried on for another 65 kilometres but were half dead when local Aboriginals showed them a hidden well. The trip was a failure.

The Duracks nevertheless tried again, and left Goulburn in 1867 for another attempt. More than three months later they reached Warroo Springs but found that the Costellos, who had left Goulburn earlier to settle there, had been beaten by drought. The parties combined and travelled to Mobel Creek. From there Durack followed a flock of birds and discovered good land, well watered, which had the native name of Thylungra. In the middle of 1868 Patrick Durack formed Thylungra station with 100 head of cattle that had survived the trip from Goulburn.

Journeys like this were repeated many times as people pushed into the remote country of the north. Brunette Downs in the Northern Territory was started in 1883 and it was several years before the land of the Kimberleys in Western Australia was settled, and then very sparsely.

This venturing went on for years and was mostly unrecorded. Ernestine Hill, in her book *The Territory*, describes how she suggested to Harry Condon, who had been in the Northern Territory from the 1880s, that he must have been the first European to see much of the country.

> 'Ah,' said Harry, 'now I'll tell you. Through all them creeks and hills on the head of the Fitzmaurice, or the Kathe-rhyne, or the Victoria, or the Goyder, or anywhere else you like to name, there was fellers long before me, an' there was fellers before them. Back in the eighties I could ride for a month, an' I'd come to gorges so steep you couldn't ride no longer, an' I'd climb them cliffs an' crawl through holes in the rocks an' go down the cliffs, an' into another gully an' on for two days with a bush net an' a bit o' tucker, an' I'd come to a waterhole I'd swear I was the first to see. Blow me if I wouldn't find a rusty old match-box, or a button, or a sauce bottle of a shape an' brand you never see for years, or initials an' a date of the sixties or seventies cut in a tree.
>
> 'There ain't no such thing as the first white man, missus. They was everywhere, looking for waters and gold in the very earlies, but they didn't think to talk about it then. There ain't no creek or gully or hill or pocket of country in the island [Australia] where a bushman hasn't been before you.'

No matter how long it took the squatters to find their land, no matter how much hardship they had to endure, if they planned to settle on virgin ground their efforts and hardships were only beginning when they first marked their boundaries.

3

Setting up a station

T HE satisfaction of finding a new run in virgin country soon gave way to the realisation that it was a long way from being a station. The squatters were looking at a wide expanse of open country, happy that it had good pasture, water that seemed to be permanent, and land that was not too heavily timbered. But that was all they had other than what they had brought with them.

They now had to make this land capable of supporting themselves, their hands and their livestock, and they had to do this fairly quickly. Precisely what they did depended on what they had with them. If they had travelled lightly they could probably support themselves for a few weeks but they would not be able to do anything of great use during that time. In that case, then, they usually returned to their starting point to organise supplies, buy a dray and bullocks, perhaps engage hands, buy tools and arrange to move their stock.

If they already had stock they would have kept them on some kind of agistment while searching for land. Most squatters were prepared to run stock belonging to other people on their property on a system known as thirds: the squatter did not charge a fee but was entitled to a third of the increase of the stock while it was on his land. If the new squatter did not have stock, however, then stock had to be bought and this represented the squatter's first major investment. Most were advised to buy stock from a nearby property on the grounds that it would have adapted to the local climate and there was more chance of being treated fairly by a future neighbour than by someone in a distant town.

Having accumulated all that they might need for perhaps twelve months, the squatters then returned to their land.

They might, on the other hand, have travelled with their stock while looking for land. If so, they needed to accommodate them fairly quickly and they also had to send back for supplies and perhaps another dray and some bullocks. If they had a dray and bullocks with them, they usually kept them on the land so that they could start work while waiting for their stores to arrive. The extra expense involved in bringing up another dray and team was well justified as they could hardly have too many of such things.

The way people started to establish their station depended as much on temperament as on the circumstances. Certain things had to be done, but the order of doing them varied from one to the other. They had to build a hut for themselves and their hands, they had to build yards for cattle and pens for sheep, they had to clear enough ground to do all those things, and they needed at least a minimum of fencing. If they were lucky they might not have to do much clearing, but they still had to fell trees for timber.

Many squatters did not build a hut immediately. Some continued to camp or live under the dray, but most spent the first day or two building a couple of bark huts. Cutting bark was, therefore, one of the first skills they had to learn, and it was one that they continued to use for a long time.

At its most basic, cutting bark simply meant removing a sheet of bark from a living tree by cutting a zig-zag shape of the size required around the trunk with an axe and then peeling the bark off with a spade. The bark was then dried by a fire and weighted to make it flat. It could, however, be much more skilled than that. The expert looked for a tree which was more than a metre in diameter and preferably a stringybark, messmate or other variety which had bark that stripped readily. The squatter made the first

A substantial hut made entirely from bark.

23

cut close to the ground and the top cut as high up the tree as the length of sheet that was wanted. An adze was then used to insert wedges under the bark which was then worked clear with a pointed stick. The sheet that came away could be quite heavy and care was needed to lower it to the ground without damaging it. It was then uncurled in front of the fire and laid smooth-side-down under weights for flattening and drying, which also made it lighter. However carefully the bark was removed it resulted in the death of the tree if the cut area encircled the trunk, which was usually the case.

The first humpy was made by laying sheets of bark over a small structure of saplings to make what was no more than a bark tent. A decent sized one needed about 25 sheets of bark, but two tents this size could be cut and built in no more than two days. They were snug, sometimes weatherproof, and provided basic accommodation while something more substantial was being built.

The first step in building a more permanent hut was to decide where this should be, and this was no easy matter. It had to be close to water otherwise carting would be an endless and time-consuming chore, but the question was how close the water might come to the hut. The debris of earlier floods provided some clues but if the water was surrounded by acres of flats the whole area might be inundated periodically.

The ideal was to have the creek or waterhole surrounded by high banks, which fell away in other places so that the stock had access to the water, and with a section of higher ground, preferably gravelly, not far away. In those circumstances the squatter built on the high ground and felt reasonably secure, knowing that the banks provided protection from rising water and also against an attack by Aboriginals from that direction.

In situations not so well blessed as that the squatter had to accept a compromise. It was not unusual for a squatter to build three houses in succession, as floods repeatedly proved that the original assessment had been wrong.

Having determined the site of the hut, the land around it was cleared of almost everything. The reason was that an unprotected tree close to the hut was likely to fall in a gale with drastic results. Grass was also burnt off so that it did not become a fire hazard. The result was usually practical but unattractive. Louisa Meredith, in *Notes and Sketches of New South Wales*, said:

> The system of clearing here, by the total destruction of every native tree and shrub, gives a most bare, raw and ugly appearance to a new place. . . unless a settler can see an expanse of bare, naked, unvaried, shadeless, dry, dusty land spread all around him, he fancies his dwelling 'wild and uncivilised'.

Having settled on the site for the hut, the squatter then started to gather timber, which was needed regardless of which building technique was to be used.

Trees for timber were felled, not ring-barked. An axe was used to cut a notch in the trunk and if two people were available a cross-cut saw was used to complete the cut. But there was a way of avoiding having to do that with every tree. The squatter looked for a row of trees that were fairly close together. Each tree was cut half-way through and the one at the end of the row felled so that it fell on the second, which fell on the third and so on. It was the domino theory applied to bringing down timber.

Felling enough trees to make a decent sized hut was heavy work however it was done. Harris describes how he and a mate started at dawn each day and worked for two hours before stopping for breakfast. They then worked until midday before having another break which lasted until about three o'clock, when the heat of the day was diminishing. They then did another hour and after a short break continued to work until nightfall.

When the trees had been felled they were cleared of branches before being split. This was done by selecting a good line and then hammering in wedges to open a crack. Only two wedges were needed, each being leap-frogged over the other as the crack proceeded along the length of the trunk. If it was well done the tree split in half and could then be split into quarters if required.

In the early days this was all the squatter needed. Later, however, the process was taken a step further and logs were converted into sawn boards. This was usually done by a contractor as the skill required was considerable. The contractor selected the best trees, stringybark if it could be found, and after they were felled bullocks were used to drag them to a sawpit that had been prepared. Wedges were used to split the trunk and then the contractor and a mate used a long two-handled saw to cut the planks. The contractor stood on the top of the log and was the 'top-sawyer'. The contractor guided the long saw blade along the line of the cut while the mate, below in the pit, simply pushed the saw back up for the next cut.

If the squatter was building a bark hut, four stout poles about 3 metres long were planted, one at each corner of the hut. Slightly thinner poles, about 25 centimetres in diameter, were then sunk at intervals of 1.5 metres along the line of the walls. Alternatively, if the walls were not too long a trench was cut in the ground and horizontal saplings fixed between the corner poles. Lengths of timber were fastened across the top of the poles and more timber might be laid across these for bracing. With the frame complete, openings for doors and windows were cut out and framed with light saplings. The roof was then erected, with small saplings making

25

the rafters and a strong tree as the ridge pole. This might also have to be supported by additional uprights sunk in the ground along its length.

All that remained was to cover the entire frame with sheets of bark, starting at the bottom and overlapping each sheet over its neighbour and the one below. The soundest sheets were used to cover the ridge pole and were laid along its length. All the sheets were kept in place with pegs or by tying them with greenhide. Finally, logs were laid on each side of the roof and were held in place by tying them through the bark to the rafters or by securing them with stringybark to the ridge pole.

If a bark hut was built with care, and the bark itself well cut, the result was a comfortable and weatherproof hut that could last for decades.

A slab hut was much more substantial, but it required more material, more labour and more skill. The success of a slab hut depended almost entirely on the first stage of construction, which was the erection of the corner posts. These had to be substantial, certainly no less than 30 centimetres in diameter, and sunk at least a metre into the ground. If these posts were not completely rigid the hut was unlikely to be a success.

If the slabs were to be used vertically, which was the easier method, a trench was cut in the ground along the line of the wall and the ends of the slabs sunk into it. The top of each slab was fixed to a length of timber that ran across the top of the corner posts. The slabs were placed with the curved side on the outside of the wall and the cracks between them filled with clay. A variation of this

A slab hut. The walls are vertical slabs of timber and the roof is bark. The ridge pole is covered by a single sheet and the other sheets have been carefully overlaid to keep the rain out.

method was to pare down the slab at each end and to lay a log along the ground and across the tops of the corner poles. These logs were mortised to take the shape of each slab.

A more substantial method was to lay the slabs horizontally between the corner posts. Intermediate posts were planted in the ground if the wall was longer than the length of the slab. The slabs were held in place by two vertical battens that were fixed to each post and spaced wide enough apart to receive the slabs. The slabs were then inserted between the battens at either end, one on top of the other. The advantage of this method, which was called 'drop-log', was that each slab added its weight to the one below so that the wall was more substantial than when the slabs were vertical.

In both cases the roof was usually built in the same way as for a bark hut, although shingles were sometimes used. This was a laborious process, however, because if the shingles were cut too wide they curled and became useless. Shingles were fastened in place with a single nail because they would always curl to some extent and would split if held too firmly.

The only maintenance a slab hut needed was periodic filling of the gaps between the slabs, which shrank as they dried. If this were not done the inside of the hut soon become infested with insects and even small animals.

Bark and slab huts were so common and in use for such a long time that they have become part of the Australian legend. But they could be built only where there was an abundant supply of bark and timber and while that was the case in much of south-eastern Australia it was not always so elsewhere. Areas that were drier and sparsely timbered did not lend themselves to these techniques and the bark and slab hut was almost unknown in those parts.

One method that was used when there was a shortage of heavy timber was known as wattle and daub. The corner posts were sunk as before but they did not need to be as substantial or sunk as deeply as they did for a slab hut. Upright saplings were then erected along the line of the wall about a metre apart and these were secured to cross poles that were placed between the corner posts. Light brush or saplings were then woven horizontally through the uprights to give a basketweave effect. The walls were then covered by kneaded clay which became weatherproof as it dried. The roof, as before, was made of bark.

There were two variations of this technique. One was to make the frame a little more substantial and then to fix the horizontal saplings to it by nailing or tying. This avoided the laborious job of weaving the saplings and was therefore quicker, but the finished wall was usually thinner. The other method was to make panels of basketweave, each within a frame, which were then dropped into

27

grooves in the uprights. This method was more laborious and required more accuracy.

R. D. Murray described a typical wattle and daub hut in *A Summer at Port Phillip*, which was published in Edinburgh in 1843:

> The walls are constructed of that material known in the colony as 'wattle and daub', or, in other words, a frame of wicker-work overspread with mud, and supporting a roof covered with rolls of bark which the wooden stretchers which keep them down can scarcely keep them from resuming their original circular shape. Two or three windows, or port-holes, admit the light, while a huge misshapen chimney of turf flanks one end of the building in front, which on the whole, may be considered a pretty fair specimen of a bush hut.

Another method used when timber was scarce was pisé, or rammed earth, which did not require a timber frame. Instead a form, a box without a top or bottom, was made of timber so that it was about a metre wide and a little over 3 metres long. This was placed on the ground along the line of the wall. Wet earth was put into the form until it was about 100 millimetres deep and was then compacted very firmly with a ram made for the purpose. Another layer was added on top of the first and the process repeated until the rammed earth was at the top of the form. The form was then moved to make the next section of the wall, and eventually to make successive layers on top of the first. Openings for doors and windows were left as gaps as the wall was being built. If necessary, a foundation of stone was laid beneath each wall.

The success of pisé depended almost entirely on having the correct soil, and on ramming it very firmly. The best soil was a mix of about one-third clay and two-thirds sand or gravel and with no animal or vegetable matter. It had to be kept moist but not wet. If it was not rammed firmly the resulting cavities became homes for countless insects which were impossible to remove.

The roof timbers were erected on top almost as soon as the walls were finished. Wide eaves were thought necessary to keep the rain from the walls, although when they had dried for six months or so they were very hard. The walls were then sealed with a mixture of linseed oil and whitewash or roughened and covered with a mixture of mortar, water and lime.

Patrick Durack built the first homestead at Thylungra in this way. It was single storey with a thatched roof which extended out over wide verandas. This house was in use for 70 years, when it was demolished to make way for a modern building.

Whatever method was used to build the huts, their interiors were all fairly similar. Rough timber and bark was used to make

simple furniture, for there was usually nothing else available. Chairs were often no more than a sawn stump, but ingenuity and skill could produce something more comfortable. One improvement was a triangular frame with a protuding ledge for the seat. An animal skin was laced to the frame and as it had only two legs it was simply leant against a wall. A bed was a low frame with a sheet of bark on which the blankets were spread. At first the floor was left as it was but eventually it wore into hollows that could be dangerous. The easiest way of improving it was to cover it with ash or gravel. The fancy way was to use sawn planks. In the north, dirt from ant hills made a very sound floor that lasted for years.

Sheets of bark were used to cover the door and windows, although shutters were sometimes used to keep the heat out. Squatters in the north were advised to do without windows if they could as this kept the hut much cooler. Inside walls were usually left as they were, but in time might be covered with calico or newspapers.

These huts were undoubtedly crude; although when women arrived in the bush they improved considerably. At first, though, they simply provided shelter and basic comforts to the squatter and his hands. They did not see them very often in the daylight hours, and in the darkness their shortcomings were not so noticeable. If the squatter prospered, and if he did not marry, he often continued

A group of station buildings at Seven Creeks station, near Longwood in Victoria.

to live in a hut of this kind long after he could afford something more splendid.

George Dunderdale, in *The Book of the Bush* published about 1870, described a slab hut with a shingle roof that was probably typical of many:

> It had two rooms and the furniture did not cost much. At Adams' stores he bought a camp oven, an earthenware stew-pot, a milk pan, a billy, two pannikins, two spoons, a whittle, and a fork. The extra pannikin and spoon were for visitors. With an axe and saw he made his own furniture—viz., two hardwood stools, one of which would seat two men; for a table he sawed off the butt end of a messmate, rolled it inside the hut, and nailed on the top of it a piece of pine packing case. His bedstead was a frame of saplings, with a strong canvas nailed over it, and his mattress was a sheet of stringy bark, which soon curled up at the sides and fitted him like a coffin. His pillow was a linen bag filled with spare shirts and socks, and under it he placed his revolver, in case he might want it for unwelcome visitors.

Much depended on the living habits of the people in the hut. If they maintained their standards, then the hut could be a comfortable place. If not, it could be abominable. There were many huts of this kind and many writers shuddered at the thought of them, especially if they had actually lived in one. This description comes from Commissioner Parry and was quoted in the *First Decade of the Australian Agricultural Company 1824 to 1834*:

> Nothing in the shape of description can possibly convey any adequate idea of the state of dirty wretchedness and want of comfort in which they live for several of their first years . . . No floor; the fireplace a recess made of slabs; their beds a sort of cot slung with bullock hide to the rough rafters, and everything giving the idea of filth and wretchedness.

As well as building huts for themselves and their men, squatters also had to build facilities for their stock. They often spent more care on these than they had on the huts.

For their sheep they needed a woolshed and a few railed yards alongside for drafting and penning. A basic woolshed, perhaps put up for the first shearing, consisted of posts and slab walls covered with a bark roof. The shed might have one or two walls open and some of them had no walls at all. The floor was bare earth, although this could be improved by laying a mat of soft branches over it and, later, sawn planks. This was done not for comfort but to keep dirt out of the fleeces.

Yards for sheep did not have to be very substantial. They were made of palings, piled up brushwood, or hurdles made from woven saplings. The uprights of these were sharpened to a point at the

The inside of a bush hut in 1874. The walls are lined with sawn timber but the floor is bare earth. Even at this time there were few comforts.

bottom so they could be pushed into the ground. It was important that the squatter prepared at least one yard (more if there was more than one flock) before the sheep arrived otherwise they would be decimated by dingoes.

Cattle yards had to be much more substantial. Solid posts were sunk along the perimeter and five or six rails fastened across them. Slip rails were easier to make than gates. Some squatters then filled the gaps with earth and brushwood. They would, in any case, soon find out if the yard was not substantial enough.

They also needed to build a gallows, which was used when a beast was killed for rations. It was made of two tall forked poles sunk upright in the grounds with a length of timber placed across the top of them and resting in the forks. After the beast was slaughtered the carcass was slung from the gallows so that it could be skinned and butchered.

Moving around the run was not a simple matter, especially at first. The run might cover several square kilometres and parts of it might be seldom visited by people or stock. Tracks, let alone roads, were impractical, so routes were marked by taking a chip about the size of a sheet of notepaper out of both sides of trees which were within sight of each other. The route itself might be determined by the location of the trees rather than the most direct line. If trees were not available the route could be marked by cairns of stones.

If the run was divided by a creek (and many were) then the

31

squatter needed to build a bridge across it so that sheep could be moved from one half of the run to the other. The best place for the bridge was where the ground was fairly soft. Holes were dug on either side of the creek to a depth of about 1.25 metres and strong posts planted in them. Because the earth that had come out of the holes was soft, the posts were supported by flat stones rammed into the hole. These posts had to be very rigid. They were then joined by poles which formed the path of the bridge across the creek. A mat of saplings was laid across and this was covered with sheets of bark and, finally, a few centimetres of earth. If the bridge was well built it could last for years and survive many floods. Cattle did not need such consideration as they could walk across most creeks.

The squatter also had to erect fences, although at first not very many were needed. The boundary line was often laid with surprising accuracy, although the method was quite simple. When it was dark, a fire was lit at each end of the boundary line. Two people, each with a lantern, started out, one from each end, and worked toward each other, pegging the ground as they went. If each kept the distant fire and lantern in line, the result was an impeccably straight line of pegs. The squatter did not fence this line until somebody took up the adjoining land. As one squatter advised a newcomer, '. . . when my flocks met those of my neighbour's some day in the bush it would be time enough to move on the matter'.

At first, then, the squatter put a fence around the huts and fenced a few paddocks in the immediate vicinity so that stock could be held without having to yard them. The easiest fence was made of tree trunks dragged into place and then covered with branches. This could be improved by laying wedges, called 'chocks', at right angles to the fence line, and laying the logs on these. Alternatively, the logs could be laid in a zig-zag so that each length supported the next.

The best kind of fence was the post and rail, which was pretty much as it is now. James Atkinson, writing as early as 1826, described how they were made:

> Select the straightest and freest grown trees, fell them with a cross cut saw, cut them off to proper lengths and billet them into as many divisions as the size of the tree will admit; they are then slit or run out with wedges into rails or posts. . . Posts are cut five feet six inches, and rails nine feet long. The mortices are cut quite through the posts, about four inches long, and two inches wide; the ends of the rail are sometimes placed one over the other in the mortice and sometimes one by the side of the other; which last is the neatest plan. The ends are trimmed away so as to overlap each other and project through the mortice on both sides; two pannels are

invariably put up to a rod, and the fences are always sunk two feet in the ground, which allows the fence to be three feet six inches high.

Even when wire became available in the middle of the century, fencing represented a considerable investment on the part of squatters and it was not until they had substance, and a more secure claim to their land, that they did much more than they needed to work the property.

Not all new squatters were as practical as this. Some took a long time to erect even the most basic facilities, either because they were short of funds or were simply idle. Others had no sense of priorities and spent time on work that was unnecessary while neglecting to do what was needed. Harris describes one of these:

> I heard that when he first took possession of his land he was very well off; but had impoverished himself greatly, as gentlemen settlers so very often do, by expending their capital on everything but that which really wants doing. They wish to make a complete farm at once, and spare no cost to do so: consequently great paddocks are fenced in before there is any stock that needs them; large pieces are cleared, and next to nothing cropped; cottages with verandahs are built, and the barn and dairy neglected; and even carriage walks are laid out for carriages, whose mere existence is among the most improbable of dreams.

The squatters who survived avoided such idiocies and concentrated on supplying what they needed and little more. The result looked crude to those familiar with the great estates of England and many wrote witheringly of what they saw. But those estates had been generations in the making, and in any case were not always as successful as appearances might indicate.

Australian squatters, on the other hand, had taken up virgin land about which they knew very little, stocked it with animals which they barely understood, and largely with their own hands erected within a matter of months huts for themselves and their labourers and installed the essentials for their well-being. If the result did not look elegant it did not matter. It had not been done for elegance.

4

How the stations worked

FOR a long time stations ran both sheep and cattle and the work of the station varied depending on which of the stock needed attention. Some work was constant, while other tasks might occur only once a year.

It was not until later in the century that many squatters ran cattle on their own, and that came about because the land that become available in the north of Australia was not suitable for sheep. The decision was based on geography, not choice. Until then, squatters ran sheep for their wool, meat, and for sale as stock, and cattle for meat. The importance between sheep and cattle varied as the squatter reacted to changes in the market, but sheep were usually the more important. Sheep had two advantages over cattle. One was that they needed less water and did less damage to the edge of the creek; the other was that sheep produced income from wool without having to be slaughtered. In 1840 there were 673 runs in New South Wales and between them they carried some 350 000 cattle and nearly 1.25 million sheep.

Squatters were involved personally in running their stations and they usually worked at least as hard as their hands. Nevertheless they relied heavily on an overseer, who had to be chosen carefully. As Harris said:

> An adviser of some sort you must have, or you will fall into mistakes, often of a very expensive and pernicious character: and to have an ignorant, weak minded man in such a capacity is worse than to have none; for your own mistakes alone will be preferable to your own and his together.

A sheep station consisted of a number of outstations which were usually about 6 or 7 kilometres from the homestead. The number of outstations depended on the number of sheep, or more specifically the number of flocks, and at first most stations consisted of a homestead and one outstation.

The outstation usually had two flocks of sheep, each under the care of a shepherd, and a hutkeeper who looked after the sheep at night. The flocks were not selected for breeding purposes. Indeed each flock might be identical in almost all respects. Instead they were determined by the number of sheep which one person could look after, and this in turn depended on the nature of the country. A flock could be anything from 400 to more than 1000 sheep.

Work on the outstation was repetitive, almost boring, and hardly varied for about 40 or 50 years. The routine was simple. Every day after sunrise each shepherd took his flock to the area of grazing which had been determined by the squatter or the overseer. Once there, the shepherd made sure that the flock did not wander and for the most part simply plodded behind them as they grazed at their own pace. By noon they had covered about 6 kilometres and the shepherd allowed them to camp in the shade while he had a meal.

> A few minutes suffice to light a fire and boil the water; tea is soon made, four or five chops are spitted on cleft sticks and grilled before the fire, a piece of damper is taken out of his wallet, and the

Until the middle of the nineteenth century sheep were under the care of shepherds. When the gold rushes enticed shepherds to leave their flocks the sheep continued to thrive and squatters realised that shepherds were not necessary. They were replaced by a small number of boundary riders who checked fences.

shepherd has his fill of good bush fare, mutton, damper and tea. This finished, he winds up his repast with a pipe of tobacco, by way of dessert.

After having a meal the shepherd roused the sheep and guided them back to the outstation by a different route. The shepherd arrived there about sundown, as did the other shepherd who was returning from a different direction. Each flock was counted into a separate yard made of hurdles and the sheep then became the responsibility of the hutkeeper. The hutkeeper spent the night in a small contraption about the size and shape of a sentry box which stood between the two yarded flocks. The hutkeeper's job was to fend off marauding dingoes, Aboriginals, or anything else that might threaten the safety of the sheep.

In the morning, the hutkeeper lit the fire, woke the shepherds, made breakfast, and cleaned out the hut after they had left with the flocks. Later in the day the hutkeeper moved the hurdles to fresh ground as a precaution against stock disease. It was such an unvaried routine that it was often difficult to remember what day of the week it was.

Writers sometimes described this life in idyllic terms, comparing it with that of shepherds in antiquity, but they were too romantic. Not only was it boring, but there were responsibilities that they overlooked. The squatter might complain that the shepherd was keeping the sheep too closely bunched, which made watching them easier but meant they were feeding over insufficient ground. On the other hand, if the shepherd allowed them to roam too freely, some could be accidentally left behind in gullies and hollows and the loss not realised until the count at the end of the day. In either case, a convict shepherd could be brought before the magistrate, or a free person refused his wages.

One old shepherd told Harris how he could have saved hundreds of sheep in his time, but did not do so because he was always flogged for those he lost and given no credit for those he saved. Another, who worked for a particularly ruthless man, found a novel way of hitting back. If he lost one sheep, he allowed the entire flock to disperse. The punishment could be no more severe than for the one lost, and eventually the squatter realised what was happening and became much less ruthless.

The squatter or the overseer rode to each outstation once a week with a packhorse carrying the rations for the coming week. Each shepherd was given about 5 kilograms of flour and meat, a kilogram of sugar, 200 grams of tea and a quantity of tobacco. The flour was supplied as whole grain and the hut had a small hand mill which the shepherds used to produce coarse flour for the damper.

Apart from this weekly visit, people at the outstation saw nobody but each other. This loneliness appealed to some and appalled others, but it changed nearly all of them. Some became 'hatters', because they were as mad as one, but even if they did not they were a recognisable breed, as this description of an encounter with one by George Hamilton shows:

> The first thing he did was to swear at his dogs in a loud, threatening tone, using imprecations somewhat original and terribly blasphemous. He then strolled, with that peculiar gait known and practised only by the 'gentle craft' to which he belonged, towards our party. He was a very good type of the Australian shepherd of that period—he was unwashed, unshaven, and very dirty; indifferently clothed in rags, with a limp hat on his head, and his feet shod with rude slippers made of sheepskins; he had a lighted pipe between his lips, which he smoked with exceeding relish. There was certainly something remarkable about the man. He seemed a mixture of Robinson Crusoe, Russian serf, Tartar nomade, and street-crossing sweeper.

It is not surprising that many bush workers refused to become shepherds and regarded the job with contempt. In his novel *The*

Shepherds took their flocks out for grazing each day and returned with them to the outstation in the evening. This work was repetitive, boring and despised by most station hands. Nor was it as idyllic as this picture suggests.

37

Squatter's Dream Rolf Boldrewood described the reaction of a stockman who had been asked if he was a shepherd: 'You be hanged! Do I look like a slouchin', possum-eating, billy-carrying crawler of a shepherd? I've had a horse under me ever since I was big enough to know Jingaree mountain from a haystack, and a horse I'll have as long as I can carry a stockwhip.'

What brought the shepherding of flocks to an end was the departure of the shepherds, and that was brought about by the goldrushes. Not surprisingly, the prospect of digging up a fortune in gold from a crowded river bank seemed far better than spending another day walking slowly behind a flock of sheep. So the shepherds left in their hundreds, their flocks were deserted and squatters thought they were facing ruin.

But the sheep were hardly affected. The squatter had no alternative but to let the sheep roam freely on the run, and to the squatter's surprise the sheep were no worse off than when they had been tended. Fences were built to contain them (indeed, this was the first use of fences on a large scale) and the days of shepherding were over.

The outstation that had consisted of two or more shepherds and a hutkeeper was now looked after by a solitary boundary rider, perhaps with the assistance of his wife. Instead of watching the sheep, the boundary rider checked the fences. He rode along a section of the fence each day and checked that it was still secure, repaired it if it was not, drove sheep out of the corners, laid poison bait for dingoes, checked the waters and returned at sundown after a ride of some 60 kilometres. The following day he checked a different section and so on until he had covered the whole of his area. He then started again.

Boundary riders were methodical men and worked to a routine that never varied. As Sorenson says in *Life in the Australian Backblocks*:

> He put his saddle always in one place, and when he brought his horse up in the morning he led him under the same tree, and hitched the bridle to the same limb, though there were twenty others equally as good and quite as accessible. You saw his mop for washing up hanging here, his tea-towel hanging there; and if you called six months after you would find them hanging in precisely the same places.

Unless he had his wife with him, the boundary rider was even lonelier than the shepherds. Sorenson describes one who played cards by himself. He dealt separate hands and made sure that a hand was never exposed to the rest, even though he was playing them all himself. Isolation also made the boundary rider more vulnerable to accidents. For example, in 1898 a boundary rider on

Mount Wood called M'Dermott was severely injured when his horse stumbled in a rabbit burrow. He tied a message to the neck of his dog and told it to go back to the hut, but the dog refused to leave him. Two days later a boy arrived at the hut with the rations and realised that something was wrong. He soon found the mare, which had returned on its own, and rode back to the homestead to raise the alarm. By the time they found M'Dermott he was nearly dead, with his hungry dog lying by his side with the message still around its neck.

Only two events broke the twelve-month routine on a sheep station: lambing and shearing.

Lambing was important because it increased the size, and hence the value, of the flock. When shepherds were looking after the flocks, ewes about to lamb were penned together for the night and in the morning the lambs and their ewes were placed in another pen. When the rest of the flock had left for the day, these lambs and ewes were allowed to graze close to the hut but were kept away from other groups that had lambed earlier. Each group of ewes and lambs was returned to the main flock after two or three days.

Lambing lasted about six weeks and the squatter might employ extra shepherds during this time. Great care was taken to make sure the lambs were well mothered and the ewes given any help they might need. Hand lambing by shepherds produced very high lambing rates, and this was often encouraged by a bonus paid for every lamb above 85 per cent. When shepherds were replaced by boundary riders the lambing rate might drop to between 50 and 80 per cent, but this was offset by the considerable saving in labour costs.

A few weeks after lambing finished the new lambs were marked, that is, they were castrated, earmarked, and had their tail docked. This was done quickly and with skill, so that a flock of 1000 might take no more than a few hours. Even then it was a controversial business, but experienced squatters knew how important it was. Joyce describes it:

> Our neighbour was prompted one year, by a feeling of humanity, to leave them with their tails un-docked, which gave them, curiously enough, a very unnatural and unsightly appearance and was so strongly objected to, both in the market and in the shearing shed, that our neighbour never repeated the experiment.

The tails were docked, then as now, so that the area of the breech did not become stained and so was less attractive to flies. Flies laid eggs on the skin of the sheep and this resulted in a loathsome mass of maggots that fed off the sheep itself. The wool became useless and the sheep lost condition so rapidly that death was inevitable unless the maggots were removed. The technique of mulesing, which consists of cutting the skin on the rump to produce a bare patch of skin as an extra precaution, is a comparatively recent development.

Shearing was the busiest time of the year on a sheep station and involved all the hands as well as the shearers. This was because each flock of sheep had to be brought into the woolshed for shearing. As the shed could not accommodate them all at the same time, and as the squatter did not want to have sheep off feed for more than two days, these movements had to be well planned.

Each flock could be moved only a short distance each day, so those which were to be shorn first might have to start for the shed days before the shearing started. Other flocks were brought in later, and those that had been shorn were taken back to their original paddock. Each flock spent no more time at the shed than necessary, for there was little feed there, and they were returned by a different route to the one they had come in by, so that there would be enough feed on the route for those still to come in.

For many years it was the practice to wash the sheep before they were shorn. Buyers expected to buy wool that was reasonably clean and in any case squatters were unwilling to pay high freight costs on wool made heavy by dirt and grease. Techniques varied, but most involved washing the wool while it was still on the sheep's

Shearing in Victoria in 1873. When using blades the shearer could work wherever he wished on the board instead of being confined to one position by a machine. The floor of sawn timber kept dirt out of the fleeces.

back rather than after it had been shorn. Joyce described the technique he used:

> The wash-pen, like most others at that time, was of logs laid across a convenient and suitable water-hole, and suspended across them by lashings were other and lighter logs to form square pens for holding the sheep during the operation and a race to pass them through, when finished, on to the clean grass. The race was always up-stream and was supposed to give them their final rinsing.
>
> The sheep would be thrown first from a small yard on the bank to the washers in the first pen, who stood on a suspended staging immersed up to their waists, and who rolled and manipulated the sheep to a certain extent, and passed them on, by dipping their heads under the spar, to the second pen of washers who finished them and passed them under another spar and up the race for exit on the grass.

A variation of this technique was called spout washing, in which water was poured over the sheep as if in a shower. This could be done by letting a dam overfill so that water ran over the top, or pipes could be placed halfway up the dam wall so that they ran with some pressure. The water might fall onto the sheep from a height of about 4 or 5 metres. Men stood in the washpool and held the sheep under the spout while they worked the fleece. The sheep then walked up a timber ramp to a holding pen. Another variation involved heating the water by means of a steam boiler.

Some stations in drier country washed the wool after it had been removed, a process known as scouring. The wool was soaked in large vats of soapy water and then rinsed by stirring it in clean water. It was then spread out to dry. In northern New South Wales and Queensland, where this technique was more common, public wool scours were established to carry out this operation on a large scale.

Eventually manufacturers preferred to wash the wool themselves. Wool that had been washed on the station still needed further cleaning by the manufacturer before it could be processed as there was a limit to what cold water could remove, and the use of hot water was limited to what a live sheep could stand. Washing therefore became part of the industrial process and stations then sold their wool in the grease. Until then, however, washing was an essential and time—consuming part of shearing.

Running a cattle station was significantly different from running a sheep station. Cattle were hardier, could walk longer distances for feed and water, had few predators and were generally well equipped for looking after themselves. Nobody thought they

Until late in the nineteenth century it was common to wash sheep before shearing them in order to remove dirt and vegetable matter from the wool. This time-consuming job came to an end when washing became part of the manufacturing process.

needed daily supervision as sheep did, so from the start cattle needed fewer people to look after them. One mounted stockman might be expected to look after 1000 head of cattle, and even in the 1850s there were not many stations running 5000 head.

Because there was no need for daily supervision there was less need for outstations. Instead, the station consisted of a number of distinct feeding grounds, where a mob of about 200 head had been bred and where they continued to graze. The mob rarely wandered beyond its own feeding ground, and indeed became so much a part of it that it could be difficult to remove them when they were sold.

The cattle were left to their own devices for much of the time. They were checked and counted now and again, but provided they were not struck by disease or drought they were left largely undisturbed until they had to be mustered. The fact that they had been undisturbed meant that cattle remained half wild. These were not friendly dairy cows that ambled gently to the bails twice a day, they were large beasts with most of their natural instincts still intact. Their horns, often more than a metre across and with needle sharp tips, were formidable weapons that were as likely to be turned on a person as on other beasts.

It is not surprising, then, that the stockman was of a different calibre to the shepherds he despised. The stockman knew he was different, and made sure the difference was recognised. The most obvious was that the stockman invariably used a horse, while those working with sheep usually did not. Thus his success as a skilled worker of cattle depended on how well he could ride, and from this developed a rather romantic view of the stockman's life. An uninformed observer might not understand how people were working cattle, but one could immediately appreciate that a rider was continuing to sit astride a skittish horse when most would have parted company with it.

This association with his horse, and the gear that he used with it, were part of the romance, but to the stockman they were simply essentials of his working life.

The saddle had evolved from those used in Britain, but by the time the evolution was complete it had little in common with them. The Australian saddle had a deep seat and high knee pads and could be used for long periods without discomfort to rider or horse. It was also quite different from the saddle used by the American cowboy. This saddle, which had come from Spain via Mexico, had a horn in front which held the lasso but the Australian stockman thought the horn was dangerous. Even the lasso was not popular although it did come into use later. When it did, it was secured to a strong ring in the surcingle.

Stockmen took great pride in owning a saddle. Indeed it was often one of the few things they did own. And craftsmen in country towns took great pride in making them, often in such distinctive styles as to make their origin unmistakable to those who recognised such things.

Stockwhips could be just as distinctive. At their simplest they were made from greenhide. The hide was cleaned of flesh, treated with salt and folded and left for a few days. The process was

Station hands working with cattle usually had a more vigorous life than those on a sheep station. Most of the cattle being yarded in this picture would not have seen people before they were mustered.

repeated and the hide pegged out to dry. To make a whip, the hide was laid on the floor and a knife stuck into it in the middle. The hide was then turned so that the knife cut a continuous strip of the correct width. Several strips were plaited to make the length of the whip. This was usually about 2 metres long and had a cracker fixed to the business end. Better stockwhips were made from kangaroo hide and these were prized by head stockmen.

Some stockmen became expert performers with the stockwhip—Rolf Boldrewood described one who rode at a canter then stood in the stirrups and cracked two whips simultaneously, one in each hand. Station owners preferred such demonstrations to take place away from their cattle, and experienced stockmen used the whip with care.

Some highly skilled stockmen became legends in their own time, especially those who worked in the outback. Two of these were Artie Rowland, who became head stockman at Innaminka station on Cooper Creek, and James Ledgerwood of Victoria River Downs. Unfortunately some stockmen had hardly any skill at all. W. Winter-Irving described one of these in his book *Beyond the Bitumen*: 'He was not particularly good at cattle work, his idea being to cut down an ironbark sapling, shape it into a weapon, and hammer the hell out of anything that wasn't going away from him fast enough.'

Cattle were mustered for several reasons. The most common was to sort them out so that calves could be branded and mature beasts taken to the nearest town for sale. But with cattle wandering over unfenced land without supervision they were liable to team up with mobs from neighbouring properties and then a group muster would take place so that they could be sorted according to ownership. Cattle were also mustered when the property was sold. This was usually a bang-tailed muster, where each beast had its tail cut as it was taken into the count thus making it impossible to count it more than once.

For the stockmen, mustering was the exciting part of a life that was often fairly dreary. It was difficult and dangerous work, but perhaps that is why they preferred it. The one certainty they could rely on was that these half wild beasts were not likely to give themselves up easily.

One method was to use coachers. These were fairly placid beasts that were used to being worked by people and horses and who had lost the wildness of the others. The coachers were taken into an exposed clearing and left to graze peacefully under the control of one or two stockmen. The rest rode off in their allotted directions and then turned to flush out the cattle to be mustered. When they

44

had a mob running they scouted for more until they had one large mob or several smaller ones on the move. They then steered them towards the clearing where the coachers were grazing. If all went well the wild cattle joined the coachers and settled down with them. But invariably some were reluctant to do so and these made a dash from the edge of the mob. They were chased by the stockmen and driven back into the mob. What made this dangerous was that it took place at full gallop across country that might be little known and which was riddled with gullies, creeks, trees and holes.

A slightly easier method, although only slightly, was to turn out the coachers on a moonlit night to graze near the water used by the wild cattle. The wild cattle used the water at night and hopefully joined up with the coachers. When that happened the stockmen came out of hiding and dashed across to cut off the retreat.

Not all musters were done with coachers. If the paddock was not too large and if there were enough stockmen, they started at one end and hunted across to the far end. Natural water provided the collection points and more beasts were run into the mob as it made its way across the country.

When cattle had been mustered they could be drafted (sorted) without the use of yards. While stockmen held the mob in a tight area, the drafter walked his horse into the mob and looked for the type of beast to be selected. Having found one, he worked it towards the edge of the mob until it could be separated from the rest and then handed over to other stockmen who supervised these smaller groups of selected cattle. This too could be exciting work but in settled areas with educated cattle it was much easier, as Anthony Trollope discovered.

> Two or three men on horseback, of whom I considered myself to be by far the most active, drove some hundreds of them into a selected corner of the paddock called a 'camp'. There was no enclosure, no hurdles, no gates, no flogging, very little hallooing, and very little work... the owner himself was the 'cutter out'. He rode in among the herd, and selecting with his eye some animal sufficiently obese for market purposes, signified to the doomed one that he should leave the herd... The beast went out and stood apart, till he was joined by a second selected one and then by a third... I had looked for racing and cracking of stock-whips, and horses falling, and some wild work among the forest trees. I would not knowingly have left my bed at four o'clock to see so tame a performance.

It might have been disappointing to Trollope, but stockmen in other parts of the country would have blessed their luck.

Branding and castrating were usually done in the yards, which

45

might mean moving the mob for many kilometres back to the station. Once in the yards the mob was drafted by the squatter or overseer. This was done by passing the beasts along the race and opening a gate according to the comment of the person doing the drafting. 'Store' meant that the beast was ready for sale, 'bush' meant it was not ready and would eventually be returned to its grazing ground, and 'calf' meant that it required branding. By the time this was finished each group was held in a separate yard.

When branding, a fire was lit outside the yard and the irons heated until they were red hot. In the early days the beast was caught by dropping a noose over its head. The noose was on the end of a rope which was attached to a long forked pole, called a roping pole. When the beast had been caught, the rope was taken around a post and the beast drawn up to it. The beast was held there and branded while still standing. In time the roping pole was discarded and the noose then became a lasso.

Ropes were used only on those beasts that were too big to be thrown. It was much quicker for two men to grab the animal at each end and throw it sideways onto the ground. The man at the rear sat down quickly, planted his feet against the under leg and pulled on the top leg with his hands while the other man applied the brand. It was better if the man holding the animal got up quickly when letting go.

Horses and working dogs were important on the stations although some stations depended on one more than the other. Cattle stations relied almost totally on horses whereas dogs did much of the work on sheep stations.

The first working dogs on Australian stations were either Smith-fields or collies but neither were very successful. Long hair was not suited to the climate and some dogs, such as the Scots collie, were good with sheep but hopeless with cattle. The problem was that they frightened cattle and were then too slow to catch them.

It was about 1830 that a drover called Timmins crossed a Smithfield with a dingo. The result was a type of dog called Timmins' biters. These were quieter than collies but their bite was dangerous to bullocks and almost lethal with sheep. Another variation was a greyhound/collie cross, known as the blue merle. The fault with these was that they insisted on working bullocks from the front as if they were sheep. A squatter in Muswellbrook in New South Wales called Hall crossed a merle with a dingo to produce the cattle dog known as Hall's heelers, but these were not much better. They attacked horses as readily as bullocks and refused to turn a mob when required.

Hall's heelers were improved by crossing them with Dalmatians, and when this cross was in turn crossed with the kelpie the result was the blue heeler, which became the standard breed for working cattle.

Meanwhile the kelpie had become the main breed for working sheep. The origin of the kelpie is still a matter of debate, but it is now thought to have originated in Scotland when a gypsy tried to breed a good poaching dog by crossing a working collie with a pet fox. The result was the fox collie. Some of these were brought to Australia and it is possible that they were then crossed with the dingo. One of these, a black and tan bitch owned by C. B. W. King of Wollongough station in New South Wales, won the first Australian sheep dog trials at Forbes in 1872. Her name was Kelpie and her progeny were much sought after. They were known as Kelpie pups, and that name eventually became the name of the breed.

Kelpies were tireless workers with sheep and the bush is full of

Branding cattle was a hazardous business. A mature beast has been caught with a rope dropped over his horns from a pole while another takes away the top rail of the yard in a bid to escape.

stories of their excellence. Ian McTaggart, in Willey's book *The Drovers*, describes how he and an old boundary rider were mustering sheep in a paddock when they noticed a mob of about 300 that had been missed. McTaggart suggested that he should get them while the other man rode on, but he was told that was not necessary. His dog could do that. And it did.

The development of the horse in Australia was a similar process of evolution and breeding to arrive at an animal that could work well in the climate.

Although draught horses were working in Australia in 1795, and carriage horses a few years later, it was a while before numbers increased. By 1800 all the horses in the colony were probably owned by less than twenty people. By 1816, however, horses were being bred for export to India and this was to continue for many years.

Although the horse adapted to Australian conditions fairly well, especially away from the coast, the quality started to deteriorate in the 1850s and this continued during the second half of the century. The tendency was for Australian breeders to breed out any distinguishing characteristics of imported horses, and the result was a plainness that eventually brought complaints from buyers in India. Committees were set up to improve the breeding and one of the results was the waler, which did much to restore the export trade.

The stock horse had emerged by the 1850s, but that was a description of an activity, not a breed. They had to have good acceleration and an instinct for working with stock. They were usually hardy geldings and their endurance was remarkable. The quarter horse is a comparatively recent development, and even the Australian stockhorse was not established as a breed until 1971.

Riding was developed as a high art by Australian stockmen, although it was hardly a classic style. They pushed their feet right into the stirrups and pointed the toes down, and held the reins, usually unknotted, in one hand and their whip in the other.

New stockmen were assessed by how they mounted their horse. They were expected to hold the reins and a clump of the horse's mane in their left hand, face towards the horse's tail, put their left foot in the stirrup, hold the front of the saddle and not the back, and swing easily into the saddle. If they mounted any other way they would be regarded with suspicion, and if they were young they were sent off to do repair work until somebody took pity on them and taught them to ride properly.

Once the station was in good working order the squatter found life a mixture of intense activity and monotonous routine. Although squatters had to be able to do everything themselves, good workmen relieved them of the need to do it, so that supervision became more important, and usually less interesting. T. P. Bernard, writing of his station near Yass in New South Wales in 1835, said:

> I visit my outstations, some of which are twenty miles off, every Saturday; when I give the men their week's rations, rest on Sunday, and return home on Monday. I generally rise before the sun, see my men get their breakfast and off to their appointed work; then mount my horse and look at my stock and crops...I have let my beard grow, for dandyfying would be here out of place.

Boredom and loneliness were as much a part of the squatter's life as hard work and many described how irksome they could be. This had nothing to do with idleness. With the shepherds watching their flocks by day there were long periods when the squatter had little to do. Curr lamented:

> Persons who have not had the experience of such situations will perhaps hardly realise how heavily time hung on our hands. We read a good deal, of course, but after one has done enough of that sort of work for the day, a weary portion of the twenty-four hours still remains to be got through. Besides, a hundred and fifty volumes do not constitute an inexhaustible supply of literary food. Conversation not infrequently halted a good deal for want of fresh subjects. Nor could it be otherwise, cut off, as we were, from the outer world. Around us was nothing but the same everlasting gum-trees basking in changeless sunshine, whilst the rarely-varied meal of tea, mutton and damper made its appearance on the table three times a day with such dyspeptic regularity that I used to loathe the sight of it.

It was the arrival of women in the bush that changed that. When the squatter married, his meals became considerably more varied and he usually built a better house to provide comforts which until then had seemed unimportant. The result was often dramatic. The wife of a squatter inland from Geelong wrote this for *Chambers' Edinburgh Journal* in 1842:

> Our station had now a great look of comfort about it. We had plastered the outside of our hut with mud, which made it quite close; we had windows and good doors, and a little flower garden enclosed in front; we had built a good hut for our servants, a new store, a large dairy under ground, a new woolshed, and had two large paddocks for wheat, potatoes etc., and we had now plenty of vegetables. We had also put up a larger stock-yard, as our cattle were increasing, and a large covered shed for the calves at night. .

A successful station was now more than a couple of rough huts and a set of yards and a woolshed. Now there were quarters and workshops for all manner of necessary tradesmen. Millers, smiths,

49

harness makers, carpenters, all were needed and in isolated areas had to be maintained full time as itinerants were unlikely to turn up when required. So the station was now a community containing 100 people or more, and its centre, next to the homestead, might be larger than the nearest town.

It might belong to the squatter, but it was not his alone. The station now provided a living for all these people, and their involvement was no less than his.

5

The station hands

MUCH of the legend that came to be associated with station life in Australia centred around those who worked on the stations rather than those who owned them. We have seen that those living in towns saw the early squatters as young men of high spirits who spurred their horses along quiet streets in a manner that was unthinkable of those who lived there. But as squatters devoted themselves to their newly established station they were seen less often in town, and as they grew older they were less dashing. They might, in time, become wealthy and influential, but they were no longer exciting.

Those who worked on the stations were exciting. There were more of them than there were squatters, many of them were young, and they lived and worked in areas that were remote, dangerous, and largely unknown to urban Australians. They had an air of independence, of freedom and a gutsy determination that was admired by those who worked in factories and did as they were told. Nor was this admiration misplaced. Most station hands did indeed possess the qualities that were credited to them. Romance and legend may have embellished these qualities, but the fact is that they were always there.

Squatters drew their labour from five types of people. There were the convicts and those who had served out their sentences to become 'time-expired'. There were those who had been born free in Australia but who, as we have seen, were not usually in a position to take up land when it became available. Although these two types were quite different in origin, in practice they had much in common and might be conveniently referred to as colonials. The third type was made up of free immigrants, those who had come to Australia in search of more opportunity but who also did not have the means of taking up land. The fourth type were the Aboriginals, who are described in detail in the next chapter, and the last type consisted of 'colonial experience' men who came to Australia with varying amounts of wealth and intelligence and who intended to take up land when they knew enough to do so. This type subsequently included native-born Australians and then became known as jackaroos.

The relative importance of these five types changed during the nineteenth century. For example, when the practice of assigning convicts to landowners came to an end in 1838 their role diminished and was taken over by others.

Squatters were major employers of labour. The 1857 census of Victoria showed that the pastoral and agricultural industries employed more than 37 000 people, which represented 16 per cent of the workforce. At that time the mining industry accounted for twice that amount, but by 1901 mining had fallen to 6 per cent and the rural industries had risen to 24 per cent of the workforce. It was probably higher in other states, as few had the industrial importance of Victoria at that time.

The squatters themselves remained numerically small. For example, the 1857 census shows that in the area of the Broken River and the lower Goulburn in Victoria there were about 400 pastoral workers, but of these only twenty were squatters.

At this time, colonial Australians (convicts, ex-convicts and native-born) made up about two-thirds of the pastoral workforce, and this remained true for a long time. Until about 1840 serving prisoners made up the largest part, but ten years later this role had been taken over by the native-born. This dominance of colonial Australians over newcomers occurred only in the bush. In towns the numbers were more evenly balanced and it is perhaps because of this that people thought that the bush contained the 'real' Australians. There were certainly more of them (however they might be defined) in the bush than in the coastal towns.

When assigned convicts had served their time on a station property they usually followed the same kind of work instead of returning to the coast. They were then free to work where they wished and moved around a great deal so that they formed a nomadic workforce on which the squatters relied very heavily. This is not to say that the squatters liked them. What the squatter looked for was a hand with the same qualities that he possessed, but he often failed to realise that those who had those qualities were more likely to want to make money for themselves rather than for him.

Many squatters even became exasperated with the time-serving convicts who were assigned to work on their properties, although they could not have developed their stations as they did without them. Under Bourke's regulations of 1835 a landholder was allowed one convict for every 65 hectares he grazed, and an extra man for every 16 hectares he had under cultivation, up to a limit of 70 people (including women, although rare). Squatters did not pay wages to these convicts but they had to maintain them according to a scale determined by the government. This required squatters to issue each convict 5.5 kilograms of wheat and a little over 3 kilograms of meat each week and to keep them in clothes. The ration was hardly generous and the quality was not subject to supervision, but in practice many squatters issued more than was required, as Harris described:

> Occasionally their master opened his heart so far as to give them a little tobacco, tea, and sugar beyond the allowance ordered by law. Altogether their cost might be about half that of free labourers; whilst between fear of being flogged and hope of getting a little indulgence in the matter of rations, their labour was nearly or quite equal—so that the master's clear gain was just the wages a free servant would have been paid over and above his ration at the same kind of work.

It was, indeed, in the squatter's interest to treat assigned convicts well, as this extract from Atkinson's *An Account of the State of Agriculture and Grazing in New South Wales*, published in 1826, shows:

Good stockmen were some of the most highly regarded rural workers.

The greater part of the settlers, however, allow their convicts a superior ration; being well aware, that, unless their servants feel that they are decidedly better off with their masters, than they would be in the hands of Government, they will invariably prefer being in the latter situation, where they have less labour to perform, and are less closely looked after.

When they used assigned convicts, the squatters became part of the penal system, and many took this role very seriously. Not only did they benefit from their labour and in return provide for them, but many squatters also thought they had to 'improve' them. They had a social role to perform, and some performed it with much vigour. One example was Thomas McQueen, who took up land in the Hunter Valley while still in England in 1823. In 1831 McQueen, then an English MP, was charged with corruption, jailed as a debtor, bailed out by his agent and immediately fled to France. It was from there that he left in 1834 to live on his considerable estate near Scone in New South Wales.

McQueen did not take long to become an expert on the treatment of assigned convicts. He wrote:

> After being sent on shore no time should be lost in forwarding the convict up the country to his assignment, where novelty of scene and occupation, the solitude of a shepherd, or the extreme labour of a farm, may create new reflections, and break up the habits of vice which have hitherto been his bane.

If that did not work, McQueen flogged them, saying that he made it a rule never to 'play' with corporal punishment, or happily herded them at night 'into a tunnel cut in a hillside'.

While McQueen might have been an exception in many ways, the view that station life was good for convicts was widely held, and with some justification. Curr, who had none of McQueen's excesses, wrote more thoughtfully and reliably: 'Station life not only put a stop to drunkenness and theft by the absence of grog and of anything worth stealing, but the constant absence of temptation had a tendency to throw the convict's mind into a better groove.'

Squatters like Curr realised that kindness was more effective than punishment and that the less they had to do with magistrates the better their hands worked. If they issued a generous ration and the occasional luxury the withdrawal of these benefits was often the only form of punishment they needed. While some squatters were inclined to be ferocious, most were not and the result was that most assigned convicts ate better and worked less than a free farm labourer in England.

When assigned convicts had served their sentence, or received their ticket of leave, they became a member of the free workforce, which consisted of others like them, the native-born and the free immigrant. The change was more or less dramatic, depending on how they had been treated as a convict. They were likely to still work on a station, but they could now drink more lustily when they had the chance and could say what they liked to the boss, especially if they were prepared to move on to another place.

Many convicts made the transition to freedom with great success, although not always quickly. Again, Curr described it from his experience as a squatter:

> After my men had realised that they were free, and found that circumstances had in great measure cut them off from drink, a desire for property sprang up amongst them; so that though the old custom of going to town once a year 'to have a spree'. . .did not go out of fashion altogether, it at least became modified, by the men investing a portion of their wages in the purchase of horses, guns, prime sheep, dogs, or something of that sort. As a rule the horse (or more often the mare) once bought was kept. . .

Unlike the squatters, most station hands were either serving convicts, time-expired or native-born Australians. These distinctions had little significance in the bush and the two men in this picture probably knew little of each other's origins.

Whatever their individual weaknesses might be, ex-convicts and native-born Australians were regarded as far superior station hands to those who arrived as free immigrants. Although their back-grounds were completely different, the ex-convicts and the native-born had this in common: they knew Australia, they knew something of pastoral life and because they did not have to adjust they became the cream of the workforce on the stations. Indeed, at a meeting on the Darling Downs held in 1850 to discuss the reintroduction of convict labour, one squatter said that he would rather have the pick of the gaols than the refuse of the workhouse.

Few migrants ventured into the bush and most preferred to remain in the towns even though they might earn a good deal less. Those who did go further afield were not much use, especially at first. As one writer said: 'The far bush is not popular with emi-grants. They are afraid, and prefer lingering at lower wages in the settled districts; if they get up, they are not of much use at first, lose your sheep and bullocks, and themselves. . .'

Not only were they useless, they were often argumentative and 'had a very faint idea of obeying orders'. The same could be said for colonial hands, and indeed their arrogance was a major problem for many squatters, but at least they could be relied upon to find their way home.

Squatters had to accept that their workers were far from humble. Colonial hands knew their importance and happily moved on if the job, the property or the boss did not suit them. Those who came as free migrants often did so to escape the restrictions of a class-conscious society in Britain. They had no intention of tugging the forelock in Australia.

Although wages fluctuated from time to time as a result of

changes to the economy or the supply of labour, they were nearly always significantly higher than in England. Farm workers in England could not afford to enjoy much of the food they helped to produce, but in Australia it was almost taken for granted. Samuel Sidney in *The Three Colonies* quotes a woman who had left the Scottish Highlands to settle at Bathurst:

> We have five children, my husband is a farm labourer, he gets twenty pounds a year; ten pounds of flour and ten pounds of meat weekly; the milk of one cow, a cottage with four rooms and a good garden, a piece of ground in which we grow wheat and millet; we have two pigs, eight cows, I don't know the number of poultry; we have milk and eggs for our own use; butter too, in plenty, for the family.

Indeed, in many cases the rations that were supplied to a station hand were worth more than a farm worker's wages in England, who then had to feed himself and his family.

The custom of supplying station hands with rations was universal in Australia. It was, of course, a legal obligation in the case of assigned convicts, but rations were also supplied to free people as part of their wages. As the station was the nearest source of rations, and as some were produced on the place, it was a natural and sensible procedure. Squatters were able to pay their hands partly with their own produce without having to send it to a distant market and paying a commission, and the station hands did not have to make their own arrangements to be supplied from the nearest town.

For the most part this system worked well, but it could fall down as a result of carelessness or greed on the part of the squatter. As Harris said:

> The Australian settler undertakes, as a matter of course, to supply his labourers with rations; but he never thinks there is the slightest obligation on himself to make that supply a constant one. Sometimes there is no tea, sometimes no sugar, sometimes no tobacco. When it suits his convenience to look after a fresh supply, he does so; otherwise all the free men on the farm may leave their work and lose their time in going ten or twenty miles to get it for themselves; and on men who are very much the slaves of tobacco or tea or sugar this bears in some cases very heavily.

Rations were also supplied to those who worked under contract, perhaps as builders, fencers or timber cutters. It was usual to stipulate in the contract for the work that the contractor would draw all supplies from the station store and the contract also stated the prices that would be charged. For example, when William Pitt Faithfull drew up a contract at Springfield in 1839 for clearing timber it was agreed that the two men would pay 9 pence a pound

British migrants were not highly regarded as station hands. Although some were successful, most were unable to adjust to bush life.

57

for flour, 6 pence a pound for meat, 5 shillings a pound for tea and 8 pence a pound for sugar. The cost of labour was therefore only a part of the deal. In this case the two men were paid 30 shillings for every acre cleared, but if the cost of rations had been greater then so might that rate. As the cost of rations changed, so did the cost of labour.

Squatters often complained that they could not get men to work on contract for them even though they were offering what seemed to be very generous rates. But experienced workers first wanted to know the prices they would have to pay for their rations and other supplies. These could be so high that they would largely eliminate the high wage rate and leave the contractor with a poor return for the work.

Greed was the problem here. Squatters knew that in practical terms they were the only source of supply and sometimes they tried to take advantage by including a very high profit. This was particularly so with goods, such as tea and tobacco, that they had to import and pay for. But contract workers had a finely tuned sense for such things and quickly determined what the net rate of the work would be. If it was not enough they refused the contract, even though the rate for the job might on the surface seem as generous as the squatter claimed.

If colonial station hands were more highly regarded than free immigrants, colonial experience men were thought to be the worst of all.

These were often from long-established and well-connected British families and had been sent to the colonies either because they were younger sons (and so would not inherit the family property in England) or so hopeless that even their own family thought life would be better if they were somewhere else. Whatever reason brought them to Australia the theory was that they would spend some time working on a station until they had learnt enough to run a place of their own.

Practically every ship arriving in Australia in the second half of the nineteenth century brought a fresh consignment of such men. They had all the superiority that the class structure in Britain could produce, they were socially accomplished and well educated, they had letters of introduction to the leaders of colonial society and some were excellent baritones. But few had any idea of what they were about and their capacity to adapt to Australia station life and to work hard was rarely very noticeable.

Even Anthony Trollope, who came from a similar background, found them embarrassing:

> I have said that the best of our labourers emigrate; but we certainly do not send to the colonies the best of our youth from Oxford and

Encroaching technology: an old boundary rider yarding sheep with a young assistant.

Cambridge, our most learned young lawyers, our cleverest engineers, or the most promising sons of our merchants and tradespeople. . . he is often listless, unenergetic, vain, and boastful.

Squatters often disliked colonial experience men as much as the station hands did. Even though squatters might themselves have arrived in Australia as reasonably affluent migrants from Britain they now had little in common with them. Their life in the bush meant that they were now closer to those who worked on their properties than to one who brought a set of values that they had long since forgotten.

It would be wrong to suggest that all colonial experience men were failures. Some acquired the knowledge they needed and went on to run their own place or manage a company property with success. But on the whole they were responsible for a degree of hostility towards people from Britain that lingered on in the bush long after they had disappeared. As late as 1909 C. E. W. Bean wrote that 'for some reason they seemed just to tolerate Englishmen in the bush. They used the word almost as a mark for incapacity'.

By then jackaroos had taken over from the colonial experience men. Jackaroos were likely to be native-born and younger and although not very competent at first, nobody expected them to be. While the colonial experience men earned dislike because of their attitude, jackaroos were treated like apprentices or officer cadets who might show promise but who were not yet fully skilled.

People worked in the bush for different reasons. For some it was a self-imposed means of removing themselves from drink or some other temptation that they suspected might eventually get the better of them. For others, it was a new start after an indiscretion elsewhere. People were not required to say any more about themselves than they chose, which might be very little.

Whatever the reason for being there, there is no doubt that station life was not only the best life in the world for those who could adapt to it, but it also changed those who experienced it for long. Those who had the qualities that suited this life found that those qualities developed even more. Courage, the capacity to work hard and survive in a hostile and harsh environment, all became central instead of peripheral.

Those who had these qualities could recognise them in others, and this recognition drew them together almost regardless of their backgrounds. Australian mateship is now a cliché, but it was an essential part of station life. Men depended on their mates, and if there was no mate around any bushman would do. The lowest form of social behaviour was to do the wrong thing by a mate. Stealing from somebody who was wealthy might occasionally be seen as excusable, stealing from a mate never was. Borrowing money and not repaying it was no great matter, unless it was to a mate. If behaviour of this kind became known, and it would, there was no appeal against the universal condemnation of the bush community. It would, in the saying, be a good day for travelling.

Successful squatters were as much a part of this community as their station hands, and this was another attraction of working in the bush. In the early days at least, squatters worked every day alongside their station hands, and many continued to do so for most of their lives. At the end of the day the squatter might return to the Big House and the workers to their hut, but nobody made great social statements out of that except the more foolish squatters. In the paddock or in the yards there was an equality that was uniquely Australian.

Station hands had other advantages over those who worked in towns. They had more freedom, for example. A man might be sent with a mate to do a job in a distant part of the station that might keep them out for days if not weeks. They were expected to do the job well and return when it was finished. Supervision was almost impossible even if it had been thought desirable.

Station hands were independent, sometimes to the point of arrogance, but they knew that they depended on others in many circumstances and that others depended on them. They were members of a shifting fraternity, and it was that fraternity as much as the squatters that developed the pastoral industry in Australia.

6

The Aboriginals

AS they tried to come to terms with the land they now worked, those who lived and worked on the stations soon realised that their relationship with the local Aboriginals was of more immediate importance.

Aboriginal society was based on a system of land use in which a group of Aboriginals was recognised as the primary owners of their region. Others might, by relationship, have some rights to hunt in the region but they were still expected to ask permission from the primary owners. Beyond their own region Aboriginals had no rights other than those that the primary owners might accord them through hospitality.

Within their region the relationship between the Aboriginals and the land was total. The land had been created by their ancestors who had then transformed themselves into features on the landscape. Aboriginals saw their ancestors in the hills, rocks and streams that were about them, and the topography of their region had a spiritual significance that the European was a long time in understanding.

What is surprising is not the subsequent conflict between Aboriginals and Europeans, but the vigour with which it was fought and the fact that it lasted until well into the twentieth century.

This was a war, although it is rarely described as such. It was fought on many small battlefields and it was fought in the bush rather than the towns. Occasionally urban Europeans feared that the Aboriginals would mount a combined attack with the intention of driving them back into the sea, but this was not how the war was fought. It was a guerilla war fought in the bush between Aboriginals and European settlers, civilians not soldiers. The Europeans received little help from the government. On the contrary

61

there were times when the government was hostile to the settlers, and urban Australians were largely unaware of how fierce and bloody the conflict was.

Although this conflict might now seem to have been inevitable, that is not the case. There was no prior intent by the settlers to annihilate the Aboriginals. Settlers went into the bush to take up land without military escorts and with no more equipment than they needed to survive in a harsh land. They did not take with them the trappings of war in the hope of achieving a speedy extermination.

There was no conflict in the use of the land itself. The Aboriginals were nomads who looked for water and wild food, while the Europeans sought to use the land for open grazing. These needs were not incompatible, and there are several examples of this. Thomas Chirnside, who took over a property in the Grampians in Victoria in 1842 after the previous lessee had been forced off by large stock losses to the blacks, made peaceful contact with them. Within a month he had twenty Aboriginals helping to wash sheep and later they worked on nearly every station in the area with no evidence of violence on either side.

What was in conflict was the concept of ownership. Aboriginals knew nothing of private ownership. Their weapons were the only thing they 'owned'. Everything else was provided by Nature and belonged communally to all in the region. Europeans, on the other hand, believed passionately in ownership. It was part of the foundation of their society, and certainly one of the reasons for the founding of Australia. Convicts were there because they had transgressed the rules of ownership and free people were there

A romantic, European view of Aboriginal life.

because it provided opportunities for ownership that were denied them in their homeland.

Conflict started over stock. The arrival of a flock of sheep was seen by the Aboriginal as another example of the vagaries of Nature, but one to be welcomed in the same way as the arrival of wild geese. That a person could claim to own each sheep was as preposterous as claiming to own the geese.

Europeans had no difficulty with this concept. They might accept that their claim to the land was tenuous, but they had no doubt who owned the sheep. They were theirs. They had bought them, bred them, and brought them here to graze so that they would produce wool and multiply.

Europeans saw their requirements as being quite simple and far from onerous. They wanted the blacks to leave their stock alone and to do their wandering and hunting somewhere else where it would disturb no one. But it was not that simple. Aboriginals could hunt only in their own region, they were tied to it and if they ventured elsewhere they would be trespassers and at considerable risk. Unable to move elsewhere, Aboriginals were faced with the choice of certain death by starvation as the wild food decreased in the region that had supported them, or a probable death in trying to drive off the settler. Not surprisingly they decided to take the slightly better odds against the settler.

The conflict that resulted lasted from a few months to several years, depending on the nature of the terrain and the number of Europeans in the area. The pioneer squatter, Edward Curr, who was a keen observer of Aboriginals, explained this in his book *The Australian Race*:

> When several squatters settle in proximity, and the country they occupy is easy of access and without fastness to which the blacks can retreat, the period of warfare is usually short and the bloodshed not excessive. On the other hand, in districts which are not easily traversed on horseback, in which the whites are few in number and food is procurable in fastnesses, the term is usually prolonged and the slaughter more considerable.

These local wars ended when the Aboriginals lost cohesion, and that was usually when there were no longer enough young males to continue the fight. Unable to resist any further, the blacks sued for peace. Squatters usually granted it by allowing the tribe to 'come in', that is, by allowing them to settle at an agreed site close to the station area. In due course the tribe worked on the station and in return the squatters provided them with the sustenance that had been deprived them by the squatters' arrival. Alternatively, squatters were sometimes unable to sustain the conflict and as their stock diminished to almost nothing they cut their losses and withdrew. So the line of the frontier ebbed back and forth as a result of these wars, although the general movement was forward rather than backward.

While the war was in progress there were no front lines. The Aboriginals were aware of the advantages that their numbers and knowledge of the land gave them. They made swift, silent attacks when they could be fairly certain of success and then withdrew to wait for the next opportunity. The Europeans were confused and frightened by the stealth, and wrongly described it as the unsporting action of a cowardly race.

The frequency and ferocity of these attacks are a matter of record. For example, the Tasmanian Aborigines Committee listed those that took place between March 1830 and October 1831, part of which read:

> 8 September. Captain Clark's shepherd attacked, but escaped.
> 13 September. One man killed and one man wounded by natives on the banks of the Tamar.
> 14 September. A man employed by government at the lime kilns, near Bothwell, chased by natives, but escaped.
> 18 September. A private, 63rd regiment, killed by natives; two sawyers speared, one of whom died of his wounds.

A similar record listing incidents over 'a few weeks' in the Port Fairy district in Victoria shows four men killed, eight wounded and the loss of about 3500 sheep and other livestock.

While these reports might have made urban Australians more aware of what was happening, those on the stations needed no reminders. In November 1838 John Hepburn was out washing sheep on his run in the West Coliban district of Victoria:

> About noon 30 natives came to the hut and asked Mrs Hepburn for powder for a musket they had. She sent one of her children to a convict hut keeper called George Cook. He loaded all the weapons he had and covered them inside Mrs Hepburn's hut, determined to defend it. Meanwhile Mrs Hepburn gave the natives some tobacco, which they threw away, and then some flour. The natives seemed friendly enough at this time and so Cook asked to inspect their musket. In doing so he opened the pan and drew his thumb across it to remove the priming. The natives did not notice. It saved his life for shortly afterwards the black with the musket laid it on top of a post and fired at Cook. It did not work, but Cook rushed for the hut as Mrs Hepburn came to the door carrying two pistols. Cook fired a shot over the heads of the fleeing natives, who in retreat took a mob of sheep and raided the men's possessions.

Because of their isolation on the outstations, shepherds were at great risk and usually in considerable fear. Alfred Thomson, who had a miserable time as a squatter in Victoria before returning to London, described it:

> Their fears magnified the danger to such an extent, that they lived in a continual state of anxiety, apprehension and alarm. The huts were loopholed to enfilade each other. They neither dined nor slept without their arms being within reach; the barking of a dog was a signal of danger which sent every man to his post; we had to place two shepherds with every flock, and when the hut-keeper went to the creek for water, a man was posted on the bank with a double-barrelled gun . . .

Meanwhile in 1838 Governor Gipps called for the protection of the Aboriginals and threatened severe punishment on those doing violence against them. In Gipps's first six years he found only ten Aboriginals guilty of crime and, in spite of the number of incidents, punished Aboriginals for only seven murders. Most were sent back to their tribes after being discharged by proclamation. The result of this attitude was described by Harris:

> Accounts of the disposition of the authorities travelled from Sydney to the out-stations; at the out-stations the extra-colonial blacks got hold of it; and presently, along the whole boundary line of the colony, the sheep are driven away, the cattle and horses speared, the men killed, and the stations driven in . . . Remonstrance after remonstrance was made to the authorities by the settlers, but all to no purpose. Indeed it was with worse than no advantage that these remonstrances were made; for they actually provoked only reiterated assurances from the authorities that the blacks should be protected . . .

It would, of course, be quite wrong to suggest that the only violence came from the Aboriginals, or that the provocation of convict Europeans was not sometimes the cause of it. Europeans were no less violent and at times equally ruthless.

In the winter of 1838 Henry Dangar's property at Myall Creek in New South Wales was managed by William Hobbs with the help of two serving convicts, who in May made friends with a group of about 40 Aboriginals and had sexual intercourse with some of the women. On 9 June a party of eleven armed men rode up to the hut. They were all convicts or ex-convicts except for their leader, who was native-born. Most of the Aboriginals were out on the property that afternoon with Hobbs, but of those who remained, 28 men, women and children were dragged a short distance from the hut and butchered to death by swords and knives. One of Hobbs's stockmen helped three young boys to escape, and two young girls were kept alive so they could be raped. The group of men spent the next day searching for more Aboriginals in the district and then returned to burn the bodies of those they had slaughtered.

Aboriginals regarded the arrival of stock as another example of the vagary of nature. Stock was legitimate game and the claim to ownership by the squatter was as incomprehensible as somebody claiming to own wild geese.

It is difficult to know how common such incidents were, but what made this unusual was that the outrage was reported to the authorities by Hobbs. The native-born leader escaped, but the rest were caught and seven of them were later hanged, to the fury of many in the colony who found it difficult to see guilt in what they had done.

It might seem that the possession of guns gave the Europeans all the advantage they needed to bring these wars to a swift conclusion. It is true that guns were an advantage, but they were not always decisive. Until 1850 guns were fitted with a flintlock mechanism, and they remained popular long after that. Unfortunately they were not very reliable. If the powder in the pan became damp the gun failed to fire— a flash in the pan'—and even if the gun went off the results could be very erratic. Hitting a person at 70 metres was a fluke. Hitting a person at 40 metres was possible with two out of three shots provided the person stood still long enough.

Curr learnt of these difficulties the hard way. One day both his guns became wet when he was out shooting ducks. On his return he was visited by two Aboriginals and he managed to hold them off with his guns until they left: After the Blacks had fairly gone I tried my guns, which both missed fire. Of course I was not long in drawing the charges, rubbing out, and reloading them. I had had a narrow escape, and took it as a warning which never required repeating...'

A skilled Aboriginal could throw a spear with lightning speed and considerable accuracy. That did not make it a match for a gun,

66

but if the gun failed to fire, or if the shot missed, then retribution could be very swift. The advantage was always with the gun, but it was not so overwhelming as might be supposed.

Some settlers preferred to respond by more stealthy means, by poisoning flour and waterholes. Stories of this kind are so numerous that if all were true the result would have been the total destruction of the entire Aboriginal race by these means alone. But although these incidents might have been exaggerated, there is no doubt that many did take place even if most accounts are second-hand. Two men in the western district of Victoria certainly made lead pills for the natives in 1837, but less certain is the story of a man at Port Lincoln in South Australia who is reputed to have filled a flour sack with equal amounts of arsenic and flour and then written a large sign on the sack warning that it contained poison. After many local Aboriginals died he was examined by a government official and then released. He had, he said in his defence, labelled the bag very clearly and it was hardly his fault if the Aboriginals could not read.

As the wars came to an end in the southern districts they continued unabated in Queensland, the Northern Territory and the Kimberleys as those areas came to be settled. Indeed, the sequence of events was practically identical whenever settlement extended into remote areas.

John Fraser had a property called Hornet Bank south of Rock-hampton in Queensland. After his death from pneumonia the pro-

Squatters and their station hands retaliated against Aboriginals for killing stock, and thus started a war which lasted for weeks or years, depending on the local terrain and how closely it had been settled by Europeans.

perty was run by his wife and nine children. During the night of 26 October 1857 the homestead was rushed by members of the Jiman tribe. All but one of the boys were clubbed to death and the woman and girls were tortured before they too were killed. The survivor was a fourteen-year-old boy who hid under a bunk. He later went insane.

In 1861 Horatio White, his family and his shepherds were clubbed to death on their property called Cullin La Ringoe, also in Queensland. Nineteen whites, including six young children, died and only one shepherd escaped.

In these, and many other cases in Queensland, retribution was swift and bloody and largely in the hands of the native police. This unusual force was originally formed in Victoria and consisted of Aboriginal troopers who revenged the killing of Europeans by carrying out punitive raids on the local tribes.

The Queensland force consisted of Aboriginals who had lost their land and sometimes their families. They had no kinship with local Aboriginals and were often merciless in pursuit of them. George Carrington, in *Colonial Adventures and Experiences* published in London in 1871, gave this account:

> On occasion, when their prey takes to the scrubs, they are willing enough to strip off their uniforms, all but their belts and cartridge boxes, and go in after them, when they seldom fail to give a good account of their errand. I have seen two large pits, covered with branches and brush, secured by a few stones, and the pits themselves were full of dead blackfellows, of all ages and both sexes.
>
> On another occasion, I was travelling along a road where for more than a quarter of a mile the air was tainted with the putrefaction of corpses, which lay all along the ridges, just as they had fallen.

A recent study of the massacre at Hornet Bank suggests that punitive expeditions mounted by the native police and squatters killed at least 150 Aboriginals, with the possibility that it was twice that number.

The blood lust for revenge was common in all parts of the frontier, especially after the killing of a popular squatter or when the dead included children. Sometimes it was restrained by those who even in those circumstances thought it unjustifiable, but on many occasions people rode out with the clear intention of 'teaching the blacks a lesson'.

The fact that some people did think it unjustifiable is a reminder that even at that time there were people who were sympathetic to the Aboriginals and thought they were unfairly treated. Many were people who had first-hand knowledge of them, such as George Dunderdale, who was a clerk of courts and customs officer in the western district of Victoria and in Gippsland:

It is absurd to blame the Aborigines for killing sheep and cattle . . .
Hunting was their living; the land and every animal thereon was
theirs; and after we had conferred on them, as usual, the names of
savages and cannibals, they were still human beings; they were our
neighbours, to be treated with mercy; and to seize their lands by
force and kill them was robbery and murder. This is the age of
whitewash. There is scarcely a villain of note on whose character a
new coat has not been laboriously daubed by somebody, and then
we are asked to take a new view of it. It does not matter very much
now, but I should prefer to whitewash the Aboriginals.

Thomas Learmonth, who founded Ercildoun station in Victoria in
1838, was proud of the fact that in spite of having a shepherd killed,
others attacked and sheep destroyed he had not been responsible
for taking a single life: 'moreover, I am free to confess that,
considering the wrong that has been done to the Aborigines in
depriving them of their country, they have shown less ferocity and
have exhibited the desire to retaliate less than might have been
expected.'

What, then, was the human cost of this war that went on for
much of Australia's European history? One study has suggested
about 1000 Europeans, Chinese miners and Aboriginal stockmen
were killed in Queensland between 1840 and 1897. In Tasmania
between 150 and 200 settlers were killed and about the same
number are thought to have been killed in Victoria. In trying to
summarise the figures in his book *Frontier* in 1987, Henry
Reynolds suggests that about 3000 settlers died in Australia and
about another 3000 were wounded.

It is much more difficult to determine how many Aboriginals
died. Their deaths were not always reported, for obvious reasons,
and not always witnessed. Reynolds suggests a figure of about
20 000 deaths, but says that it is little more than an informed guess
and the true figure could be much greater. It does, however, seem
more reliable than the usual method of subtracting the population
figure of Aboriginals in 1901 from the supposed population before
the arrival of Europeans. This leads to a conclusion that more than
200 000 Aboriginals died.

Even if this is true, it does not follow that they all died of
violence. Curr said that in ten years the number of Aboriginals
around his station fell from 200 to about 80, but during that time
only two were killed and one of those was the result of an accident. Nor was liquor the cause, as it was not in use by them during
that time. The reason, he thought, was disease that had been
introduced by Europeans.

Curr also makes the point that in his case it was impossible to
negotiate with an Aboriginal leader, even on a local basis, because
none existed:

69

When Aboriginal resistance came to an end the squatter allowed the tribe to 'come in'. Aboriginals were then allowed to camp nearby and in time many worked on the squatter's station.

Writers who have not lived in the bush...frequently describe in a very circumstantial way, and as a thing well known, a council of old men...who deliberate in company, and indeed govern the tribe. As a fact, however, as far as I could learn, nothing of the sort existed amongst the Bangerang. Usually, when matters of general interest were pending, it was the custom for anyone who chose to harangue the camp... I never heard of any special chieftainship or authority among themselves...

Even when the Aboriginals 'came in' the violence sometimes continued, and in the top end of Australia it went on until about the 1920s.

In 1895 two teamsters were attacked in the Jasper Gorge, near Victoria River Downs in the Northern Territory, by 'wild blacks' who were thought to have been encouraged by two blacks who were working with the teams. Both Europeans were wounded by spears, but they survived even though it took a month to get them to Darwin for treatment.

Even though incidents of this kind were not frequent, it was a long time before European suspicion of the blacks who worked for them diminished. As Reynolds says, one story that was almost universal described how a squatter was out with a trusted black who had been with him for years. Turning round, the squatter saw the black about to strike him a blow. When subdued, the black explained that he had experienced an uncontrollable urge to kill him, and it would be safer in future if he walked in front of the squatter. The story was published in the 1880s and has resurfaced with many variations ever since.

Although there is no doubt that some squatters exploited the Aboriginals who now worked for them, just as some had exploited their assigned convicts, others developed a good relationship with them that was based on respect and in many cases turned to affection. Unfortunately it is the excesses that are remembered longer, but good relationships were widespread and many Europeans who worked with Aboriginals or grew up with them on stations thought it a rewarding experience.

Black women and children were especially welcomed by the squatter's wife, who might have had no company since she left the coast. Kate Parker in New South Wales described in *My Bush Book* how she took in a half-caste waif, then a black child who had been half strangled by her mother, and then another girl who wanted to work for her: 'After this it became a camp fashion for mothers to dedicate their babies at birth to my service. It is fourteen years since I took the first three into the house; two of them I still have working, the third is married and on the next station.'

It is easy to be misled by a patronising air that seeps through many of these accounts, and exploitation then comes readily to the lips of some. But it is to ignore the fact that that is how people spoke of Aboriginals at that time. Kate Parker talked of her 'black-but-comelies', which came from a book by a missionary published in 1884, *Black but Comely, or Glimpses of Aboriginal Life in Australia*, which in turn was based on the Song of Solomon. If that is thought to be offensive, it was surely better than the *Bulletin*, which simply called them niggers.

Aboriginal stockmen were no less welcome. They already had highly developed bush skills that alone would have made them valuable members of a station, but to these were added an enthusiasm for cattle work which made them largely indispensable in the north. They rode well, were almost fearless, could detect cattle where none were thought to be and were never in danger of becoming lost. Europeans acknowledged that in many ways they were superior and paid tribute to skills that to them seemed uncanny.

In *Beyond the Bitumen*, W. A. Winter-Irving described how he looked for cattle in basalt country in Queensland with an Aboriginal stockman called Norman. Norman picked up cattle tracks by seeing no more than a broken twig, and from it knew that not only had cattle passed that way, but had done so within the last day or two. Later they crept up to a waterhole and Norman indicated there were two dingoes close to it. Winter-Irving read the signal that he was to shoot one of them and Norman would take the other. It was some time before he saw them for himself.

Norman looked at me, smiled, and nodded. The shot followed and I let go. Immediately another shot rang out from Norman, then a pause and another shot from him. . . . 'Nother one get away, we too slow to get him,' said Norman. Get away, I thought. I hadn't seen a sign of him. In fact, except for Norman I'd have had no hope of seeing any of the dingoes. I didn't even see the third one that Norman shot until it was dead.

Although Winter-Irving was still a young man he was an experienced bushman and was familiar with that country. When Norman asked him which way they should now go he looked around him before pointing the direction. No, said Norman, over there. Maybe ten miles. 'It was about ninety degrees from where I thought it was.'

Many Europeans learnt a great deal from the Aboriginals, others became experts in Aboriginal culture, or at least made the attempt. Many had a knowledge of them, acquired over many years, that was detailed and based on a genuine regard, but in time it was overwhelmed by those who claimed to know more and who were, it seems, more fulsome in their concern. But they were not usually from the bush, as Ernestine Hill explained:

> There are others, with far less opportunity, who appear to have been lucky in research. I have been twice round Australia by land, clockwise and anticlockwise, on varying routes in hard monotony of miles. I have been three times across it from south to north, many times east and west, and once by the diagonal, with spider-web journeys from almost every outback town as far as I could travel—all this apart from journeys by sea and air. I have spent months among some of the groups of natives, collecting vocabularies. . .and quietly looking for legend and lore. Yet never could I unearth stories one half so fashionably romantic as those I hear over the radio from Melbourne and Sydney.

In the same way, many who experienced the reality of the conflict between Europeans and Aboriginals in the Australian bush were surprised to find that their most vocal advisers and critics—the leaders of opinion, the true experts—were all in the towns.

7

The hazards

N O sooner had squatters established their stations on new land than it seemed that events were designed to drive them from it. The reaction of the Aboriginals was the most obvious, and often the most successful, but there were others which were less predictable and less obvious but which presented themselves as obstacles to be overcome before success could be claimed. Some of these events were natural, others the work of man, but they all tested the resilience of the squatters and those who worked for them.

One of these events was bushfire. The most ignorant squatter could see that Australia's hot and dry climate made fire a constant danger. Periodic growth was needed to provide feed for stock, but if it became too luxurious as a result of unusually high rainfall then the feed shrivelled in the hot winds that followed. The result was a thick carpet of tinder dry feed that covered the whole of the run. If it caught fire it was almost impossible to stop.

At first their defences were very limited, and it was a long time before they improved. Squatters depended on natural water for their stock, and also for fighting fires. The trouble was, in both cases, that they had few means of moving it. This meant that it was almost impossible to check a fire even when it was fairly small, especially if it started on a distant part of the run, and if the conditions were right it soon spread into a fire of devastating proportions.

An example of this occurred in 1845, when hot winds and dry weather continued in Victoria for three months. Alfred Joyce, in his book *A Homestead History*, said:

> The result...was that fires sprang up in every direction, travelling over the plains like a racehorse and sweeping everything before them. Our neighbour had 500 sheep burnt and nearly all his grass.

Fire was a constant hazard in the bush and people had little defence against it because of the lack of mobility and the difficulty of obtaining sufficient water. Most of the fight was concentrated on saving stock and buildings.

Others also lost sheep in considerable numbers. We were fortunate in that we lost no sheep, but three-fourths of our grass went.

The fires of 6 February 1851—Black Thursday—in Victoria were considerably worse. At 11 a.m. Melbourne had a temperature of 47 degrees Celsius. For six days fires raged from Western Port and the Dandenongs across to the Loddon and the Wimmera. J. H. Kerr included an account in his *Glimpses of Life in Victoria*:

> Among those who fell a prey to the flames was a shepherd, whose charred and lifeless form was subsequently discovered in a sitting posture reclining against a rock, and by his side his faithful dog, which had shared his master's fate. In another spot were found a woman and two children quite dead... There were many other deaths to swell the list of horrors, and many flourishing farming settlements were completely consumed with their homesteads, crops, and other scarcely completed improvements. The damage which had been wrought could hardly be estimated.

When a fire started on a station men formed a guard around the buildings and advanced towards the fire. They beat down the grass as they went and when they met the edge of the flame they tried to smother it to stop its advance. It was a desperate method and had little hope of success. Later, water carts were available which could be driven to the site of the fire, but the pumping had to be done by hand.

Fighting fires was a communal activity. Station hands received no extra pay for this as such encouragement was thought likely to produce more fires than might occur otherwise.

In his book *On the Wool Track*, published in 1910, Bean

describes how a 23-year-old manager left his station one Friday to drive 20 kilometres south to spend the weekend at the nearest town. On the way he saw smoke coming from a neighbour's paddock and drove 11 kilometres to see if he could help. He was told the fire was under control and he drove into town. That evening he received a telegram saying that the fire was spreading, so at 9 p.m. he started back for his station.

Some of his men had already left for the fire. He rode after them, leaving the others to bring up the water cart. All night a group of seven men fought the flames and by eleven the next morning they had them under control. They left the fire cart with the local men and returned home. An hour later they saw more smoke, this time from a different part of the same property.

They set off again and were the first to arrive. They fought the flames with water bags and when they could sent back two men for fresh horses so that they could bring the water cart from where they had left it. One of the men left the homestead with a led horse and returned with the water cart at 11 p.m. He was ordered to rest, so it was not until 2 a.m. on Sunday morning that he left for the fire. There, the men had fought it all through the second night and by the middle of the day they were at last able to leave it. Bean says:

> Now reflect on this. Neither of these fires was on the property on which either that manager or those men worked... They fought and galloped for forty-eight hours continuously—as a matter of fellowship; thrashing the flames till they were blacker than sweeps; rushing in upon the fire for a few moments and then retiring choked and breathless. Their clothes were burnt. The hair was singed from their faces... And most of those men would wonder why anyone

Rabbits could reduce the carrying capacity of the land by half in good seasons, and to nothing in the bad. Many squatters and station hands fought the plague for the whole of their working lives.

should bother to tell about it. For though it is fighting as hard as most in real warfare, there is nothing in it that is out of the day's work in the bush.

Droughts were less dramatic, but were just as destructive. And if squatters had few defences against fire, they had none at all against drought.

The start of a drought can only be determined afterwards. It starts as a dry spell which then goes on longer than usual and which eventually looks as if it will never end. As it developed the squatters watched as their natural water started to disappear. What had been a running creek became a series of waterholes, and as the drought continued even the waterholes started to dry out. In the early days there was no way squatters could bring water and feed from elsewhere. Their stock died, and there was little they could do other than watch.

In inland areas droughts were almost constant. A few good seasons might make the country attractive and people would move in with sheep and cattle, but as the season turned and the waters dried up the attempt to settle the land was defeated and they left with little to show for their effort. It was, in any case, impossible even at the best of times to plan more than a few weeks ahead. At least one squatter in western New South Wales saw his flock drop from 100000 to 6000 in two years.

Dunlop station on the Darling, owned by Samuel Macaughey, had four good years before the rain stopped in 1893. That year Dunlop shore 276300 sheep and marked 92000 lambs. The following year it lost 90000 sheep in the drought and lambed less than 2000. Between 1900 and 1909 there were never more than 100000 sheep on the property. In central Queensland, Lansdowne had been running more than 100000 sheep but by 1902 they were reduced to less than 40000 and produced only 700 bales of wool whereas twenty years earlier they had been sending away more than 2000. The new manager who took over in 1898 stayed for five years and the property was in drought for the whole of that time.

The effect of drought was not confined to the stations. Transport of goods depended on animals, who in turn depended on water and feed along the track. Dry spells made travel precarious and drought eventually made it impossible. Mrs Meredith in *Notes and Sketches of New South Wales* described Bathurst in the drought of the early 1840s: 'Every article of food was extremely dear, and nothing could be procured at any price. Meat was lean to starvation, and flour liberally adulterated with various cheaper ingredients; vegetables there were none; butter and milk had long been but a name...'

Coastal areas suffered less, and most urban Australians had little understanding of what those in the bush were experiencing. Bean not only described the effects of a drought at Bourke, but also how great the gulf was between those who were there and those in the towns: 'The grass had long since disappeared, the face of the country was shifting red and gray sand, blowing about wherever the wind carried it. The fences were covered; dead sheep and fallen trunks became sand hills. Millions of trees were killed; the birds had been dropping dead.'

The town received a visit from the Premier and a deputation met him to ask for a few more concessions in rail freights.

> When they had pretty well finished he suddenly looked up. 'What do you do with the country in these parts?' he said. . . They were a little surprised. They had just been telling him for three-quarters of an hour. But they said: 'Oh, well, we put sheep on it—that is, when there is any grass on it. . .' 'D'jever think of dairyin'?' asked the Premier.

The alternative to having no water at all was often to have too much of it. Droughts were often followed by higher than usual rainfall which produced floods, but they also occurred at other times and in places which seldom experienced severe drought.

Floods were not usually as serious as fire or droughts as they were generally more localised and did not last long. They also brought some benefit to the land. The immediate danger was to livestock and people. Alfred Joyce described the effect of flooding in 1845. After a run of good weather the rain came and he had his hands bring the lambing flock inside for protection. Some were put in the shed and others were yarded nearby. Then:

> We were roused by a shout that the flood water was rising in the sheep-yard, and on going out we found that we ourselves were on an island, the water surrounding us. To get to the sheep we had to cross a gully up to our waists in water before we could let them out and shift the fold further up, and then go back through the water again and get another change before turning in. On turning out in the morning and viewing the disaster we found that about sixty lambs had perished with the cold and wet.

But floods could be much more destructive than that. In 1863–64 the Darling flooded to a level that had not been experienced before. Sheep were swept away and homesteads isolated, but the resulting feed and full waterholes led to a rush to claim nearby land after it receded.

In 1882 Cooper Creek rose more than 12 metres and the manager of Innaminka station found that he could row a boat to every door of the homestead. Elsewhere, two stockmen were cut off for days by the rising water. By the time they managed to get their cattle out the mob had been standing in mud and water for

Rabbit-proof fences were built over enormous distances to contain the spread of rabbits. This photograph shows part of a fence in Western Australia.

nearly a month. They recovered 400 head, but the rest, 700, were drowned.

Apart from natural disasters of this kind and theft by Aboriginals, the most serious danger to the settler's stock was disease. As an isolated country Australia was less vulnerable to disease than European countries, but nevertheless there were a number of significant epidemics that decimated stock and ruined settlers. Anthrax broke out in the late 1840s in Queensland, New South Wales and Victoria, but ten years later it had been contained as a result of burning carcasses and crude innoculation. More serious was pleuropneumonia, a respiratory infection of cattle that broke out in Portland, Victoria, in 1858. Two years later the disease had spread through Victoria and New South Wales and a million head of cattle had died. It was brought under control by slaughtering herds until two doctors in Brisbane developed a method of innoculation in the 1880s.

In the 1830s catarrh seriously affected sheep flocks. Catarrh was a type of pneumonia which produced serious loss of condition and which was nearly always fatal. There was no known cure and infected sheep had to be killed and burnt.

Even more serious was scab. Now that it has been eliminated scab has been almost forgotten, but in the middle of the nineteenth century it was the most important single threat to the Australian sheep flock. The disease came from a tiny mite which attached itself to the skin of the sheep and caused oozing and scabs. What made it particularly virulent was that the mite remained alive even after it had left the animal, so that it survived in grass or even on rocks while waiting to attach itself to another sheep.

The discovery of scab in their flocks usually filled squatters with such dismay that the only alternatives seemed to be to sell the place and stock for what they would fetch or to face certain ruin. When Alfred Joyce discovered scab in his flock in 1853 he wrote:

> So I left George with the understanding that the concern was to be sold as soon as possible unless some other means of extricating ourselves from the difficulty presented itself in the meantime. The alternative was gloomy enough; to think that after striving for ten years...and just as I thought myself getting comfortably settled, I should have to give up all, or nearly all, and commence life again, was certainly disheartening, and yet it seemed that unless we got rid of it quickly we should have very little to commence again with.

The difficulty was that there was no known cure. Squatters treated their sheep by either scarifying them or by dipping. Scarifying consisted of scratching the infected part of the sheep with a sharp comb so that the skin was broken and blood came to the surface. A mixture containing salt and anything else thought to be effective was then rubbed in so that it penetrated the skin. The trouble was that this method was likely to kill a weak animal, and in any case it took as long to carry out as it did to shear a sheep, and so was virtually impractical.

Rabbit-proof fences were successful provided they remained secure. Boundary riders such as this one were employed to inspect the fence constantly over a certain distance and to keep it in good condition.

Dipping was easier and safer, but no one knew what to dip them in. Joyce tried lime and water but found it useless. He then tried a mixture of arsenic, sulphur, tobacco and salt but found this very expensive and not very successful. New recipes for dips appeared constantly, such as one recommended by a country doctor in Victoria which consisted of 50 kilograms of flowers of sulphur, and 25 kilograms of quick lime boiled up in 450 litres of water.

The successful cure, when it was discovered, was close to that used by Joyce and consisted of a dilute mixture of tobacco and sulphur. This dip was made compulsory in New South Wales in 1865 and it was illegal to use any other treatment. The result was spectacular. Within three years scab had been eliminated in New South Wales, and shortly afterwards elsewhere. But the toll had been very high. Out of a flock of 10 000, for example, Joyce lost 2500 within a matter of weeks.

Later in the century and further north a cattle disease appeared that was to be almost as devastating. It was caused by a small bloodsucker no bigger than a bug—the cattle tick—and the disease it caused was redwater fever. The tick was first noticed in 1880 at Glencoe in the Northern Territory and the fever killed half the stock there within a week. The following year it was on the Roper River and it quickly spread east and west until by 1883 it was across the Queensland border in one direction and approaching the border of Western Australia in the other.

Many people gave up in the face of the disease. Dr Browne sold Newcastle Waters and obtained only 3 shillings and 6 pence a head for the stock, while the North Australia Pastoral Company gave up 26 000 square kilometres of country in one day. Those who had to stay watched their cattle die, and cattle that lived were prevented from reaching markets because of quarantine laws.

Fortunately the cure, when it was found, was relatively simple. It consisted of running the cattle through a dip of carbolic acid and then innoculating them. But it was less simple in practice. Cattle in the north were not used to being yarded, let alone being made to swim through a dip, and the action was often fast and very furious.

As if this was not enough, there was by now a plague on most of Australia which was of Biblical proportions. It was the rabbit. Relatively harmless in Europe, in Australia the rabbit became so uncontrollable that only modern science was able to contain it.

Domestic rabbits that arrived with the First Fleet were all eaten and some imported by King from the Cape remained placidly around Sydney. In the mid 1820s domestic rabbits were being kept by settlers in Tasmania, but these were no threat either. A settler in South Australia released rabbits on his property in 1854 and although these went out of control they were soon mopped up by dingoes and did not spread far.

Then in 1859 Thomas Austin imported wild rabbits from England and turned them out on his property of Barwon Park near Geelong. The original twelve breeding pairs multiplied and three years later Austin was hunting them for sport. By the time the Duke of Edinburgh visited the property in 1867 he and four friends were able to shoot more than 200 rabbits by simply waiting for them to pop out of their burrows. A few years later Austin's property had been eaten out even though he had killed more than 20 000.

From then on the invasion was rapid and relentless. They were in the western districts and the Wimmera by the end of the 1860s. They reached the Murray in 1872, fourteen years later they reached Queensland and by 1894 they were at the border of Western Australia. The effect was serious in some areas and quite disastrous in others. In good times rabbits could reduce the carrying capacity of the land by half and in bad times they reduced it to almost nothing. In a parliamentary debate in 1883 the Victorian Minister of Lands described the effect on the Mallee:

> The rabbits began to invade the district in 1876, but the effect of that invasion was not seriously felt until 1877. In the following year the abandonment of runs commenced, and since then no less than 62 once prosperous runs, each carrying from 20 000 to 40 000 sheep, have now been absolutely abandoned. . . And name after name might be given of persons who have lost enormous sums of money through their flocks not merely being decimated, but obliterated altogether.

The most effective method of controlling rabbits at that time was by poisoning their water with strychnine or arsenic, but this had to be done carefully and the water had to be securely fenced off so that it could not be used by sheep. Because of this the poison cart became more popular. This ingenious machine consisted of a hopper that was filled with a phospherised material. A belt drive from one wheel of the cart forced this material out of the hopper in a continuous length about as thick as a finger, and a knife automatically cut this into short lengths. These were dropped into a trench cut in the ground by a knife on the bottom of the cart.

In 1894 Otway Falkiner spent £120 000 in the fight against rabbits on his famous property of Boonoke near Deniliquin in New South Wales. One of his sons wrote later: 'One of the worst jobs I had to do was to clean out the rabbit bays along the fences. Dead and stinking rabbits were waist-high around me as I worked.'

This battle went on until the discovery of myxomatosis, and is still well within living memory.

By contrast, the dingo was less serious. One reason was that they had always been in the bush and their population varied only with the nature of the seasons rather than exploding by sudden adaptation. They were a danger to lambs, and this is why shepherds were at first thought to be essential. Later, dingoes were kept down by highly skilled doggers who laid strychnine baits, used guns or set traps. Fences, both on the properties and along state boundaries were effective so long as they were well maintained.

Nor was the dingo the major predator that the squatter had to face. That was, as usual, man himself. Man the predator took two forms of activity in the bush, and indeed sometimes combined them. One was bushranging and the other was cattle-stealing.

Bushranging, that most typical of Australian activities, was a rural activity. Crime was not uncommon in the coastal towns but that is not where bushranging flourished. It flourished on bush roads and occasionally within station homesteads. Travellers were not safe, and neither was the mail. Indeed the loss of mail became so common that people sending cheques by mail cut them in two and sent them a week apart.

Stations were particularly vulnerable to bushrangers. Even if there was not much money there the bushrangers were attracted by the horses, often of very high quality, which could be used or sold. In 1865 four of William Pitt Faitfull's sons drove out of Springfield on their way to Goulburn, but as they turned onto the main road they were accosted by Ben Hall and two of his companions, who fired two shots to make them stop. Instead of doing so, one of the boys whipped the horses to a gallop and drove them across a paddock towards the homestead while one of his brothers returned the fire. When they were stopped by a fence, this boy urged the others to run while he covered their retreat. After firing his last shot, he too ran for the house and the bushrangers retreated. Some 94 shots had been fired in the encounter and the only casualty was one of the bushranger's horses.

An even more dramatic encounter took place in Victoria later that year. After a long career as a bushranger in New South Wales, Dan Morgan crossed the Murray to look for a man in Victoria with whom he wished to settle an old score. Failing to find him, Morgan robbed a teamster near Benalla and the following day rode towards Peechelba station. He ordered two station hands to accompany him to the homestead. Once there, he ordered the family and servants into one room and demanded tea for them all. When a child in the house started to cry, Morgan allowed the squatter's wife to leave the room to attend to it. Instead she sent the nursemaid to alert the police in Wangaratta.

Morgan spent a pleasant evening listening to the squatter's daughters take it in turns to play the organ. Eventually he allowed the women to leave, but kept the men in the room with him. By then the police were in hiding outside.

At eight in the morning Morgan, pistol in hand, drove the men out of the house and they started to walk to the horse paddock. Near the gate the men split into groups, leaving Morgan separated for an instant. It was enough. One of the policemen fired a single shot and Morgan fell to the ground mortally wounded. Before he died he complained that he had not been given a chance.

While contact with bushrangers was always a possibility, contact with cattle thieves was almost a certainty. Cattle-stealing was universal in the bush and even people of undoubted integrity in every other respect were not above keeping cattle that they knew were not theirs. But at least that passive form of theft was likely to balance out in the end, for what could walk through a fence in one direction was likely to be passed by others walking in the opposite direction. Others took a more active line and searched runs for stray cattle to stock a new property.

None of this was regarded very seriously. Rolf Boldrewood described this attitude in *Robbery Under Arms*:

> Any man might take a turn at that sort of thing, now and then, and not be such a bad chap after all. It was the duty of the police to catch him. If they caught him, well and good, it was so much the worse for him; if they didn't, that was their look-out. . . And a man that wasn't caught, or that got turned up at his trial, was about as good as the general run of people; and there was no reason for anyone to look shy at him.

Cattle-stealing was carried out on a bigger scale than that, and perhaps the most famous case was that of Harry Redford. In March 1870 Redford and four associates (two of whom left him soon afterwards) yarded about 1000 head of cattle on a remote part of Bowen Downs station in central Queensland and then walked them off. Helped by good seasons, they drove the cattle south to Cooper Creek on a 2500 kilometre treck to Adelaide over country that had hardly been seen by Europeans.

Meanwhile a stockman on Bowen Downs, William Butler, noticed the tracks and reported the loss. He was ordered to follow them and when he reached Walleldine in the north-east of South Australia he recognised a white stud bull which Redford had sold there. The rest of the cattle, which Redford had sold further down, where soon identified. Redford was arrested and stood trial at

The four sons of William Pitt Faithfull who fought a running battle with Ben Hall, John Gilbert and Johnnie Dunne on Springfield station in 1865. Nearly eleven years later the government presented them with gold medals for their gallantry.

Roma in Queensland. In spite of overwhelming evidence the jury returned a verdict of not guilty, to the fury of Judge Blakeney, who told them acidly, 'I thank God, gentlemen, that this verdict is yours, not mine.'

This was certainly not the only incident of cattle-stealing on such a scale. Ten years later 500 head were stolen from Bulloo Downs in western Queensland and driven down the Darling and Murray Rivers before being sold to an agent at Morgan in South Australia. The thieves were not caught, but the owner of the station tracked them as far as Morgan and then hurried on to Adelaide where the cattle were to be sold. He subsequently was able to prove ownership and received the proceeds of the sale, to the undoubted fury of the agent.

Stealing calves was relatively easy and this activity, known as poddy dodging, was practised on a wide scale. An unbranded calf could not be claimed by anyone, and once the thief had put his own brand on it there was no way to prove that it was not his.

Mature beasts that carried a brand could be identified unless the thief 'faked' another brand. This was done by covering the existing brand with another so that the new brand, while retaining the features of the original, was undoubtedly different. Among the fraternity, designing a cross brand to serve this purpose was a high art, and the experts were very scornful of those who used a hot frying pan to botch the original. Thomas Elder's famous E brand was perhaps even more famous than he realised because it could be easily converted to a B, or have a reverse B added to it or made into a double B. The brand of Ord River, 055, was almost an insult to the professional. It could be converted with little effort into any combination of B, P, Q and 3 and 8.

With such a catalogue of potential hazards it might seem that a squatter would be called on to face only a few of them in one lifetime. But that was not so. Nearly every squatter experienced fire, drought and flood, coped with stock disease, fought rabbits and lost stock to thieves. The least likely was to be accosted by bushrangers, especially in Queensland where they were not common, but even that was not impossible.

Some squatters were driven off their land by these misfortunes, but even those who survived were very familiar with them. They were an inescapable part of running a station.

8

Making it pay

WHILE most squatters enjoyed the freedom and independence of life in the bush, that is not why they took up land. They were the benefits, not the reason. The reason was to make money.

Almost from the start the station and stock represented a considerable investment, not only in effort but in hard cash. No matter how wealthy a new squatter might be, a profit had to be made in order to survive, and if the squatter was not very wealthy a profit had to be made fairly quickly. Running costs were high and if the income did not exceed the costs the station would fail. This was no different from any other business, but the point has sometimes been overlooked since. Squatters were not there to preserve the land, to employ labour, to look after Aboriginals or to improve the standard of breeding stock. They were there to make money. They would preserve the land, employ labour and so on only while those things were not in conflict with profit.

Nor is that as mercenary as it sounds. Squatters have often been described as ruthless seekers of fortune, prepared to sacrifice anything, and especially the land, for that ambition. Perhaps some did. But the squatters were there on their own account and financial success was the only means of staying there. There were many factors likely to drive them off their land and the only thing that could protect them was profit. Even that did not guarantee survival, but without it the squatter was finished.

The economics of running cattle were relatively simple. Until the last quarter of the nineteenth century there was no way of exporting meat and the produce of a cattle station was limited to the Australian market. At first squatters walked their cattle to the nearest town and took their chance in the saleyards. They were often at the mercy of wholesale buyers who might have decided collectively to bid no higher than a certain level, and they were certainly vulnerable to oversupply. But at least squatters had a product that could be sold at any time. If they had beasts that were ready for the market they could sell them if it suited them. If it did, they took them to the market and came home with the money.

Squatters were also vulnerable to bad seasons and disease. They could do little about disease, but they could protect themselves against the seasons by establishing runs in different parts of the country. Or they could if they could afford to do so. The most obvious examples of this technique were Tyson and Kidman. Tyson established a string of stations in areas of high rainfall, while Kidman did the same further inland.

The advantage was that they could move stock from one property to another as the season dictated. Squatters who did this have often been criticised for 'raping the land', for moving stock onto a property and then grazing them heavily until the land was exhausted and then moving them to do the same elsewhere, thus leaving a trail of destruction behind them. It may have been so, and to a casual observer it would certainly have looked so. But it may have been no more than sensible husbandry. The station was used because the season had provided it with the means of supporting stock. When the seasons changed and the carrying capacity was reduced the stock had to be moved elsewhere. In this case it was not that the stock had eaten out the country, but that the country could no longer support the stock. At that point the country would certainly be damaged if the stock remained. They

Unlike wool, selling cattle was relatively easy: the squatter took them to the nearest town and came back with the proceeds. The journey might be difficult and the prices depressed, but at least it was quicker than sending wool to London.

were moved for economic reasons to be sure, but moving them also lightened the demand on the country and gave it a chance to revive when the seasons improved. It was grazing by rotation, albeit on a massive scale.

A large amount of capital was needed to acquire enough stations to make this work, and for this reason large pastoral companies were formed and capitalised for the purpose. Although many of those companies subsequently took up sheep properties, the economic benefits were less and most sheep stations continued to be owned by families rather than companies. Nor is that to suggest that all cattle stations were eventually owned by companies. Obviously they were not. Many were privately owned by the people who had founded them and who managed to survive without the benefit of large capital.

The economics of running sheep were more complicated than cattle. Sheep required more labour, which was a continuous cost, and the income came from the sale of wool and surplus stock. Surplus stock could be sold at any time (although the price varied enormously), but wool could be sold only once a year. This presented a cash-flow problem of some magnitude, especially in the first few years, and explains why squatters without capital were rarely successful. Even those with money usually had to raise more, and those without had to raise nearly all of it. The level of this debt was of great significance in the profitability of the station.

With wool prices consistently high until the late 1830s, many who started before then did very well in a short time and this led others to believe that making money from sheep was easy. But as prices fell and costs remained the same, many became disillusioned.

When Curr started in Victoria in 1841 his running costs for the year were £1071 15s. He expected to produce about 2½ pounds of wool from each sheep and this would result in an income of £262 1s, leading to a deficit in the first year of more than £800. In fact, by the time he had completed his first shearing he had lost £1000, the value of the property had dropped and he was unable to sell his lambs. He did not, however, have any debt and in time, and after moving to a better property, Curr became moderately successful.

Another set of figures was provided by Hodgson in his *Reminiscences of Australia*. He invested just under £8000 in stock which included 20 000 sheep. His costs for a year were £3058 6s 4d, which included interest on the cost of the stock of £632 13s. In return he received some £3000 for his wool. From this two important points emerge. The first is that in his first year he had invested £11 000, which was not all his, and had a deficit at the end of £8000. Nevertheless, given good seasons, no disease and good prices he could

87

expect to recover this in the coming years and then start to show a profit. The second is that the income from the sale of wool was roughly equal to his running costs for the year.

This was one of the fundamentals of running sheep. Rachel Henning, in a letter written from her brother's station in Queensland in 1865, said: 'When a station is in working order, the improvements etc. done, the price of the wool is supposed to pay all the expenses, and the increase of the sheep is the squatter's profit. . . Therefore a bad lambing destroys his profit.'

A flock of, say, 15 000 sheep would contain about 7000 breeding ewes and a lambing of 70 per cent would result in an increase of 5000 sheep. If the squatter eventually decided to sell them about £3500 would be received although that could vary considerably depending on the market. The original flock would have cost about £15 000, so the return on the sale of the surplus was about 20 per cent. This was reduced if money had been borrowed to buy the flock in the first place and a return of about 10 per cent was more likely. If the return was applied to reducing the debt, eventually an annual profit from the sale of surplus sheep of the full 20 per cent was possible. This was in theory, for it depended on the squatter selling all the increase at stable prices, on a constant lambing of 70 per cent from a flock that did not diminish, and on the sale of wool covering the running costs for the year.

The price received for wool was therefore crucial to the squatter's success. With a flock of 20 000 sheep a difference of 6 pence a pound in the price meant a total difference of about £3000, up or down depending on which way the price moved. As Trollope said:

> It will at once be seen how rich the poor man may at once become by such a change in the circumstances of the wool trade. And it will be seen also how speculative and precarious such a business must be. The wool-grower in Australia watches the price list in England with an intense and natural anxiety. He can do little or nothing to regulate the market. He cannot understand why it is that the fluctuations should be so great. But he obeys the market, too often with an implicit confidence that it does not deserve.

The squatter could sell wool in Australia or send it to the London sales. At first most wool was sold to dealers who waited to meet it on the outskirts of town, but as the number of squatters grew this became impracticable and firms were set up by people such as Thomas Mort and Richard Goldsbrough to handle it on a larger scale. Wool sold locally was eventually sent by the buyer to the London sales, who hoped to make a profit in the process. The benefit to the squatters was that they received their money much sooner than if they sent it there themselves.

This needed fine judgment, although if the squatter needed

money quickly there was little choice. What made it difficult was that news of wool prices was already three months out of date by the time it reached Australia, and if wool was sent immediately to London it would be three months at least before it was sold. Trollope thought that if prices were low it was better to send the wool to London, and if they were high 'he had better take the ball at the hop, and realise his money in the colony'. The opening of the Overland Telegraph Line in 1872 meant that news from London could be received within a day or two and the benefit of this was considerable, even though the bales still took three months to get there.

If the squatter decided to sell the wool in London, it was consigned through a broking company in Australia. This company paid the squatter an advance on its value, arranged the shipping and sale, and subsequently sent an account of the transaction and the balance of the proceeds to the squatter. For example, in November 1876 William Pitt Faithfull sent 120 bales to his broker, Gilchrist, Watt & Co., for shipment to London. Gilchrists paid him an advance of £2484 15s, from which £42 was deducted for rail freight. The wool was sent on two ships and was sold in separate lots for a total of £3435 4s. Selling costs, interest on the advance and other charges amounted to £355 1s 2d, so the net proceeds were £3080 2s 10d, or £637 7s 10d more than the advance. The final account was dated November 1877, twelve months after the wool had left Springfield.

A squatter in the back country might have to wait much longer than that. On 30 September 1899 John Conrick dispatched 117 bales from Nappa Merrie on Cooper Creek to the railhead at Charleville

While the sale of wool paid most of the costs of running a sheep station, the profit came from selling sheep that had been born there. The increase in the size of the flock was therefore of great economic significance.

89

some 800 kilometres away. By the time the teams reached Mt Howitt drought made it impossible for the horses to continue and the wagons had to be abandoned for eighteen months. The clip finally reached Charleville on 25 July 1901, but it was still a long way from the sales.

Whatever the market prices might be, the squatter's debt still had to be repaid, or at least the interest had, and it was the size of the debt that drove the unsuccessful to eventual ruin rather than the variations in prices or seasons. The debt was usually raised with a merchant or broker because banks were reluctant to finance pastoralists. The reason for this is not clear, although it may have been because squatters rarely had freehold title to the land they occupied. In any case, the debt was nearly always on the value of the stock and not the land.

When money was readily available the debt seemed unimportant and if times were good the squatter would not hesitate to increase it. Trollope describes how:

> When prices are high he increases his flocks,—and with his flocks he increases his debts also. He is almost negligent how much he may owe if wool be high. The temptation is so great that if his credit be good he will almost assuredly increase his flock to the bearing capability of his run. Three years of high prices will, perhaps, make him a rich man. But a fall again,—a speedy fall,—will bring him to the dust. . . When the large squatter really owns his flocks . . . then even at the worst of times, with wool even at 8d, he does well; and in that condition, when wool rises he becomes a millionaire.

It was an inescapable truth that debt raised in the good times could not be sustained in the bad, especially if the bad came early. From being an independent businessman the squatter then became little more than a manager of the station. The debt increased because the interest was not fully paid, and this in turn created more interest. Sometimes both the squatter and lender found themselves locked into a position that was financially hopeless: the squatter had a debt that was greater than the value of the assets, and the lender would lose money if the debt was foreclosed.

The collapse could be dramatic when it came. In a letter to England on 12 December 1857 Joyce said that he now had at Norwood 8000 sheep and 300 acres under cultivation. He had a staff of 22 plus their families and his gross receipts for the year were about £6500 against working expenses of £3000: 'My last balance showed the value of all the property I now possess to be about £20 000. I find from a careful examination of accounts since I first arrived in the colony that I have doubled my capital every two and a half years.'

Twenty-one years later, on 8 August 1878, Alfred Joyce met his bankers for a distressing interview. The result of that meeting was confirmed in a letter from the bank later that day:

> In view of your long and favourable connection with this bank, I shall be pleased to recommend the following as the basis for a settlement.
>   That in consideration of your reducing your present debt (say £28 350) to £23 129 by a cash payment, the bank will release its claims upon your wool, wheat and chattels, and write down its debt to £20 000, accepting in satisfaction an absolute transfer of all this landed property, houses, mill &c which it now holds, and will then as proprietor let to you the same at a rental of £1000 per annum . . .

Joyce accepted these terms on a three-year lease and in 1881 the lease was renewed. But he was barely hanging on and when drought came in 1884 it was the beginning of the end. On 26 November 1886 the local newspaper carried an announcement of the 'absolute clearing sale at Norwood'. When it was over Alfred Joyce drove away, crossing the bridge he had built across the creek when he first arrived.

Squatters were also affected by events which they could not control. In this sense they were little different from those in any other business, except that they had the climate to contend with as well. The drought of 1828 had effects that were to be repeated with practically every drought since. J. D. Lang described them:

> Month after month herds of cattle and flocks of sheep were seized and sold for payment of debts incurred by their original purchase; and this process was so frequently repeated, and the price of sheep and cattle consequently fell so rapidly, that when the original stock, with its whole increase during three successive years, failed to realize any thing like the original price, which very soon proved to be the case in many instances, the settler's farm was seized and sold also, and himself perhaps ultimately lodged in jail.

There was another bad drought in 1839 and this was one of the causes of the widespread crash of the 1840s. Since the passing of the Squatting Act in 1836 the colony had been gripped by land fever. With land available to anyone who took the trouble to find it, capital poured in from England to finance it all. The country was awash with imported capital, inflation was soaring and optimism was unbounded. It all had to come to an end, and the drought was a major factor.

Wool prices fell sharply in 1839 and at the same time the flow of money from England came to an end. By the end of 1842 ruin was almost universal. Debts were called in, the price of wool continued to fall and sheep were worth next to nothing. At the end of that year the *Sydney Morning Herald* said somewhat ponderously: 'Commerce, agriculture, and even the great staple in which we

91

Wool from a station was sold once a year, and if it was sent to London it could be another twelve months before the squatter received the proceeds. This photograph shows a shipment of wool arriving at Carnarvon in Western Australia for the next stage in the journey to the sale room.

once exulted as our 'golden fleece', were alike laid prostrate by the blasts of pitiless adversity.'

In the eleven months from February 1842, the number of declared insolvents was 600, and of these 78 were described as settlers, farmers and graziers, which was nearly twice that of any other category. In 1843 the owner of Yarralumla, who was in Sydney, wrote to the manager of the property: 'I must ask you, my dear boy, not to draw upon me on any account whatever until I write to you to do so. You are not aware of the state of money matters here . . . sell anything you can get an offer for.'

A few months later he sounded even more desperate: 'I wish you to discharge all the men you can, and to hire no more. In these days money is everything—sheep, cattle and land are nothing, absolutely nothing.'

By then sheep were worth about 6 pence each for mutton, but only if a buyer could be found. Surely, the *Sydney Morning Herald* wondered, there must be enough on or in a sheep to make it worth more than that. Henry O'Brien of Yass replied that there was. The answer was tallow.

Tallow was used to make soap and candles and was worth between £2 and £3 a hundredweight in London. O'Brien had found that if a sheep was boiled down it produced between 12 and 25 pounds of tallow. Boiling down 800 sheep and sending the tallow to London would cost about £109, but the tallow would fetch about £350, or about 6 shillings per sheep. It was a good deal better than 6 pence.

This simple arithmetic saved the Australian sheep industry from oblivion. Nearly a quarter of a million sheep were boiled down within a year, and three-quarters of a million the year after that. Factories were built so that the process could be carried out quickly and economically and squatters sent the flocks that they had nurtured to these communal boiling vats.

Fifty years later, in the 1890s, the Australian economy crashed again, and this time the result was even more disastrous.

For twenty years the country had enjoyed a prosperity that it had not seen before. Individuals and governments had raised money easily, seasons were mostly good and wool prices high. But again much of the capital had come from England and when the supply was reduced the problems began to appear. The weakness was that much of the capital had been used in land speculation by companies who had little backing and who could not meet the growing number of lenders who now wanted their money back. In 1891 several of these 'land banks' failed, but worse was to come.

On 28 January 1893 the Federal Bank of Australia closed when it ran out of cash, and the Commercial Bank of Australia suspended trading on 4 April. In the next two months fourteen of the 25 leading banks suspended payment. Soon 1000 branches had been closed and the banks were in liquidation.

Thirteen of these banks were able to come to life again by means of a curious technique called restructuring. They reopened with a slightly different structure, but with identical or similar names, and called in unpaid capital from the previous shareholders. A third of the depositors' funds were converted into shares in the new bank and the remainder frozen. Customers with current accounts were allowed to use only half of their deposits. The system worked, and the banks revived, but the financial consequences were horrific. Large sums of money that had been lent to the banks for a short period were now tied up indefinitely, while the compulsory call of unpaid capital ruined thousands of shareholders.

These consequences were felt by almost everybody, rich or poor, town or bush, but the effect on squatters was particularly dramatic. Of the £73 million owed to the banks on overdraft ten years earlier, £55 million was owed by squatters. Much of this was debt of long standing which had excited little concern, the rest had been incurred to build homesteads and to finance improvements. When it was called in, many squatters were ruined after nearly a lifetime on the land.

In 1892 R. H. Kennedy had a huge run that carried 92 000 sheep and he told a friend that he would have 100 000 the following year. But when the next shearing came he no longer owned Wonnaminta. The owner of Tinapagee on the Paroo had borrowed from Dalgety's to finance improvements but in 1892 the company took over and appointed his son as manager. John Rule of Aramac station in Queensland was sold up without warning even though he had enough wool on the way to London to cover his mortgage in full. And Patrick Durack, who had pioneered Thylungra and, through his sons, the Ord River saw an empire that had been worth £750 000 suddenly become worth next to nothing. Not all his mis-

93

fortune was a result of the crash but in time the bank took over Thylungra and his house in Brisbane was sold. The properties in the Kimberleys were in the name of his sons and so were immune. When he was 56 years old Durack wrote to them: 'So ye're Mama and me must now come to Kimberley to live at Argyle for ye understand that we have not at present any home of our own... For myself I have only now my old moleskins, riding saddle and pack and what experience I have at your disposal.'

It was the end, too, for Kate Parker and her husband Matah in New South Wales, where they had been in drought for seven years:

> Later in the evening came many men, old hands from far and wide, the bush telegraph having spread the news of our projected departure. These men made a torchlight procession round the homestead, singing in many keys, 'For he's a Jolly Good Fellow', and cheering in finale for 'The Whitest Boss the Back Creeks ever knew.'
>
> Next morning, off we started in the waggonette, which had superseded the old Abbott buggy, behind four good horses, as we had arrived over twenty years earlier... A chorus of 'Good Luck' and cheers echoed after us as we drove away...

As Trollope said earlier, 'the growing of wool is at the best a precarious trade'. And so it was. Most squatters committed everything they had to their station and flocks, making no attempt to spread the risk by investing in other ventures. They rose or fell as the case may be, believing that wool would pay and wethers were profit. And so they were, provided the wethers kept appearing, wool held a price and the flock did not die from disease or drought.

One cannot say that the squatters who failed always did so because of bad luck or because of circumstances they could not control. Some did, but others failed because of bad management and reckless spending. What one can say, though, is that those who made a fortune and held on to it did not do so easily. The remarkable thing is that any did.

9

The shearers

S HEARING was always the most active time of the year on a
sheep station. It was the time when the squatter saw the result of a year's work and assessed how successful it had been.
Output was measured in bales, and when they left the station on a
bullock dray it was the start of a process that produced most of the
squatter's annual income. It was also the point when the wool that
had been produced ceased to be an agricultural product and became
the raw material for an industrial process.

Squatters had to choose their shearing time with care. It was
always carried out at the same time each year, but the reasons for
selecting that time were far from casual. First, they did not want to
shear during lambing. If they started a month before lambing they
ran the risk of having ewes giving birth to early lambs while in
the shed. And they did not shear until two or three months after
lambing so that the lambs and ewes could put on condition. As
most squatters had an autumn joining to produce a spring lambing,
this largely determined when they would shear.

The second consideration was grass seed, or more accurately,
the time when it fell. Washing sheep before shearing removed dust
and some grease, but it did little to remove grass seed, which was
a major fault in the wool as far as the manufacturer was concerned.
If sheep were in full wool when the seed dropped, their fleeces
accumulated large quantities of seed and the ultimate price
suffered. If, on the other hand, they shore them before the seed
dropped, the short wool left on the sheep did not pick up so many
seeds and the wool was cleaner.

The arrival of spring weather, and therefore the lambing, and
the dropping of grass seed, happened at different times in different
regions and so, therefore, did the shearing. The result was that
teams of itinerant shearers could move around a large area of the

country from one shed to the next by following the season. If shearing had taken place in the same few weeks in all regions of Australia the economics of the wool industry would have been considerably different. A great number of shearers would have been needed at that time, and there would have been little for them to do for the rest of the year.

In the early years of squatting shearing was relatively informal. Flocks were small and the shearing was done by the squatters and their hands with whatever help might be available. Station hands were expected to be able to shear, as were the itinerant workers. It was a basic skill rather than the specialised one it became later.

At first the facilities were crude. Squatters provided no more than was necessary to remove the fleece from the sheep's back. In time the facilities become more permanent, but in the early years squatters managed as best they could, as Joyce describes:

> The usual time for shearing now approaching pretty close, it became necessary to make some preparations for it. On the adjoining and most other stations, wash-pens and wool-sheds had been constructed a year or more, but in our case everything in the way of improvements had to be begun. Seeing we had no time to erect anything of a permanent character for this shearing, and also that our funds were exhausted, we decided to get through with only the most temporary conveniences, which consisted of a rough structure of posts and plates covered thickly over with boughs and hurdled in, and with our tarpaulin laid upon the ground to shear upon . . . For our limited stock, four shearers sufficed, who were also required to assist in the washing, as no shearing could go on on the days of washing . . .

At first, fleeces were simply rolled and loaded on to the dray, but the weakness of this method was obvious, especially after taking so much trouble to wash the sheep before shearing them. In spite of his lack of funds even Joyce preferred to put his wool in bales. This was done by hanging an empty bale inside a timber frame that was built to contain it. Eight fleeces were placed in a layer, and then a spade was used to lever space around the edges so that another eight fleeces could be squeezed in. The full bale contained 80 to 100 fleeces. This method was in turn replaced by the lever press, which was more efficient but difficult to operate, and the screw press, which was expensive.

Before long shearing became the work of specialists and at first there were two distinct groups. There were the Derwenters, who came from Tasmania, and the Sydneys. The Derwenters crossed the Bass Strait each season and were recognised by their tall hats and kangaroo knapsacks, called Derwent drums. The Sydneys carried quart pots and blankets rolled into a swag. The Derwenters were regarded as the better shearers, but the Sydneys were faster.

Shearing was also carried out by Aboriginals, while in South Australia much of the shearing was done by German settlers, as described by J. W. Bull in *Early Experiences of Colonial Life in South Australia*:

> The shearers were principally young women, who were waited on by the men of the village, who, when called on, caught and carried the sheep to the shearer. The sheep was carefully laid down on its side; the young woman, without shoes and stockings, had a piece of thick soft string tied to one of her big toes, the other end was then tied to the hind foot of the sheep; her knee or left hand was pressed on the neck or shoulder of the animal which was then left to her charge, and she commenced clipping. . . most carefully avoiding any snips of the skin. The number shorn by one never exceeded thirty a day. At first I was inclined to laugh, but I was soon pleased to see how tenderly the sheep were handled. The wool was not taken off very close.

In the more conventional way of shearing with blades shearers sat the sheep on the board between their legs with the forelegs held under the left arm. The belly wool was then removed and the fleece then opened from the brisket to the left ear and clipped down the left side to the tail, taking the cut well past the spine. The sheep was then turned and the wool removed from the other side, finishing at the thigh.

Three movements of the blades were made with each cut. At the start of the cut the shearer's hand was close to the skin so that the cut was started with the widest part of the blades. The shearer's hand was then raised so that the cut was continued by the middle of the blades, and at the end of the cut the hand was raised higher again so that the cut finished with the points. These actions were carried out in one continuous movement. As the blades came together they were prevented from crossing each other by the knockers, large lumps of metal on the shaft of each blade. The sound they made when they came together was the clicking of the shears. Although much loved by poets, many shearers found the sound annoying and lessened it by putting leather facings on the knockers.

Competition between shearers to shear the most sheep was intense, as a man's skill was measured by how many he could push down the chute to the counting out pen. Sydneys boasted of doing 100 a day, but Derwenters usually did from 60 to 80. The man who shore the most in a day in the shed was called the ringer, and he retained the title until somebody bettered it. A man who could consistently shear a large number of sheep in a day was called a gun, and this title was recognised beyond the confines of the shed.

This emphasis on speed was a mixed blessing to squatters. They certainly wanted their sheep shorn as quickly as possible, but they also wanted all the wool off and the sheep intact afterwards. The

Shearers made up an independent and itinerant army of highly skilled workers. Many walked from one station to the next, although in time the bicycle became almost universal.

97

cutting edge of the blades was not protected and a close cut was liable to cut the skin as well. The cut was treated by an application of tar which was brought up by a boy as soon as it was called for by the shearer. If the shearer did not cut close enough, however, some of the wool would be left on the sheep and that which was removed was shorter in the staple than it should have been. The main consideration was that the shearer was paid for the number he shore, and this was balanced by the squatter refusing to pay for sheep that had been shorn badly.

Shearers did nothing but shear sheep. Others in the shed made sure that they were supplied with sheep, kept the board clean of locks and carried away the fleeces to the classing table. While others removed dirty and stained pieces from the fleece, the classer assessed the quality of the wool and allocated it to its appropriate bin. Each bale contained wool of similar quality and this was identified on the outside of the bale.

The classer was a very important part of the team and highly regarded for his skill. But the classing was perhaps not as important as they thought. In 1873 Trollope wrote: 'But I am told that in England very little is thought of this primary sorting, and that all wools are re-sorted as they are scoured. The squatter, however, says that unless he sorted his wool in his own shed he could not realise a good price for a good article.' By this time, shearing was entirely in the hands of professionals and was highly organised.

The squatter rarely advertised for shearers, or even announced

Before shearing started the squatter called the roll. Shearers often wrote ahead to book a place in a shed and the rest were taken on from those who turned up in the hope of obtaining a place. This photograph shows a roll call at Wilcannia in 1902.

when it was to take place. Shearers either knew when it would be through custom, or learned of it as they travelled. A shearer wrote to the station weeks or months ahead to book a stand in the shed, and often sent a sovereign as a sign of good faith. This was returned when the shearing was finished. If the shearer was unable to turn up at the shed, through accident or a change of plans, he might sell the booking to a mate, who then assumed his identity while he was at the shed. If not, the squatter retained the deposit and usually donated it to the local hospital.

Shearers were responsible for making their own way to the shed and did so as best they could. At first, successful shearers travelled on horseback and the rest, the footmen, walked. What changed that was an event in Belfast in 1889. At a cycle meeting at the local track the crowd roared with laughter when one of the competitors rode into the arena on a bicycle which had two wheels of the same size, and which was dwarfed by the more conventional penny-farthings. The strange new bicycle, which silenced the crowd by winning, was fitted with pneumatic tyres which had been developed the year before by Dr John Dunlop for his son's bicycle using a length of garden hose.

This invention transformed life for Australian shearers. The bicycle was cheap, it could be ridden over almost any type of country, it was light enough to be lifted over fences, it did not need feeding, it could carry as much gear as a footman and nearly as much as a horse, and it could be repaired if necessary. About the only thing that crippled it was damage to the front forks—anything else could be fixed with sacking, fence wire and ingenuity.

Although some continued to use horses, the bicycle was soon almost universal among shearers. Singly or in groups, they rode vast distances with such lack of concern as to imply that it was no more than a social ride in a park. As Bean wrote:

> For exactly the same trip the average European would probably requisition a whole colonial outfit, compasses, puggaree, sun-spectacles and field glasses. The Australian shearer didn't even change his hat. If he wore a 'hard hitter' [bowler hat] back in his home town or city, well then he rode off with the hard hitter on his head, as many snapshots of that era show.

On arriving at the station the shearers either camped by the creek or claimed a bunk in the hut, depending on their inclination. They included men who had already booked a place in the shed and those who turned up in the hope of being taken on. The roll was then called and the terms of employment read out. Those who were engaged asked to see the price list of station stores and signed on. Those who had been unlucky were given rations before they moved on to the next shed.

The shearers then elected their cook and spent the rest of the day preparing their equipment. They were usually issued with two pairs of blades, an oil stone and a bottle of oil. Men adapted the shears to suit them. Some put leather on the knockers, others filed them down so they could make a wider cut. Most fitted a strap to the blades which passed over the hand, and some cut strips off the bow with a cold chisel to weaken the spring.

Those who had camped when they arrived now usually moved into the hut. This consisted of a long narrow building with tiers of bunks along each long side. The dining table was a rough structure fastened to the floor in the aisle, so that a man might have to squeeze between it and the bunks.

The following day the men filed out to the shed after breakfast and drew lots for their stand on the board. Each shearer then arranged his equipment: water bags were hung, oil and stone placed on a shelf and a can filled with water so that the blades could be dipped from time to time. Facing the board was a row of catching pens, each of which supplied two shearers. The shearers examined the sheep before the work started to see how difficult or easy the job was to be. Then the overseer came into the shed, the bell rang, and there was a scramble as the shearers went to the pen to remove their first sheep in the hope that they might be the first to push a sheep out into the catching pen.

The working day was split into four 'runs' which at that time were from 75 to 90 minutes each. At the end of each run the shorn sheep were counted and a list posted showing the number shorn by each man.

The tallies achieved by blade shearers were often remarkable. In September 1895, 26 men at Barenya station averaged 172 each in one day, and of those, eight men averaged 236 each. The record for blade shearing was set in October 1892 at Alice Downs in Queensland by Jack Howe, who shore 327 ewes in seven hours and twenty minutes. Most of the big tallies took place in Queensland because the sheep there were lighter and the wool not as dense as in Victoria and New South Wales.

Shearers preferred the shed to start work on a Thursday or Friday, so that they had the weekend to recover from the exertion. Similarly, squatters preferred to have shearers who had recently worked at another shed so that they were broken into the task. The physical effort was enormous and even those used to it needed a day or two to adjust to it if they had not worked for a few weeks. Nor was the shed designed for their comfort. Sheds were known to shearers as good or bad depending, among other things, on how hot they became.

Once work started in a shed it continued day after day, apart from the weekends, until all the sheep had been shorn. Or at least the squatter hoped it would. What prevented it was wet sheep.

Shearers refused to shear wet sheep, believing them to be a danger to their health. Tales of illness when this rule was ignored were frequent and convincing. Medicine has failed to establish the truth either way, but shearers never had any doubts and they alone decided whether the sheep would be shorn. Not surprisingly this led to antagonism between the shearers and the squatter, especially as it was difficult to tell if the sheep were damp. In the moist atmosphere of the shed the greasy wool on a sheep's back rarely felt totally dry and squatters told how shearers, when given a sample of wool from a bin and one from a sheep and asked to say which was wet, would often pick the sample from the bin as being unacceptable.

There is no doubt that shearers did claim the sheep were wet because it suited them—before the weekend, for example, or after a few days of hot weather. On the other hand, sheep rarely became wet within a couple of days of the job finishing. When the sheep really were damp, though, the squatter stood to lose little when the shearing stopped as damp fleeces packed tightly into a bale were likely to start to smolder in spontaneous combustion.

When shearing was in full swing the squatter's wife was expected to visit the shed and in some districts was expected to 'shout' the men a drink, which was called 'wetting the board'. Kate Parker described one of her visits, although wetting the board was not the custom in her part of New South Wales:

> The finish up to a shed visit is tea in the overseer's quarters.
> Brownie, buns, flaky turnovers and jam tarts to satisfy your hunger, and tea to quench your thirst. But it is hard to forget that smell of hot workers, sheep, tar and oil which reeks in the shed, and also the set-on-edge feeling of your teeth after the noise of men sharpening their shears...

It is often said that women were not allowed to enter the shed while the shearers were working, but this was rarely the case. If a woman arrived the first to see her would announce 'Ducks on the water' or some other local warning so that the rest would know she was there and behave in a suitable manner. What the shearers did resent, however, were visits by people from the local town. 'Flash' shearers dressed well when visiting town and cut a good figure there. They did not like to be seen in shabby working clothes sweating profusely over a sheep that was difficult to hold, or hearing the mutterings of sympathy if they nicked the skin.

The main objection to visitors, however, was that the shed could not accommodate them. As each shearer finished a sheep he pushed it into the counting pen, wiped his face, and crossed to the catching

101

Shearing with blades. Each cut required three movements of the hand. A great deal of skill was needed to cut the wool close to the skin without damaging the sheep. The significance of machines was not that they made the job quicker—they made it possible to obtain a good result with less skill.

pen for the next sheep. Others would sweep the board and collect the fleece so that the stand was clean by the time the shearer was ready to start again. This happened continuously along the board throughout the run, and a visitor could hardly avoid being in the way most of the time.

Before the coming of the union the shearers worked on the terms that the squatter laid down in the agreement which each man had to sign. Some agreements were sensible, others were heavily weighted in favour of the squatter. Men were not paid until the work was finished, although this in itself was not inconvenient as men needed little money while they were on the station. At the end of the job the tally for each man was reckoned, a deduction made for what he had drawn from the store, and the balance paid by cheque. But one agreement insisted that payment was to be made by money order payable in Adelaide, which was 1200 kilometres from the shed.

In her book *The Shearers*, Patsy Adam-Smith quotes the agreement used in 1887 at Meteor Downs in Queensland:

> Shearing to begin at time appointed by person in charge of the shed and continue till sunset if necessary.
>
> Any shearer absent from the shed during working hours without permission will be fined a score of sheep.
>
> Any shearer using obscene language or swearing will be fined a score of sheep.
>
> All sheep not shorn to satisfaction of person in charge of shed not to be paid for.

These agreements, which the men had to accept before starting work, were one of the reasons that led to the founding of the union. But they were probably no more onerous than those which applied to people working in factories. In 1888 in Adelaide the workers in Fulton's foundry sometimes worked from 6.30 a.m. one day until 5 p.m. the following day and might have to do 84 hours in the week. Also in South Australia, a Royal Commission reported in 1892 'an entire absence of any legislative provision for the protection of women and children in relation to their hours of labour'. An Act to remedy this was passed in 1894 but children of thirteen could still work a 48–hour week.

But there were other problems that affected shearers which led to the founding of the Amalgamated Shearers' Union in 1886. One was the exhorbitant prices charged by some squatters for store goods, and another was the way payment could be suspended. W. G. Spence, one of the first organisers of the union, described this in his book *Australia's Awakening*:

> In the pre-Union days not only did the squatter offer low rates for shearing but he took advantage in many other ways. A favourite

method was known as 'second price'. The squatter would provide in the agreement which shearers had to sign that he would pay for all sheep shorn to his satisfaction the sum of 17s 6d per hundred, but if at any time the shearer failed to do his work in a manner satisfactory to the employer or his agent he would be paid at the rate of 15s a hundred—not only for the sheep alleged to be badly shorn, but for all those previously and already passed as well done. Under this clause men have had their work condemned during the last few days of the shearing, and have been victimised to the amount of 2s 6d per hundred on thousands of sheep, which had been shorn satisfactorily. Another scheme was known as 'raddling'. This meant that a whole penful of sheep would be marked and not paid for because the last one or any other one was not done to please the boss. As the employer was sole judge, he had the men at his mercy.

The relationship between the squatters and the new union came to a head when the squatters, under financial strain of the late 1880s and early '90s, announced a reduction in the rate to be paid. The union did not accept this and in Queensland in 1890 announced that its members would not work alongside non-union labour. The result was a strike by shearers that was marked by threats and violence on both sides and which created much bitterness. In 1891 many union shearers were close to starvation and the union finally gave in and accepted that its members would work alongside non-union labour. The strike had not been entirely in vain, however, for it established the union as the shearers' negotiator with the squatters and a steady improvement in conditions was brought about.

At about the same time shearers were confronted with a new machine which was to revolutionise the way they worked. The machine was not popular with them at first, but in time it completely replaced blades as the tool for removing wool from the sheep's back.

Several people had tried to invent a machine to shear sheep. In 1868 James Higham of Melbourne invented a machine which he patented but did not put on the market. In 1870 J. E. A. Gwyne invented a machine with flexible joints, but it was the work of Robert Savage and Frederick York Wolseley that made possible the first commercial machine.

Their first patent, dated 28 March 1877, was titled 'Improvements in apparatus for shearing sheep and clipping horses, and in contrivances for driving them, which latter are also applicable to other useful purposes.' Later that year Wolseley was granted a further patent for a new kind of drive

> by means of a round belting, such as cord, passing over, around, and between pulleys suitably arranged for the purpose, the length of which cord is capable of being increased or decreased at pleasure, so as to permit of the free use of the machine on any part of the animal

103

to be shorn or clipped, and from one part to another, without any extra effort on the part of the operator.

By 1885 John Howard had invented a handpiece that was little different from that in use today. Using the drive that had been developed by Wolseley they demonstrated their first machine in 1887 at Goldsbrough's wool store in Melbourne. A gun shearer, Dave Brown, shore three sheep with blades, and then one of Howard's assistants, a man from Khartoum called Hassam Ali, went over the same sheep with the machine and took off another kilogram of wool.

That kilogram was more than enough to convince the squatters and the more forward-looking started to equip their sheds with the new machines. The first to be ready was the shed at Dunlop, where 184 000 sheep had been assembled for shearing in June 1888. After signing on 40 shearers from the considerable number that had arrived at Dunlop, the manager took them into the shed and confronted them with 40 machines.

The shearers refused to have anything to do with them. They picked up their gear, crossed the Darling and set up their camp on the other side. The sheep waited on one side of the river as the men waited on the other and it seemed that only the removal of the machines would lead to the shearing of Dunlop sheep that year.

Every day John Howard crossed the river to talk to the striking shearers, and when they would listen no more he joined them in whatever they did to pass the time. This went on for three weeks. Then the shearers challenged Howard to swim across the flooded Darling. He swam it twice before breakfast, and the strike was over. If Howard was prepared to do that, they would try out his machines.

A team of shearers at Currawillinghy in New South Wales. The man on the extreme left is the cook.

Even so, the experiment became something of a shambles. Some of the combs were upside down, men let go of the handpiece while it was in gear so that it lashed around on the floor, and the main drive belt was cut in several places. Nor were the tallies encouraging. Men who could shear nearly 200 sheep a day with blades struggled to do 50 with the machines. It might have been the end of machine shearing had not a small group of men started to think they could master the technique. At the end of the fifth week a New Zealand shearer shore 100 sheep in one day. Howard offered a bonus for every sheep over 150 a day and before long the shed was averaging 120 sheep a day per man. If the extra wool had impressed the squatters, it was that tally at Dunlop that reassured the shearers.

The benefit of machine shearing was not that it was quicker. It was that the wool could be taken off near the skin without the high skill needed to do so with blades, and that instead of physically cutting the wool the shearer now only needed to guide the handpiece while it did the cutting. The disadvantage was that sheep and shearer had to remain within reach of the machine.

Shearers found this difficult at first. With blades a shearer could work from any position he liked provided he could reach the part of the fleece to be cut. If the sheep moved, the shearer also moved. Neither had the same freedom with the machine and at first shearers used a lot of energy in trying to restrain the sheep so that they could use the handpiece in the correct place.

In time, shearers developed a different sequence of movements in order to remove the fleece quickly with a machine. As with the blades, he started by cutting off the belly wool so that it dropped on the floor in one piece. He then worked up the inside of each back leg and continued up the flank furthest from him to work over the rump. He left the wool hanging there and cut the topknot, the area between the ears. He then held the sheep with its chin raised and cut upwards from the first cut he had made down the belly. Working upwards, he worked around the neck and face to join up with the cut he had made across the topknot. From there, he opened up the wool across one side of the ribs and then moved the sheep onto its side for the 'long blow', the first of a series of sweeping cuts that ran from the rump to the back of the head. He then worked round the ear and down the neck to the shoulder on the other side and made a series of cuts from the spine and round the far ribs to the belly. Finally, he made a series of short cuts down the flank, called the 'whipping side', and finished at the hind leg so that the fleece came away in one piece.

With the coming of machines, and the growth of the union, the organisation of the shed started to change. A man known as the

105

'expert' was required to run the machinery, and this skilled man was often the 'boss of the shed'. Contractors also started to offer squatters a complete team of men to do the shearing, so that the squatter no longer had to pick each man and shearers no longer had to write ahead to book their stand.

But throughout all these changes shearers remained the most highly skilled and highly regarded of all bush workers.

10

The drovers

DROVERS moved mobs of sheep and cattle, and sometimes both, overland. They did this by walking them because apart from the small network of railways there was no other way, even though the distance to be travelled was often very great.

There were three main reasons for moving stock overland. One was to take stock up to new country when it had been taken up by a squatter, and in this case the squatter was often the drover. Squatters might, indeed, have their stock with them when searching for land, so that their journey of exploration was a drove as well. This type of outward droving went on for many years as country in the north was brought into use long after the south-east was well settled.

The second reason was to bring stock from the station for sale on the coast. This applied particularly to cattle, which had to be taken to the centres of population for killing before refrigeration made it possible to kill them at regional meatworks, but it also applied to sheep that were to be sold for meat. At first the stock was walked to the coastal saleyards or meatworks but later they were walked to the nearest railhead and completed the last part of the journey by train.

The third reason was to move stock from one station to another, either because they had been sold, because the owner was moving to the new station, or to fatten them on better feed before they were sold for meat.

In most cases the drover was an independent contractor who specialised in this work. Sometimes he took a share of the profit on the sale of the stock he had moved, but the more usual method of payment was a fee based on the number of head and the number of kilometres. In return for this the drover supplied his own equipment and men and was responsible for the stock while it was in his care. The stock was counted over to him at the start of the journey and counted out at the end; and the value of any stock lost on the way was deducted from the money due to him. Once the drover had handed over the stock he was 'empty'. He paid off his men, who either went on their way or stayed with him and waited for the next job.

The drover's equipment was called a 'plant' and it represented a considerable investment. The plant consisted of his horses (of which he might need a great number), riding gear, pack gear, cooking equipment and rations, and a wagon to transport them, and all the bits and pieces needed to support men and stock for several months. However, not all drovers made long journeys. Some, known as 'smoke-stack' drovers, worked within a limited area and their journeys might be no longer than two or three weeks.

The drover was always an accomplished stockman and most had worked on stations for a number of years before setting up their plant. With the extra experience they gained while travelling with stock they became highly skilled and treated with nonchalance achievements that would have taxed most good stockmen on stations. For example, in 1872 D'Arcy Wentworth Uhr took 400 bullocks from Charters Towers in Queensland to Darwin, a trip of some 2500 kilometres through largely unknown country. Nobody in Darwin knew he was coming and a surprised friend he met there asked him what he was doing. 'I just came across the Gulf with cattle.' 'Go on! Have much trouble?' 'No. Got along well.'

Perhaps the first true drover in Australia was Joseph Hawdon, who in 1836 helped to overland the first cattle to Melbourne on a 500 kilometre trip from the Murrumbidgee. Two years later he took a mob of 340 head of cattle from Port Phillip to Adelaide. The journey took a little less than three months and was repeated by many others in future years.

As droving became common, regulations were introduced to govern the movement of stock. Sheep had to travel at least 9.7 kilometres a day and cattle had to travel 12.9 kilometres a day unless flood made either impossible. Drovers also had to give notice to property owners of their intention to move stock over a route that crossed the property owner's land, and drovers had to keep their mob within a width of about 800 metres.

Squatters frequently sent one of their own men to accompany a travelling mob as it crossed their land. They made sure that the mob travelled the minimum distance and that they grazed no more country than the regulations allowed. Without this supervision the squatter might find that the mob had left the paddocks bare and the water exhausted and that the drover had preferred to use the resident stock for rations instead of his own.

Cattle droving. Cattle were moved for three reasons: to stock a new station; to move them to the coast for sale; or to move them to another station for fattening or restocking. Although squatters sometimes moved stock themselves, most droving was carried out by specialist contractors.

This relationship between squatter and drover was not always friendly, especially in poor seasons. The drover had to keep his mob alive but squatters might be having great difficulty doing the same. In due course squatters might contract the same drover to move their stock, and then they expected the drover to feed and water them with abundance as they travelled through other properties.

Town people saw little of the drover, especially after railheads became the end of the trail, but they enjoyed the romance of it all. When George Hamilton took a mob of cattle to Adelaide in the 1840s he was disgusted to find that among the noisy groups in the Southern Cross Hotel

> the most uproarious, the most swaggering, and the most
> objectionable in the assemblage, were some young men in red serge
> shirts, corduroy breeches, and gaiters. These were the dilettante
> South Australian bushmen—fellows who had penetrated the country
> as far as Mount Barker, and possibly the Lower Gawler, who carried
> about in their hands long stockwhips which they could not use.

Curr described how, when travelling, he had come across a drover's camp:

> Altogether the scene was picturesque enough, and the overlanders
> seemed to be enjoying themselves. The camp-fire, made against the
> butt of a fallen tree, was on the brink of the river, which ran
> noiselessly through the towering gum-trees which overshadowed its
> course. Around the fire were the shepherds and bullock-drivers of
> the party, seated...at their suppers, each expectant sheep-dog
> waiting for his share from his master.

109

Life for the drover was rarely that idyllic. Feed was often uncertain for much of the trip, and in this case the drover was probably working out how to get the sheep across the noiseless river in the morning. And apart from the difficulties of the journey, bad weather could make life miserable. George Hamilton was familiar with this situation:

> Sudden gusts of wind swept through the forest, driving pelting showers of rain before them. Men crept out one by one from their sheltered places, and looked forth on the gloomy, uncomfortable prospects with anything but pleasant countenances... The cattle stood with drooping heads, turning their tails to the drifting rain. Many vain attempts were made to kindle a fire—the wood was thoroughly soaked and would not burn. At last, after many failures, a weak sickly flame struggled into existence, which strengthened and grew into a blaze. This important feat having been accomplished, preparations for breakfast were made.

But those living on stations also saw the romance in droving. There was, after all, something exciting in seeing a small group of men take a large mob of stock and disappear over the horizon on a journey that might keep them in isolation for months. Kate Parker, who knew all the hardships of rural life, wrote:

> Travelling cattle thrill me still... I liked to see Queensland drovers bringing in their cattle. They were such typical bushmen, the bushmen of romance... I liked to hear the distant roar of cattle voices. I liked to hear the cracking echo of the stock-whips as the drovers drove the cattle into the water... I liked to see the careless, sort of born-in-the-saddle seat of these men on their horses, lithe, spare bushmen mostly, keen and alert...

When droving cattle, the men arranged themselves around the mob and rode easily alongside while the cattle moved at their own pace. One man, the lead, rode in front to steady the mob. On either side of the mob were the wing men, the points were at each rear corner and the tail was between them. Cattle took up the same place in the mob when it formed up, so that if men rode in the same place each day they were in the company of the same beasts and got to know them well.

While the mob was on the move the cook took the wagon ahead to the next camping place, while the horse tailer, a most important member of the plant, took along the unused horses, often more than 100, in a separate mob. The number of men varied with the size of the mob. A mob of 1500 bullocks needed about eight or nine men as well as the cook and horse tailer.

Given good feed and water along the route, moving the mob during the day was relatively simple, especially when the cattle

Crossing a river with a mob of cattle was a difficult exercise. This picture of the Murray River in 1865 shows that the punt could cross in a straight line but the cattle had to enter the river upstream in order to arrive safely at the exit point.

had settled down after the first few days. It was during the night that the difficulties arose because the cattle had to be held without the use of yards.

Until the 1840s cattle were not watched at night. The men drove them into an open space, preferably one that had a natural barrier on one side, and held them in a tight group while others lit fires around the mob at intervals of about 10 metres. The men camped on the other side of the fires and one of them stayed awake to keep the fires burning. Any cattle that strayed through the circle of fires had to be found in the morning before the mob could be moved off. Later, more men remained awake at separate fires and walked a beat to the fires on either side, pushing back any beasts that wanted to stray.

This in turn gave way to a system of night watches. For the first few nights a couple of men circled around the mob from opposite directions in shifts of two hours. Later, when the cattle were more settled, only one man stayed on watch and his shift was determined by the number of men in the camp.

The man on watch rode around the mob on the night horse. This horse was kept specifically for this purpose and did not work during the day. The night horse had an instinct for cattle and even in the dark could take the watchman to a part of the mob where a beast was trying to stray. This was an important skill as cattle often tried to drift off from the mob in a quiet trickle. If this was not stopped the mob was much smaller in the morning and time was lost in finding them.

What was considerably worse was when all the cattle decided to leave at the same time and at full speed. In Australia this was called a rush, not a stampede. A rush could start out of nothing. A camp fire might flare, or a man walk between the fire and the mob. This

111

might happen on several nights without disturbing the mob, and on the next night or the next week cause a rush.

Whatever the cause, the mob suddenly rushed at full gallop in the direction that most suited it. At the front of the rush was a small number of fast beasts who led the way, while behind them came the bulk of the mob, jostling each other in their anxiety not to be left behind.

The man on watch had one duty to perform, but he had to perform it at all cost. He had to turn the lead. In order to do this he first had to gallop the night horse alongside the fast-moving mob because the lead would not have started where he was. He relied implicitly on the night horse to find its way in the dark, and it was this ability that qualified the horse for the job. When man and horse were alongside the leaders he rode as close to them as he could and tried to make them change direction, if only slightly. He could only hope to turn them away from him. He could not hope to cross to the other side of the leaders and he had to turn them from where he was whether he liked it or not. If man and horse were lucky the leaders turned and then slowed down until the whole mob was milling around in confusion. When that happened no attempt was made to return the mob to where it had started. Instead it was left where it was and quietly tailed for the rest of the night.

Although the days were usually less eventful, moving the mob was not as simple as it seemed. The boss drover relieved the last man on watch at about 4.30 a.m. and usually took the mob off the

Swimming cattle across the River Darling in 1878.

112

night camp while the men were having breakfast. When they joined him he had his own breakfast before returning to the mob or riding ahead to scout the route. Some drovers moved the mob along smartly in the morning so that most of the day's stage was completed before the heat of the day, leaving only a short distance to do during the late afternoon. Others kept an even pace all day and let the mob graze all the way. If the stage was a long one he might have to push them on for the last hour to reach camp, but this was no hardship to a mob that had grazed at its own pace until then.

While on the move most of the drover's problems were associated with water—sometimes there was none and at others there was too much. After a long dry stage the mob could become almost uncontrollable when it smelt water and the skill of the drover and his men might be tested to the full. The danger was that they would rush towards it and those in front would be trampled by those behind. One night in 1883, for example, 600 bullocks out of a mob of 1300 died, smothered, at the Wonnamitta waterhole in the north-west of New South Wales.

The drover had to prevent the mob from making a concerted rush for the water, which meant that he had to know that it was

A flock of sheep travelled slower than cattle and could be followed on foot. Two men with dogs could handle about 3000 sheep.

there before they did. He stopped the mob before they detected it, and then took the cattle to it in small groups. He could then safely leave them there while the men brought up another group, and this was done until the whole mob was safely at the water.

If there was too much water, if the country was flooded, he could do little but keep his mob on high ground and wait for the water to go down. Provided there was sufficient feed all he lost was time.

Crossing rivers was more routine, but it was never free of risk, especially if the river was flooded. In 1904 a drover lost 300 head out of 1470 at the Georgina when the mob started to circle in mid-stream instead of going straight across.

When faced with a river, the drover looked for a good entry point on the near side and a good exit point on the far side. If there was a strong current the exit point needed to be downstream. These entry and exit points were well known on most rivers, but those venturing into new country had to find them for themselves.

The usual method of getting cattle across was to swim a few across first and then let the remainder swim across to join them. At well-known crossings the landowner often kept a decoy cow that was hired by drovers to lead the mob across. Otherwise the drover sometimes put his loose horses into the mob. The horses swam straight across and took the cattle with them.

Once there were cattle on the far side the rest usually followed without much difficulty. If the leading cattle stopped or turned before they were across, men rode quickly into the water and tried to move them in the right direction by cracking stockwhips or even tugging on horns.

For all the skill, though, crossing a big river was a major problem. It took Hamilton several weeks before he successfully moved 500 head of cattle across the Murray:

> Thus ended the battle of the Murray. On mustering my forces it was found that eight horses were more or less gored, all the men had received casualties, the leader [himself] had lost his voice and a great portion of his good temper; on the other side one of the enemy had fallen a prey to the wild dogs. . . and the other had fallen from the cliff. The rest of the enemy were suffering from horn-wounds inflicted by comrades. . . However, we were now all on the western bank of the river, and the road to Adelaide was open to us.

Sheep were generally easier to drove than cattle and it was perhaps because of this that cattle drovers were inclined to look down on those who drove sheep, just as stockmen did with shepherds.

Sheep were required to travel a minimum of 10 kilometres a day, and the pace was slower than with cattle. Because of this sheep drovers followed the flock on foot and at first were little different from the shepherds who did the same each day on the station.

Later, when sheep drovers used horses, the distinction between cattle drovers and sheep drovers became less obvious.

Sheep could also be handled by fewer men. Two men with dogs could look after about 3000 sheep, and the same ratio could be applied to bigger mobs. Travelling sheep were not steadied at the front as cattle were. Instead there was a man on either side of them and one (or a dog) behind and they let the sheep graze as widely as circumstances, and squatters, allowed. Alfred Joyce described the day's routine:

> It was necessary, in order to get the sheep along as easily as possible, to keep them going smartly for the first six miles after starting in the morning, while they were somewhat empty, until they drew into the mid-day dinner camp, and then to feed them slowly the remaining two miles of the average eight and into the night camp. Being thus pretty well filled, they rested quietly in the night camp. There being no paddocks to turn them in, a watch had to be kept through the night, which we all took in regular turns in front of a rousing fire.

If the mob was travelling in separate flocks, fires were lit around each flock and dogs posted to keep watch. Sheep drovers soon discovered an improvement in this method, borrowed, perhaps, from those who rounded up brumbies. It consisted of strips of calico stretched from one tree to the next or supported on posts planted

Drovers settling down for the night. Sheep were held for the night by dogs and watchmen, and later with portable fencing.

115

for the purpose. Sheep refused to go near the calico and this proved a most effective method of containing them. This in turn was replaced by a type of fence made from rope, usually five strands laced at intervals into a kind of netting. When erected on posts this made a very successful night yard and made night watching unnecessary.

Dogs were essential when droving sheep. Indeed it was because of dogs that a large flock could be handled by so few men. The dogs patrolled the perimeter of the flock and immediately drove back any sheep that were inclined to stray. A large flock spread out while travelling and a couple of agile kelpies were far better at this work than men.

As with cattle, it was the lack of water that presented most problems. Sheep had less endurance than cattle and suffered from lack of water much sooner. When that occurred they were very difficult to keep moving and the drover then had to push them on as best he could. In 1899 a drover lost 800 sheep out of a mob of 2500 at Gilgandra, New South Wales, through lack of water. There was also the same danger of them rushing water after a dry stage. Sheep could also be lost as a result of less obvious dangers. Sheep that had become overheated during the afternoon could die by the score during the night, and the loss was even higher if they were camped in too small an area on the hot ground. Another major cause of losses was when sheep overgorged themselves when suddenly coming onto green feed. The drover had to guard against these dangers all the time, but he was not always successful. In 1899 a drover reached the tank a few kilometres from Rockhampton after the fairly short journey from Evesham station with only 3000 sheep alive out of the original mob of 14 000.

When the sheep drover had to move sheep across a creek he swam his horse across while trailing a rope behind him. The end of the rope was tied around the horns of a sheep and it was pulled across the creek in the hope that the rest would follow of their own accord. Sometimes they did, but not often.

If that did not work there were two alternatives, both of which were time consuming. The drover built either a bridge or a boat. Both were basic to the point of being crude, but they worked. A bridge was built by laying tall trees across the creek parallel to each other and filling the gap between them with poles and branches and a covering of earth, twigs and leaves. Men clung to the side of the bridge along its length concealed by bushes so that they could reach up and prod the sheep if they stopped. This had to be done with care because if sheep jumped off the bridge the rest were likely to follow. Some of these bridges were extremely successful. In 1906 a drover called Stuart Field spend a fortnight, and £43, in erecting a bridge across the deep water of the Koopa in Queensland. Within

A sheep bridge at Tirrana, near
Goulburn in New South Wales.

two days of completing it, 22 000 sheep had crossed to the other
side.

Boats were made from logs tied together and were pulled across
from the far side. Landowners on rivers often made boats available to drovers as they did the decoy cow, although in settled areas
squatters were likely to bridge the river for their own convenience.

Once the sheep were across, the plant had to follow, and this
often took nearly as long. Hamilton describes how he did this on
his journey from Port Phillip to Adelaide in 1839, after he had swum
his sheep across:

> The drays were then crossed over; the box dray . . . had been sunk in
> the river for a few days, so that the woodwork might swell and fill up
> the crevices, and it had a tarpaulin fastened to the bottom and sides
> in the inside. The wheels were then taken off, and the body floated
> in the water; it was then pushed across by poles and paddles, the
> wheat and dry stores having been placed in it.

Some of the journeys made by drovers are almost difficult to credit
now, and some of the most amazing were made by those going to
new land. They crossed country that was barely known, if at all,
with no prior knowledge of feed or water or even the route, and yet
it hardly seems to have occurred to them that they might fail.

In 1863 George and John Sutherland took 8000 sheep from
Rockhampton on the Queensland coast to Rocklands on the
Northern Territory border. The journey covered nearly 3500
kilometres and took seven months. In 1872 John Conrick and three
friends, all less than 21 years old, took 1000 head of cattle with
them when they set off from Warrnambool in Victoria to find land
on Cooper Creek not far from where Burke and Wills had died in
1860. The 1900 kilometre journey took eighteen weeks.

117

These men were droving their own stock, but perhaps the most famous contract drover was Nat Buchanan, Old Bluey. Buchanan was born in Dublin in 1826 and came to Australia with his parents. He took up land of his own but had to walk off when cattle prices collapsed in the 1860s. He then took up droving and became a master of it. Much of his work involved taking Queensland cattle to the huge stations that were being formed in the Northern Territory and beyond. One of his major jobs was taking 20 000 head to stock the new run of Victoria River Downs that had been leased by Charles Fisher and Morris Lyons in 1879.

The journey was planned with great care. The mob was assembled at Leichhardt Crossing on the Gulf of Carpentaria, although getting each mob there was itself a feat of droving. Then, under the care of 70 stockmen, the mob left in small groups at intervals of two days. Progress was slow as much of the route had not been explored, Aboriginals were a constant threat, and part of the mob went down with redwater fever. But the trip of 3000 kilometres was completed successfully.

When Nat Buchanan died at Tamworth in 1901 the *Bulletin* said that he had helped to settle more country than any other man in Australia.

And there were others. On 12 June 1883 a party which included the Duracks left Thylungra with 2000 head of breeding cattle for their new station in the Kimberleys. Two days later another party left with 1270 head and another party left Galway Downs with 2000 head that had been bought there. This mob rushed two weeks after setting out and 300 were lost or killed. By the time the journey ended at Ord River on 25 September 1885 the mob had been reduced to less than half. The journey covered nearly 5000 kilometres

Travelling sheep had to cover at least six miles each day. Drovers with sheep or cattle had to notify station owners of their intention to use a stock route which crossed station land.

and the total cost was more than £70 000. The homestead that the Duracks built at Argyle Downs stood until it was covered by the waters of the Ord River irrigation scheme in 1971–72.

Equally impressive was the journey of the MacDonald brothers, who left Goulburn in the middle of 1882 on a trip of 5600 kilometres to a new property near the junction of the Fitzroy and Margaret Rivers in the East Kimberley. Many of their cattle died as a result of drought in Queensland and had to be replaced. By the time the party reached Arnhem Land two and a half years after leaving Goulburn the men were too weak to repair a damaged wagon. Charles MacDonald fell ill with fever and it was decided that his brother Donald would take him into the new settlement of Darwin while Will MacDonald and the men continued with the cattle.

It was a gruelling journey across the Territory to the border of Western Australia. Will MacDonald decided to make for Wyndham, and there he received help for the last stage to the Fitzroy. By the time he reached it he had only 327 head of cattle and only thirteen horses left out of the original 100. The journey had taken three and a half years. The local newspaper said: 'Barely able to realise that it was all over, Will slumped from his horse and squatted on his heels. In every direction, as far as he could see, were green flatlands and gentle slopes. Birds whisked overhead. Game abounded.'

It is not surprising that journeys such as these became legends in their own time, although many are barely remembered now.

But for the most part drovers saw themselves as ordinary people with a job to do. That job was to deliver their mob in good order and without taking too long to get them there. If they had a few problems on the way, they were hardly worth talking about.

11

The bullockies

WITHOUT the bullocky and his team of bullocks many parts of Australia would have been almost impossible to settle. When choosing land squatters rarely thought of the difficulty they might have in servicing it. The quality of the land and its ability to support stock were far more important than its convenience. They simply assumed that if they had managed to move their stock onto the land, then any self-respecting bullocky should be able to follow. They were rarely wrong.

While the bullock team is now remembered as a means of transport they did much more than that. They were used to clear land, scoop out tanks, bring in logs for sawing or building, and a thousand other things that people could not do themselves. Bullocks, often working without a vehicle, were the tractors of their day. For this reason most squatters regarded at least one team of working bullocks as essential equipment for station work, and the bullocky who drove them was part of the assigned or employed labour on the property.

Their role as a means of transport was no less important. Transport was essential to the squatter. Stores had to be brought to the station, and if growing wool the bales had to be sent away every year. But the nature of the country and the business of the squatter made transport difficult. The squatter might, for example, be in a very remote region with few neighbours and even fewer roads and a considerable distance from the nearest service centre.

The other consideration was that the goods that had to be transported were either heavy, bulky, or both. Wool bales are the obvious example, but stores imported from the nearest town were no less impressive. Individual items might be small, but when they were brought in sufficient quantities to last six months or more their bulk was considerable. When large items such as fencing wire, machines and even pianos were added the load became awesome.

Most squatters relied entirely on the ability of the bullock driver for their supplies and if he was unable to get through, the station was soon in a state of siege. Items such as tea, sugar and tobacco which the squatter could not produce were carefully husbanded until they were either exhausted or replenished by the arrival of the team.

In some parts of the country squatters relied on other forms of transport. The Murray–Darling system meant that squatters in that area could be more easily serviced by river traffic, the very heart of Australia relied on camels rather than bullocks, and more settled areas could be serviced by horse teams. Elsewhere, though, and especially in black soil country, the bullock was the main form of transport, and often the only one.

Travel of any kind was difficult in those areas. Roads were little more than beaten tracks that could be made impassable by flooded rivers and distances were great enough to challenge the most adventurous. The only thing most travellers knew with any certainty was the time of their departure. Their time of arrival could be affected by so many factors beyond their control that it was pointless speculating about it until the destination was almost within sight.

Bean, for example, describes how a woman went to the local forwarding agent because she had heard that her husband, who was bringing wool down from Thargomindah in Queensland, had been held up by a flooded river. The agent told her that the journey of nearly 400 kilometres involved crossing two rivers, the Warrego and the Paroo, both of which were usually dry:

> What had happened on this occasion was that one of these two rivers had come down. The boss had seen the streak of it miles ahead, and when he reached the water he found it—as he had expected for several weeks past that he would find it—too fast or deep or wide, or the bottom too soft, for crossing. So he camped on the bank, and was now waiting three or four weeks till it subsided. As to which river it was there did not appear any definite information. He was somewhere out there, on one or the other—didn't matter which. They were only ninety miles apart.

In spite of their tendency to disappear like this, bullockies were probably the most visible of rural workers. There were many of them and even after railheads became convenient depots the bullocky remained a familiar feature of town life. Shearers, although itinerant, were based in the bush, and if they had families in the town they were nevertheless away for much of the year. Drovers could be heaven knows where, and after the railheads were established rarely came into town anyway. But bullockies were in and

This photograph shows how bullocks were harnessed. The wooden yoke went over the necks of a pair of bullocks and was held in place on each bullock with an iron bow. Each yoke was fastened to the next with a length of chain.

out of town all the time. They might not be the same bullockies, but as one left with a load of stores he was likely to pass another arriving with a load of wool.

To the town-dweller, the bullockies were a distinct and rugged breed: 'dressed in a red shirt, with the sleeves tucked up and the collar open, displaying a broad hairy chest. On his head was a venerable ragged straw hat, over the rim of which fell the ends of a broad black ribbon, obscuring one eye; his trousers were greasy and his feet bare.'

That image of the bullocky is still with us, but it is based on those who saw them in the town rather than those who knew them in the bush. Dirty, tough and noisy they might have been in the town, but bush people saw beyond that. In a letter to England in 1863 Rachel Henning said:

> Since I last wrote the drays have come in again and started once more with their second load of wool. Biddulph has nearly always two drays on the road going down with wool or bringing up supplies. The bullock-drivers are almost the best-paid men on the place. They get 40s a week, as much a year as some clerks and curates have to live on at home. It requires a great deal of skill and practice, though, to make twelve or fourteen bullocks all pull together.

She could well have added that it took even more skill to make them go in the right direction. As Sidney said, 'Any man can knock bullocks about, but very few can drive them.'

Bullocks were being used in Australia shortly after the arrival of the First Fleet and although the convicts probably had no previous experience of them they later came to be regarded as the best bullock drivers and were much sought after well into the nineteenth century.

At first bullocks were driven with horse harnesses made of leather but these were soon replaced by simpler and more specialised harnesses that had been developed for bullocks. These were not an Australian invention. They had been used for a long time in America and had probably been developed from those used in Mediterranean countries for centuries.

Bullock harness consisted of a wooden yoke which fitted over the necks of a pair of bullocks. An iron bow, like a horsehoe with long legs, was fitted under the neck of the bullock and the ends of the legs pushed through two holes in the yoke and fastened. A large ring, called a start ring, hung from the centre of the yoke and this was connected to a length of heavy chain that ran the length of the team. The last hook in the chain, at the rear of the team, was fastened to the vehicle.

When yoking the team, the driver first laid the yokes on the

ground about two metres apart, corresponding roughly to the position they would be in when the team had been yoked. He then laid the chains diagonally between each of the yokes. Going to the front of the line, he took the first yoke and stood it on end. He removed the nearside bow from it and placed the bow upside down over the neck of the nearside bullock. He then lifted the yoke onto his shoulder and removed the offside bow. This he placed correctly on the offside bullock, that is, with the curve under the animal's neck. He passed the yoke over the top of the neck and fastened the legs of the bow to it. He then reversed the bow that he had hung over the neck of the first bullock, pushed the legs through the yoke and secured them.

He then hooked one end of the chain onto the start ring that hung from the yoke and laid the other end over the flank of the nearside bullock while he yoked the next pair. When he had done this he connected the rear end of the first chain and the front of the second to the start ring on the second yoke. When he had finished yoking the team, the end of the last chain was fastened to the vehicle.

At first this chain was made of round bars of iron about 30 to 40 centimetres long and these bars were connected with forged links. The links at each end of the chain were fitted with hooks. As iron-work improved a new type of chain became available and this was made entirely of links. Many drivers used this type of chain on the leading bullocks, which had to be able to turn sharply, and used the old bar chain at the rear of the team where the strain was greater.

The front pair of bullocks were called the leaders, the back pair were the polers and the pairs between were called body bullocks. Bullocks were selected with great care. They had to be sturdy animals with broad chests, straight legs and good hooves. The nostrils had to flair in a wide nose and the under jaw had to be strong.

Apart from those common requirements, the bullocky looked for specific features in bullocks depending on where they worked in the team. The leaders did not normally have to pull a great deal, but they had to walk well. This meant they had to be long in the leg

The front pair of a team of bullocks were called the leaders and the rear pair were the polers. Those between were called body bullocks. Each pair of bullocks was closely matched and always worked together.

123

and active and, as they steered the team, they had to be intelligent enough to understand the driver's commands.

Body bullocks were arranged in order of size, with the tallest pair at the front and the smallest at the rear. Polers needed very strong necks and had to be fairly short as the chain from the start ring on their yoke dropped to the fastening on the vehicle. Polers might be bulls or stags (bulls castrated when mature beasts) rather than young bullocks.

Bullocks were matched in their pairs and always worked together. The pairs that made up the leaders and polers had to be particularly well matched, although the pairs themselves were quite different. When yoked the bullocks in the team became progressively smaller towards the rear of the team. Some drivers went even further than this and matched their pairs for markings and colour, but getting a pair that had the right physical attributes and which worked well together was enough for most people.

Bullockies drove their team by a combination of spoken commands and the use of their whip, although the precise combination varied depending on the temperament of the driver and the situation he found himself in.

Bullockies usually made their own whips. The whip itself was about two metres long and was made by plaiting lengths of hide. This resulted in a whip that was light and flexible and although many preferred this, others liked their whip to be heavier. In that case they prepared a piece of leather so that it was about 60 centimetres long by just over a centimetre wide and tapered at each end. This was used as a core inside the plaiting and was invisible when the whip was finished. Whichever method was used, the whip was fitted with a piece of leather on the free end. This was 60 centimetres long and was tapered so that that the end that was tied to the whip was about a centimetre wide and the other end came to a point.

The handle of the whip was the same length as the whip itself, about 2 metres, and was broader at the bottom than at the top. The top was forked to make the fastening secure. The whip was fastened to the handle by means of a keeper, which was a strip of leather about 50 centimetres along and a centimetre wide. The keeper was doubled on itself and the loose ends tied to the whip. The other end was doubled again, passed over the fork in the handle and pulled tight.

Not many bullockies used a cracker on the end of the whip, although they were much favoured by stockmen because the noise they made frightened the beasts and made them more responsive. Bullockies had little to gain by frightening their bullocks, however, and in any case the whip they used was not as suitable as a stockwhip for cracking.

A bullock team consisted of between one to twenty bullocks depending on the job. In practice, though, twenty bullocks were difficult to handle except in the best of going and the largest teams usually consisted of fourteen or sixteen bullocks. The first bullock drays had two wheels and could carry about twenty bales of wool or a load of two tonnes. The wheels and pole were made of hard timber and the tray was made of wooden slabs with gaps between them. The load was held on with ropes and covered with a tarpaulin in wet weather. These vehicles were not very efficient as they were liable to tip when going up a steep rise and bore heavily on the polers when going downhill. They were replaced by four-wheel wagons which could carry about seven tonnes.

Bullock wagons had a single pole in the middle and this was fixed to a turntable on the front axle. The front end of this pole was connected to the start ring of the polers when the team was in place. The early wheels of solid wood were not suitable for rough tracks and were replaced with spoked wheels with iron tyres. Wheels were fitted directly to the axles and had to be greased regularly. The grease was retained by leather washers cut to an accurate size with a brace and bit.

The bullocky did not ride on the wagon, but walked beside the team. His usual position was alongside the nearside poler and it was from there that he controlled the team. He had no reins, of course, and he drove the team with only his voice and the whip.

To start the team, the bullocky, from his position beside the poler, held his whip high and vertically and told them to 'get up'. He then swung the whip forward so that it was horizontal and parallel to the team. As the team moved off he put the whip over his shoulder and carried it like a rifle.

In order to turn the team to the left the driver called 'whoa back and come here'. On this command the nearside leader backed off and his offside partner came around. It was much easier to turn to the left than the right. When the driver was standing by the nearside poler he could watch how the leaders made a left turn, but a turn to the right took them away from him and as they were then on the far side of the team he had no means of knowing precisely where they were. If he had enough room, a driver would rather take the team in an almost complete circle to the left rather than make a right turn. If a turn to the right was unavoidable, his command was 'get off'.

Even turning to the left required a high degree of skill, especially if it meant taking a team of twenty bullocks and a heavy dray through a narrow gate. The team had to approach the turn as far to the right as the road allowed, and the turn had to start at exactly the right place so that by the time the dray reached the gate it was able to pass through it cleanly. The leading bullocks would have passed

125

Flooded rivers or wet black soil made life difficult for the bullocky. If his dray became bogged he hoped that other travelling teams might help to pull it out, as in this case. Otherwise he simply waited for the conditions to improve.

through the gate before the vehicle started to turn and the driver had to decide then whether the vehicle would pass through or not. If he misjudged the turn he had to unhook the team and hook them to the rear of the vehicle so that it could be pulled out and repositioned for another attempt.

Because of the method of yoking, the team could be reversed only when it was not hooked to a vehicle. The driver did this from his usual position by the near poler, but this time he turned to face the rear and said 'whoa back' as he thrashed his whip on the ground. Stopping the team was done from the same position (facing to the rear). The driver lifted the whip high over his shoulder and told the team to 'whoa'.

The team was unyoked in the opposite sequence to yoking, that is, from the polers to the leaders. The chains and yokes were left on the ground in the sequence that they were removed so that they were correctly positioned for re-yoking. Yokes and bows were fitted for each pair of bullocks and were not interchangeable.

Although bullockies were famous for their colourful language, and with good reason, this was not universal. There were two kinds of drivers: those who drove with the voice and those who drove with the whip. Voice drivers were the ones who used colourful language, although not all of them swore at their teams. It was the tone of voice and the volume that conveyed the commands, and these were just as effective even if the words were the essence of decorum. Whip drivers achieved the same result but gave their commands by holding the whip in different positions, or using it. This was another reason for not using a cracker on the whip. The whip was for hitting, not for cracking.

It is not surprising that the more vocal drivers came to be regarded as typical because they were much more noticeable. Bean described how he saw a driver arrive at a railway yard after a journey of several days. The railway porter, no more than a boy, opened the gate and stood near it to watch. The team had to turn right to pass through and the driver could not understand why the leaders kept shearing away. After several attempts he went across to the offside of the team to have a look and found the boy standing near the gate.

> He put his hands on his hips, and drew in one long, slow breath. Then he opened. 'You brass-buttoned, blanky, qualified, asterisked Government official,' he began—it was five minutes before he drew breath again. The boy did not wait. He gave one cowering, shrivelled, bewildered glance at the big man, and then made for the station house as fast as his legs would carry him. He was not frightened of being physically hurt—the big man would no more have thought of hitting a boy than of hitting a woman. But the boy shrank and fled under the sheer force of that language. That was how it affected a human being. Bullocks haven't the power to realise that he is not going to hit them; besides, he may be. So the effect of language on them is not really so strange a matter.

On the other hand, Bean also described how he saw another driver manage his team for half an hour without using a single swear word. '"You fool" was about the strongest expression that man used in twenty minutes. Some people, on being told this story, have plainly disbelieved this.'

Railway yards were the focal point of bullockies in the bush and there were strict regulations to control them. If a bullocky arrived at the yard before 6 p.m. he was allowed to enter and unload, no matter how long it might take. If he arrived after that time, how-

A bullock team at Mitchell in Queensland. The load consisted of 123 bales weighing 12 tons and it was pulled by a team of 26 bullocks.

ever, he found the gates closed and he had to wait until they re-opened at six the following morning. This also applied after the weekend break, so that a busy centre might have twenty teams waiting for the gates to open on Monday morning. The teams were unloaded in the order in which they had arrived, and this was policed by the drivers.

Inside the yard was a high platform called the wool bank which could take two or three wagons at a time. As long as there were railway trucks on the other side, unloading the wagons and loading the trucks was a continuous operation. If there were no trucks available, drivers were allowed to unload onto the wool bank if there was room. If not, they unloaded onto the ground and covered the load with a tarpaulin supplied by the railway.

The wagon was weighed as it came into the yard with its load, and reweighed when it left empty. The difference was the net weight of the load and this appeared on the receipt given to the driver. Drivers also tried to obtain a clean receipt, that is, one that said that the load was received in good order, but few succeeded.

A travelling bullock team made about 16 kilometres a day, so that out on the western plains a bullocky might be able to see his next camp before he left in the morning. As with all travelling, water was the most important factor. The bullocky could not expect to have water on every camp, as they were relatively close together, and at the end of the day he often had to drop the dray at the camp and then walk the team back, or ahead, to the nearest water. This meant that his mileage for the day might be considerably higher than the distance covered by the dray.

On long dry stages, or in drought, the bullocky's job was even

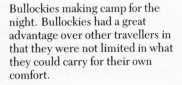

Bullockies making camp for the night. Bullockies had a great advantage over other travellers in that they were not limited in what they could carry for their own comfort.

more difficult than the drover's. He not only had to keep the bullocks alive, but he also had to keep them pulling the dray. In extreme conditions he left the dray on the road in order to save his team. Not surprisingly, his team did not work well without water and some of the weaker bullocks might refuse to get to their feet. There are eye-witness reports of bullockies lighting small fires under such bullocks, although this was probably not a common practice as the animals were the bullocky's biggest asset. There was also an account of how a driver with a small load and a pair of bullocks lit a fire under one that refused to get up. The bullock got to its feet and with its partner moved just enough to pull the wagon over the fire and then stood immovably while the driver tried to save his load.

Mud was another major hazard, especially in black soil country. A heavy dray could sink up to the axles very easily and be impossible for the team to move. If the road was well travelled the driver might be able to use a passing team in tandem with his own. Otherwise he had to unhook his team and take them to firm ground and wait until the mud dried sufficiently to release the dray.

Bullockies had one great advantage over other travellers. They were not limited in what they could carry for their own comfort. Some bullockies were even accompanied by their family, and with them went dogs, a few sheep for fresh meat, and even chooks. Other travellers were always pleased to fall in with a bullocky's camp because of the superior rations, which drivers shared willingly in return for a night's company.

Not all the comforts actually belonged to the driver. Their load often included kegs of rum and other spirits on their way to station stores, and bullockies were expert at enjoying the benefits without leaving a trace. The simplest way was to pour boiling water on the top of a wooden keg and leave it overnight. By the morning this water was well worth bottling. If that took too long, or the result was uncertain, a driver might ease one of the bands of the keg slightly out of position and then drill a hole just big enough for some of the contents to trickle out. He then inserted a slither of wood in the hole, cut it flush, and moved the band back to its original position. One settler who cut an old keg in half to use for storage described how the inside was a veritable forest of little wooden spikes, testimony to countless bullockies who had enjoyed its contents during its well-travelled life.

Most bullockies were so enthusiastic about their job that it bordered on fanaticism. They knew the pedigree of not only every beast in their team, but also every team that worked the same roads. The knew their abilities and shortcomings and these were discussed with other drivers at night camp with the same intensity

129

that car enthusiasts displayed in a later age. One traveller who spent a night with a number of drivers asked them what they would do if they were rich. The answers consisted of lengthy and detailed descriptions of the marvellous teams they would buy. Not one contemplated doing anything else.

It was well for the squatters that this was so. They might abuse the bullocky for arriving late with their stores, or for being slow to deliver their wool. They certainly became angry with any bullocky who held a team for long while on their good grazing land, or who flattened one of their fences during the night so that his team could drink at a nearby tank. But they knew that the bullocky was their lifeline. Without the support that he provided, the squatter could not hope for success.

12

The cooks

APART from the boss, no single individual had so pronounced an effect on the lives of those working in the bush as the cook. The climate had to be endured, but in most places it changed with the months and so could be expected to improve, and dreary work had to be endured in the hope that the next job might be more interesting or exciting. But if the cook had to be endured there was little to look forward to and life was bleak indeed.

Bad cooks are well established in Australian legend. To such an extent, indeed, as to suggest that all cooks were bad and one of the hazards of bush life was to survive the burnt offerings of a cook who was dirty, incompetent and drunk. But not all cooks were like that. Many were extremely good and the best could become legends in one dinner time.

Practically all bush cooks were men, and cooking was a recognised trade that was followed with some pride. Most cooks were so by choice, not by default, and some were well-trained in more conventional forms of cooking. They lived and worked in the bush for the same reasons that others did, but many were quite capable of holding down a good job in the kitchen of a city hotel. Indeed, many bush cooks returned to such jobs for a spell between trips to the bush.

But there is also truth in the legend. Many cooks were bad tempered, lazy and ready to drink or fight as circumstances allowed. That did not always make them bad cooks, but it did make them difficult to live with.

Cooks in the bush worked under such difficult conditions that some of these characteristics are not surprising. Lack of varied rations and poor equipment might make a cook bad tempered, especially when he was blamed for the results. He might then be inclined to defend his reputation by fighting those who complained the loudest, although most cooks were not as fit as the stockman they confronted.

As for drinking, the cook was unique in bush life in that he had access to drink in some form during each working day and the temptation to use it was often too great. That well-known ingredient, essence of lemon, is a good example. Many cooks were addicted to it and no wonder, for this was no modern chemical concoction depending on colourings and preservatives. Essence of lemon was made by cutting thin strips of lemon rind and putting them into a bottle filled with spirits of wine or brandy. It was ready for use after three or four days and could be used straight from the bottle or the liquid decanted into another bottle and the rind discarded.

There were several different classes of bush cooking and a cook usually followed one of them in preference to the others. There was the cooking for the Big House, cooking for the station, cooking for drovers and stock camps, and cooking for shearers.

Cooking in the Big House depended on the lifestyle of the squatter, but the cook's work was little different from that of a cook in a similar house in the city. He had a well-equipped kitchen and probably staff as well and his only inconvenience was that his larder might lack the luxuries or variety of the city.

For the squatter, or more typically the squatter's wife, the trouble was finding a good cook, and then keeping him. Many were ill-suited to bush life. Previous work with the gentry of Europe or the notables of Australian cities made them arrogant in the bush and they usually moved back to those environments and shuddered as they told stories of their experiences 'out there'.

Kate Parker, for instance, had a cook called James who left when she failed to comment on some French roles he had made. His replacement was not much better:

> The next man had a presence which showed a white apron to
> perfection. His manner was awe-inspiring. When I ordered dinner,
> he gazed abstractedly round, occasionally said, 'Yes, Madam,' or
> 'No, Madam,' but never by any chance cooked what I ordered,
> though what he did do was well done. We all so rejoiced in getting
> decently-cooked food, that I refrained from complaint. However he
> began to average three days a week off work, being indisposed! The
> indisposition was a craving for drink, which he endeavoured to
> quench with numberless bottles of Lea and Perrins' sauce. He had
> to go.

This was one kind of bush cooking that was sometimes done by women, but even this had its problems, as Kate Parker found on another occasion:

> Next came a stop-gap couple, one of our boundary riders and his
> wife. Their romance was that they were bride and bridegroom,

A station cook in 1882. His reputation was largely in the hands of the squatter, who decided what stores and rations could be used. Cooks with a good reputation usually insisted on having the run of the store, meathouse and garden before starting work.

though both over fifty... But love-making, though delayed, was not left out of their scheme of life... She was the cook. He worked outside, driving bullocks, and so on. It used to take him half a day to get away, he came up so often from the yoking of the bullocks to say goodbye. Evidently parting was such sweet sorrow. And when he did get his bullocks yoked up, there was a terrific lot of whip-cracking and side about getting off, for his antique Juliet stood watching his departure from the kitchen verandah; sometimes, if he were to be away a night or so, quite tearfully.

Station cooks might also cook for the Big House, but their main job was to cook for the station staff. Their kitchen was part of the dining room and was a separate building which stood near the men's quarters.

The success of the station cook rested almost entirely in the hands of the squatter, for it was the squatter who determined what stores and rations the cook could use. If the cook was badly rationed the men complained that the meals lacked variety, or that luxuries such as jam were not always available. Whatever his skill might be, the cook could soon get a reputation for being a 'poisoner', and travellers who called in for a meal spread this undeserved reputation far and wide.

Those cooks who already had a good reputation took a job at a new place only on the understanding that they had the run of the store, meathouse and garden.

Many of these cooks were outstanding, and some worked at the same station for most of their lives. Ernestine Hill quotes a description of the cook at Pigeonholes, an outstation on Victoria River Downs:

133

He was a little man with brown silky beard an' dorg's eyes, always in a long white sheet of an apron an' a cocky little flour-bag cap that sort o' surprised you in that old bark kitchen. They reckoned he'd been cook an' bottle-washer to a duke, an' he came out to Australia as a chef on a liner. Any rate, he was a white-tablecloth cook. He could dress a bush turkey so you'd think it was the real thing, an' knock up a duff or a curry with caroutes an' canapes an' all them French an' Hindu sauces. For a golden pudding of his made with a dipper of flour an' a tin of golden syrup I seen the boys back up a dozen times—as light as cotton-wool. He was alone out there nearly all the year, sixty miles off the head station, an' his trouble was that he had nothing to cook.

As this description suggests, many station cooks had far more skill than the job required, and some had found their way into the bush for reasons known only to them. Cooking was one of the few skills needed on a station that could be acquired in the city, and those who had it, and could adapt to the bush, were able to start a new life in a way few others could. Doris Blackwell, who spent her childhood at the Alice Springs Telegraph Station where her father was superintendent, described in *Alice on the Line* how she visited Undoolya station only to find that the manager was out mustering:

> But the cook, Charlie Towers, entertained us that afternoon in the kitchen. From there I could just see his small adjoining room, which to my fascination was lined from floor to ceiling with beautifully bound books. He was a tall, bearded man, one of those mysterious Englishmen who drifted to the outback...and stayed there... I had seen enough to know that Charlie had the benefit of a superior education. That rough stone homestead at Undoolya must have been a humble place after the great halls he had been used to [Towers was thought to have renounced a claim to an English title]. And one knew just by speaking to him that his rank was Gentlemen as well as Camp Cook.

Others were eccentric, and some were simply bad cooks. One who was thought to be eccentric, and who was certainly drunk, ran out of his kitchen one day saying he was leaving because there were too many snakes in it. The men thought they were all in his mind until they went into the kitchen and found three huge snakes in residence. One cook who was bad served a pudding on his first night that was covered with ashes but which was uncooked in the middle, so that when it was cut it oozed off the table and had to be caught in bowls. He remade it several times over the next few days without success, until he finally served it as a passable plum duff. But he made the mistake of telling the men that it was still the original pudding, and none would touch it after that. As one of the men said, 'It was a puddin' with a past.'

On the whole, squatters got the station cook they deserved, and the men got him whether they deserved him or not. One squatter,

134

for example, asked his city agent to send him up a new cook and when asked what sort of man he needed, he said, 'Oh, well, just a man who can kill a sheep and cut wood. An' do a bit of milkin', and perhaps fetch water. It might be a good thing if he was a good hand with a horse...'

The man who cooked for a drover probably had the most difficult cooking job in the bush because the rations were even more restricted and his kitchen had to travel each day. The small advantages that compensated for some of the difficulties were that he rarely had to serve more than two meals a day and never had to lay a table.

The cook was usually the first man up on the camp each day. He attended to his fires and made the breakfast, and while the men were eating he packed the midday dinner onto the packhorses. These were taken along by the horse tailer with the rest of the horses.

When the men had left the camp for the day's stage, the cook put out the fires and packed his gear into the wagon, which he then drove to the next night's camp. Once there, he set up his kitchen again, lit his fires, and started to prepare the evening meal.

A drover's cook needed ingenuity above all else. He had few cooking utensils and apart from fresh meat his rations were limited to what he could load onto the wagon at the start of the trip. He had to cook on open fires, even though the rain might be teeming down, and he had to produce meals that were acceptable to men who had been working hard all day.

Many did this very well. If he was given some wild game, for example, he wrapped it in well-greased brown paper and buried it in the ashes of the fire. A pie could be cooked by encasing it in clay from the nearest waterhole. After cooking in the ashes, the clay was knocked off with a stick. Pies could also be baked in large shells or even in hollow stones.

In spite of their expertise, drovers' cooks were not highly regarded and many cooks refused to have anything to do with this work. A good shearers' cook, for instance, would have worked for a drover only in the most desperate circumstances, and then would probably have changed his name.

Shearers' cooks were in a class of their own. Like some of the shearers themselves, many shearers' cooks were based in the cities and worked as cooks there until shearing time came around again. They were as itinerant as the shearers and worked nearly as hard as they did.

The cook was selected by the shearers after they had arrived at the shed. Some of the shearers might have worked as a team at a smaller shed before arriving at a bigger one, and each team would

135

have arrived with their cook. Other cooks would have turned up in the hope of being taken on. Some cooks were known by their reputation, although union rules insisted that no cook could be given a reference, good or bad. Those that were not known, or known to be bad, had little hope of being voted in unless there was no other cook available. If a cook proved to be hopeless he could be removed by a vote of the shearers before the shed cut out, but this was an extreme measure because it might be impossible to replace him. Even a bad cook was better than none at all.

Although the shearers' cook had the benefit of a kitchen this was always fairly basic as it was used for only a few weeks of the year. In a big shed the cook also had an assistant called a 'slushy' who was expected to do at least half the work and all the unpleasant parts.

Cooking for a shed that had 90 people to feed was hard work. The cook and slushy got up about four in the morning to restart the fires and to bake bread for breakfast. This meal consisted of chops, tea and bread. At morning smoko he might serve tea, coffee, bread of some kind and possibly scones. Lunch was mostly mutton in some form or another, afternoon smoko was the same as in the morning, and dinner was mutton again, preferably in a different form to that at lunch.

While any cook worthy of the name could work to this routine, what distinguished a good one was the ability to add variety. Many were excellent pastry makers and served mutton as a pie or as a stew with a top of suet pudding. They also baked a range of cakes, breads and scones for smoko, and made puddings for the evening.

Every bushman was expected to be a cook of sorts. In this engraving of 1881 a team of fencers prepare their tea and damper, a diet that often remained unvaried for weeks.

And when they had time they used offal and small pieces of meats for brawns and soups.

Shearers' cooks were probably more prone to fighting than most, and many believed that the sooner they established their superiority in this respect the better. One very large cook always served the first dinner by saying, 'There's your tucker, gentlemen. You can have a piece of that or a piece of the cook.' Another well-known story describes how a shearer wanted to know what the stew was. The cook said it was a ragout. The shearer said it was hash. After they had made their assertions several times they went out to settle the matter. A few minutes later the shearer returned with a swollen nose and a bruised eye and said, 'He's right, lads. It's ragout.'

On the whole, shearers disliked cooks who were too ready to fight. A good cook had no need to fight, so a cook with a reputation as a fighter was assumed to be short of the necessary skills as a cook. Drunken cooks were also unpopular. Meals became unpredictable in content and could also be late, which was worse. What shearers wanted was a cook who was a 'decent sort', was punctual and generous, and who could provide the variety and treats that made life pleasant. Cooks who met this specification were always in demand, and many became fairly affluent in the process.

While food on the stations might be good and plentiful it did not vary much. John Sherer, in his book *The Gold-finder of Australia*, published in 1853, described a monotony that was a long time changing:

> Truth to say, at most stations the bill of fare is reduced to two dishes and no more. You have mutton and damper today—mutton and damper will appear tomorrow; and from that day till the end of the year your dinner is mutton, boiled, roasted, or stewed, or otherwise dressed as seemeth good to the hut-keeper.

Trollope in the 1870s found station food very substantial but said the most distinctive feature was the similarity of meals. Breakfast was nearly as substantial as lunch or dinner, and lunch and dinner were so nearly identical that it was some time before he discovered the difference between them. Both consisted of two or three hot joints and four or five dishes of vegetables, but lunch, he eventually realised, never had more than two puddings whereas there might be considerably more at dinner.

One thing all bush cooks had in common was that they were professionals who earned their living cooking for others. But every bushman was a cook of sorts. Shepherds and boundary riders were expected to cook for themselves, bullockies did so as a matter of course and others, especially when travelling, might do so out of necessity.

Cooking of this kind was done in the open over over a wood fire, with whatever equipment was available. A bottle was used as a rolling pin, a toasting fork was made from fence wire, a skimmer was a piece of tin with holes in it fixed to a stick, and the dish cloth was a piece of moleskin fastened to the end of the stick and cut into strips. This also served as a weapon which could be used to swipe anybody who complained.

The most basic requirement was to make tea and damper, those staples of bush fare which, with the addition of salt meat, might make up the entire diet for a considerable time. Tea and damper had the advantage of needing few ingredients (and they were light and easily carried) and the only liquid required was water. If the water contained sediment it was removed by throwing in some ashes or a little flour, both of which took the sediment to the bottom.

Originally the quart pot was used for making tea. This was a tin jug with a handle at the side but it was replaced by the more convenient billy about 1850. The billy had a lid and a handle made of wire fixed across the top so that it could be suspended over the fire. Little skill was needed to boil the billy assuming one could light a fire, but there were a number of wrinkles that bushmen used. One was to make sure the billy was full of water if it was to be placed on the fire, otherwise in time the top half of the container would burn through.

The tea was thrown directly into the boiling water and the billy allowed to stand for a while. Those who objected to floating tea leaves either tapped the side of the billy with a stick or whirled the billy by windmilling one arm. The tea was then poured into pannikins and usually drunk black. Milk was rarely available when travelling and sugar was kept for those uses where it was essential.

The quart pot was not entirely replaced by the billy, however. The quart pot became oval-shaped and the side handles were hinged so that they folded against the side of the pot, which was then stowed in a leather container. Those on horseback preferred the quart pot to the billy because the container could be fastened to the saddle so that it did not move. A noisily swinging billy, on the other hand, was often irritating to the rider and frightening to the horse.

The damper consisted, at its most basic, of flour, salt and water mixed into a dough and cooked in the ashes. The result was a heavy bread and was, according to Louisa Meredith, 'the worst way of spoiling flour'. Alfred Joyce, on the other hand, made it sound more pleasant and showed some of the care needed if the damper was to be a success:

> In the forenoon the flour for the damper was mixed in the iron pot and when thoroughly kneaded the hearth was prepared by carefully

setting aside all unburnt wood and embers till nothing remained but the clear, glowing ashes, which were then well opened out leaving a hollow to the middle for reception of the dough, the drawn up ridge around it being ready to cover it when placed in its bed, which latter was finally prepared by flattening it down smoothly with the bottom of the frying pan. The damper dough, in the shape of a flat, round cake, about two or three inches thick and about fifteen inches across, was then laid carefully in its place and finally covered up with raised ashes round the edges, where it was allowed to remain till a knife inserted in it showed no signs of unbaked dough. It was then taken up and thoroughly dusted with a cloth to remove any adhering ashes and set aside to cool.

When travelling, the dough could be mixed on a piece of bark, on a stone or in the flour bag. This was done by punching a hollow in the flour and pouring in the water. The mixture was stirred with a stick so that more flour was brought in from the edges. When the dough was the correct consistency it could be lifted out of the remaining flour in the bag.

This basic damper was used only when there was nothing to improve it. A rising agent such as bicarbonate of soda made the damper lighter and more digestible and there were other variations of this mixture. Johnny cakes were small dampers about the size of scones which could be cooked, with care, in a frying pan. If the cakes were made still smaller they were known as devil-on-the-coals. They were about the size of a biscuit and as they cooked very quickly they were made when there was no time to produce a more

Teamsters at a meal break. Like bullockies, teamsters could carry ample supplies, even down to bottles of sauce.

139

conventional damper. Johnny cakes could also be fried in any fat that might be available, when they were known as leather jackets. Finally, lumps of damper dough could be thrown into a stew to become dumplings, or boiled in water containing a little fat and then eaten with golden syrup. Both were known as sinkers.

Camp ovens made for much more varied, and cleaner, cooking but were too heavy for most travellers. They were, however, much used by bullockies and drovers' cooks. Early camp ovens were made of iron, although steel ovens were popular when they became available. The camp oven had three short legs and a flat lid on top. It could be stood in the fire or suspended above it, with ashes laid on top of the lid for an even heat. A better method, though, was to dig a hole in the ground a little larger than the oven and line it with hot ashes. The oven was placed in the hole and more ashes spread over the top so that the oven was completely covered.

All cooks, professional or not, had to cope with the effects of climate on food. Before refrigeration, meat had to be cooked almost as soon as it was killed, which meant there was little hope of it being tender. Meat that had turned could be made useful again by a little artful ingenuity. One method was to wipe the surface of the meat with a cloth dipped in vinegar, which not only removed the smell but also got rid of the slimy feel. Another method was to soak the meat in running water for anything up to two days or until the cook thought it might escape detection. Herbs and curry powder were also used to make suspect meat presentable.

Curing meat to preserve it was an almost constant task in any kitchen. Bacon, for example, could be cured by stabbing the rind side with a sharp point and then rubbing coarse salt into the holes. Salt was then sprinkled liberally on the meat side and the piece covered with a cloth and left for two days. This was repeated three times and the meat then hung up to dry.

A variation of this method, in this case to cure mutton, was recorded by Mrs Mitchell in her handwritten book of 'receipes' in 1827:

> It is necessary that the mutton should be very fat. Two ounces of raw sugar must be mixed with an ounce of common salt and half a spoon full of saltpeter. The meat is to be rubbed well with this and then placed in a tureen. It must be beaten and turned twice a day during three consecutive days. And the scum which comes from the meat having been taken off, it is to be wiped and again rubbed with the mixture. The next day it should again be beaten and the two operations should be repeated alternately during ten days, care being taken to turn the meat each time. It must then be exposed to smoak for ten days.

It was the combination of ingenuity and skills that are now almost forgotten that made a good cook. It is not that cooking was a thankless task. On the contrary, good professional cooks would be applauded every day if that was what it took to make them stay. It was that the ability of cooks varied so hugely that those facing his first meal knew that the next ten minutes would determine their well being for some time to come.

13

Travelling

THERE is the story of two brothers who ran an isolated
station in northern Australia. During a quiet time one of
the brothers decided that as the wagon needed attention
he would drive it to a station some 400 kilometres away which employed a blacksmith. He ran some horses in from the paddock and
started to harness them, but they had been untouched for months
and refused to co-operate. After they had tangled themselves in
the harness several times, with the wagon lurching spasmodically
on the rough ground, he yarded the horses for the night with the
intention of setting off in the morning. In the morning the horses
behaved perfectly and he was on his way in less than an hour.

Three days later a pastoral inspector for one of the big companies
called at the station while en route for the same distant one. When
he was told that the man was also on the road he asked if he would
be able to catch up with him. The brother said he didn't think that
would be at all difficult. 'He only made eighteen inches the first
day.'

Travelling in the bush was so rough and hazardous that it was not
to be undertaken lightly, although of course many people did. Those
travelling between what are now state capitals preferred to make
the trip by sea rather than overland, and one can hardly blame
them. By 1840, for instance, there were still only five police stations
on the main track between Melbourne and the Murray and the
road was quite empty for most of the way.

But people who lived and worked in the bush had no choice.
Many station workers were itinerant and had to travel from one job
to the next, and the squatter needed to travel to other properties or
to the city from time to time. The difficulties were well-known but
they had to be faced. Often they were faced with characteristic
nonchalance, and sometimes with tragic results.

On an isolated station the only link with more settled areas was the track the squatter had made when he first arrived. It became defined with use but in the early years it was barely visible to those without local knowledge. Indeed, a good road at that time was one that was so clearly defined that you always knew you were on it. But roads of any description were rare and travellers often found themselves crossing open country with little to guide them. Harris described the problem:

> We had heard of a piece of unoccupied ground some distance off the road to the eastward, and rode across to examine it. Our directions to it (there being no roads across the country, except the two or three great ones to the principal points) were up a certain hollow, through a gap in the range, and then across to a mountain on the distant horizon, by riding over which at the easiest acclivity we could find, a creek would be reached, and this creek followed down would lead to the run. Travellers in England would probably think such directions as these poor guidance for a distance of many miles; however, we were successful in our search. Practice in bush travelling gives great address in tracing such natural landmarks . . . The infallible accuracy with which some men will hit a point several miles off in a dark night, and all the way through thick forest, is quite amazing.

Not everybody had this accuracy, however, and those who did sometimes found it was not as infallible as they thought. Getting lost was only too easy and by no means restricted to those who were unfamiliar with the country. Newcomers were, of course, most at risk. Nehemiah Bartley described a Yorkshire man called Mr Stokes who he was taking to his run:

> Next morning Mr Stokes, taking one of the best horses, started out to look for water, declaring he would take the cattle on at all hazards. That night he did not return. The next morning I rode out with the blackboy to follow Mr Stokes' track. It led us to a patch of stony desert, the whole covered with flat waterworn pebbles of red sandstone. Tracking was impossible there. We returned to camp. Mr Stokes was never again seen alive or dead.

Getting lost was that easy. Riding out for a few hours from a group of men with 1500 head of cattle, Mr Stokes simply did not come back.

Good bushmen got lost too. Harris found himself lost when he rode around a small hill while his friends rode over it and it was only by shouting loudly that they were able to find him. And as late as 1894 a man was reported lost near the rabbit-proof fence which he had helped to build in south-western Queensland. A search party failed to find him and it was only by accident that a boundary rider found his body years later hidden by a bush only 40 metres from the fence.

143

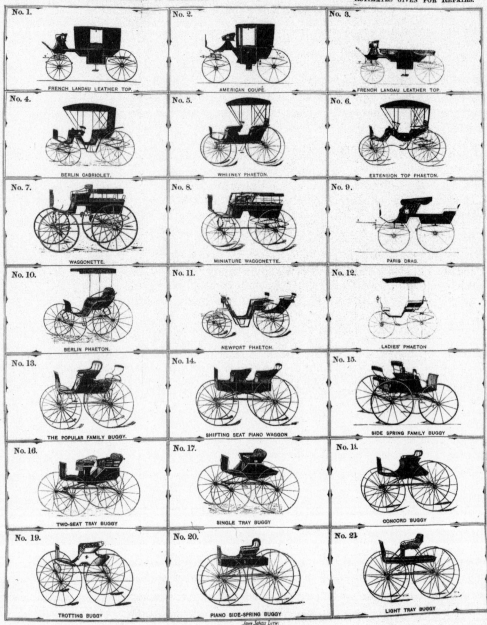

An advertisement from a famous carriage builder in Goulburn, New South Wales, showing a wide variety of vehicles.

As roads became more extensive and more clearly defined, travel became slightly easier. Those who could travelled by horse or bullock dray, and those who could not had to walk. A survey of road traffic between Junee and Wagga Wagga in New South Wales over seventeen days in 1861 showed how light the traffic was, and how most of it was on foot. During that time the survey reported seven horse teams, four bullock teams, eight passenger vehicles, 43 people on horseback and 500 on foot.

Many writers commented on how far people would take a horse in a day, saying that it was considerably further than would be the case in Britain, even though the horses there received more constant attention than those in Australia. A journey of over 100 kilometres in a day on the same horse was not uncommon, and William Kelly in *Life in Victoria* described how a party of three driving a pair of horses went from St Kilda to Kyneton and back in one day, a distance of some 180 kilometres.

Most journeys were, of course, much shorter and slower. Katie Hume described how she and her husband rode a distance of 65 kilometres when returning from a neighbouring property on the Darling Downs:

> We started at 9.30, Walter riding and leading my horse, which I mounted at King's Ck. We then rode a few miles into the Bush & halted in the middle of the day at a spot where the grass seemed good for the horses, which were soon unsaddled, hobbled, & turned adrift while we sat down under the shade of a Gum tree and 'recreated' on sandwiches & sherry provided by our hosts... The solitude here is so striking to one not accustomed to it. In the course of a 20 mile's ride on the *high* road you may meet one dray & team— 2 flocks of sheep, one cart, one horseman! After resting the horses about an hr. Walter caught and saddled them & we proceeded on our journey & I did not dismount until we reached Drayton before 5 p.m. about 18 miles!

Men travelling together often did not have a horse each, but sharing was better than walking all the way. The method was known as 'ride and tie'. One man rode ahead for a prearranged distance, then dismounted, tied up the horse and started walking. The man behind mounted the horse when he reached it and rode ahead for a similar distance (passing the other man on the way), when he too dismounted and tied the horse before walking ahead. If there were three men and two horses, one walked while the horsemen rode ahead. But in this case one horseman rode on as far again after the first dismounted. Those walking mounted the horses as they came to them.

The arrival of children, or of a wife who could not ride, meant that the bullock dray had to be used instead of horses. The inside of the dray was covered with a layer of straw and boxes used for seats.

145

Coach services made long-distance travel much easier and those with no transport of their own now had an alternative to walking. This engraving made in 1888 shows the 'Great Leviathan' coach in Victoria.

Four bullocks were sufficient for this purpose and although the journey was slow there was the advantage of being able to carry a good load of stores.

The four-wheeled buggy was a considerable improvement on the bullock dray and was widely used in the bush by those who could afford them. Rachel Henning described the buggy bought by her brother in 1865:

> We have the buggy up at last and it will be very convenient for travelling to the Port in. It is a very pretty one—double-seated, runs on four very high, light wheels. The whole thing looks too light to be of any use, but it is the strongest of all carriages for a bush road, as it hops over gullies and holes where a heavier machine would break to pieces.

This lightness was a disadvantage when crossing a flooded creek. If the horses started to swim the buggy floated downstream and started to pull the horses. It was vital that the horses were made to walk and pull the buggy, even though the water might be deep and their inclination was to swim. It needed a good driver to do this.

On a journey of any great distance, travellers had to be prepared to spend at least one night in the bush, and a major journey would certainly take several days if not weeks. Those travelling alone or in groups nearly always camped on the way, and indeed there was often no alternative. But men travelling with wives were often required to face the rigours of a country inn if one was available.

Very few travellers ever spoke well of such places. Their prime purpose was to relieve travelling station hands and shearers of as much money as possible in the shortest possible time. Consequently they were usually noisy and dirty and the provision of accommodation and good food was not a high priority as most of their customers had little concern for those services.

Even those who could afford them and had their wife with them often preferred to camp even when an inn was available. But sometimes the prospect of hot water, a served meal and a real bed was too tempting, even though they knew that they would also probably be illusory until the bill was presented.

One Victorian squatter said, 'Of all the impositions inflicted on mankind an inn in the district is the most dreadful abomination. It appears to me the licensee considers only one duty, that is, to persecute and victimize the traveller.' Edward Curr, travelling in the bush for the first time, described an inn that was little more than a day's ride from Melbourne:

> Having got rid of the horses, a step took us into the sitting room, which opened on to the verandah. The building was of slabs, roofed with shingles in the usual way; its dimensions were about thirty-five feet by twelve, with a skillion in addition in the rear, which ran the whole length of the structure... In the middle [of the sitting room] was a deal table, one end of which was laid with washing utensils for the morning... There were also in the room four sofas, of the poorest sort, on two of which beds had been made, the one having an occupant who was already asleep... Supper being desirable after our ride, the startling sound of the big brass bell, which stood on the table, brought the barmaid into the room, who having promised us some bacon and eggs and tea without milk, and tried with a spoon... to stop the candle from guttering, removed the washing utensils to a corner on the floor, and proceeded to lay the table.

Curr spent the night on one of the sofas and was delighted to leave the place the following morning.

Some inns made an attempt to provide a higher degree of comfort and service, but they were not always successful. Kate Parker stayed in one that had antimacassars on the chairs and a bunch of woollen flowers under a glass on the table. The parlour was, she said, full of furniture and gimcrack rubbish, but the bedroom was worse: 'A little stale water sweltered in the jug; a much-used piece of soap clung to a dusty soap-dish, and dirty towels hung dejectedly, as if ashamed.'

The introduction of coach services made long-distance travel much easier, and those who had no transport of their own at last had an alternative to walking.

Although coach travel had been available on a limited scale, the first extensive network of services was that run by Cobb & Co. This was started by an American, Freeman Cobb, and three friends who, after running a coach between Melbourne and its port, in 1854 introduced a service to the goldfields. Cobb left the company two years later, when it was already successful, and in 1861 the firm was bought by another American, James Rutherford, with five partners. The following year Rutherford moved the headquarters

147

to Bathurst in New South Wales and in 1865 services were introduced in Queensland. By 1870 Cobb & Co. were harnessing 6000 horses a day in the three colonies and their coaches travelled more than 40 000 kilometres a week.

Although there was an obvious need for these services, much of the success of Cobb & Co. came from the coaches they used. They introduced the American Concord coach, a large, heavy vehicle in which the body hung on huge leather straps. Even so, the ride they offered was not always comfortable, as Louisa Meredith discovered:

> Not the most pleasant things in the world to climb into by the way, these American coaches! especially in the dark, or darkness made visible by a lamp or two—as they are one indistinguishable mass of mud, with no steps to speak of. But we are in . . . and off we go —bounding, bumping, knocking about—jolting every instant as if a dozen bones were broken in each concussion, and every tooth in one's head jarred and splitting. 'Hold on, or you'll pitch out,' cries my husband, as I suddenly make an involuntary plunge to leeward. 'Hold yourself down to the seat with both hands.'

The best seat was outside on the box and Trollope, who was often offered this position as a courtesy, found it much more comfortable once he got over his fear of being smashed against every passing tree. This seat also had the advantage of being next to the driver, so it was possible to admire his skill and listen to his conversation.

Coach drivers were highly regarded, and were indeed highly skilled, but most had all the nonchalance of the bushman. William Kelly described one he travelled with: 'He sat, rather leaning forward, with his arms distended like a spread eagle, a pair of reins in each hand, and his right foot hanging loose over the side to press the break at any instant. And on we raced, up hill and down dale, in perfect safety, but considerable anxiety . . .'

Trollope, too, was impressed by these men:

> On this road there is a place called the Glue Pot, extending perhaps for a furlong, as to which the gratified traveller feels that now, at any rate, the real perils of travel have been attained. But the horses, rolling up to their bellies in mud, do pull through. This happens in the darkness of night, in the thick forest, —and the English traveller in his enthusiasm tells the coachman that no English whip would have looked at such a place even in daylight. The man is gratified, lights his pipe, and rushes headlong into the next gully.

The conversation of coach drivers was no less impressive. As one traveller said, 'Everyone can lie, and everyone does, more or less, but few rise above the amateur stages: coach drivers are professionals.' In their role as entertainers, coach drivers drew on a considerable repertoire of stories and anecdotes which hardly varied and which were often told by other drivers as if they were theirs.

A coach of Cobb & Co. at a breakfast stop in New South Wales in 1878. Travellers often complained vehemently about the quality of roadside inns.

In this they were rather like music hall comedians before the invention of radio in that both were travelling constantly and the chances of the same person turning up in the audience were negligible.

One of these communal stories told by coach drivers, always with themselves in the lead, described how a parson was on the box next to them. The road was difficult and the driver, hours behind schedule, forgot the parson was there and started to swear. The parson said, 'Please do not use such language, driver. Christ Himself might be listening to you.' 'No fear of that,' said the driver. 'He would know enough to go by Wagga and give this road a miss.'

Drivers also described in vivid detail the smashes they had seen (but never caused) and the miraculous escapes they had had. When told on a dark night when the coach was rushing down a hill they concentrated the mind of the passenger remarkably well.

Nor were they all fictitious, for crashes and accidents did occur in spite of the driver's skill. In 1902, for example, a coach crashed into a tree between Albury and Howlong in New South Wales when the horses were frightened by a goanna. And in 1905 a coach on the Glen Wills line in Victoria was destroyed when it was caught in a bushfire. The driver escaped, but one passenger and three horses died.

Coach services gradually gave way to the railway, but they lingered on for many years in the backblocks. The last Cobb & Co. service was between Yeulba and Surat in Queensland and it operated until August 1924.

Railways themselves had little effect on station life. Development was slow and largely restricted to the settled areas except for

A group of shearers walking to
their next shed.

the main services which eventually joined the major cities. In 1861
there were only about 400 kilometres of railway in the whole of
Australia, and the first through train between Melbourne and
Sydney ran in 1883, although because of the difference in gauge
passengers had to change trains at Albury. Sydney and Brisbane
were joined in 1888 and by May the following year it was possible
to travel by train from Adelaide to Brisbane, a distance of nearly
3000 kilometres. From these main routes other lines branched off
to country centres, but many parts of the country were so far from
the railway that it brought hardly any benefit.

Shearers used the railway for the first part of a journey that usually extended far beyond the railhead. When the tracks stopped, they
took their bicycles out of the freight van and started the journey
proper. Other travellers used them when they could. Doris Blackwell, for instance, describes how a traveller who arrived at Alice
Springs was asked if he had walked the 1600 kilometres from Adelaide. No, he said indignantly, he had taken the train to Gawler,
which was 40 kilometres north of Adelaide.

The main benefit of the railways to squatters was that they carried
freight, which meant that stores could do at least some of the journey by train on the way out, and wool could do the same distance
on the way in. William Pitt Faithfull at Springfield had paid between £3 and £4 10s a ton to send his wool to Sydney by road on a
journey that took between five and ten days. With the coming of
the railway in 1869 the cost fell to £1 7s 6d a ton and the journey
took only fourteen hours. When the line was extended south from
Goulburn, however, it ran through the middle of his property and
he lost about 16 hectares which, he said, would 'ruin the property
forever'.

A station overseer and his dog moving sheep in the early morning in western Queensland. It was in this way that men of similar age travelled in search of new pastoral land.

The station buildings at Undoolya, near Alice Springs. The original homestead, which is the tall building to the right, was built in 1872 and is the oldest building in central Australia apart from the telegraph stations.

An early timber hut at Elgin Downs in central Queensland stands as a reminder of the people who pioneered the land.

A station horse waits for the day to begin at Rocklands station on the Queensland–Northern Territory border. Many stations used thoroughbreds to improve the quality of their working horses.

A dog moving a mob of sheep at Boonoke, near Deniliquin in New South Wales.

The earliest part of the homestead at Springfield in New South Wales, built by William Pitt Faithfull in 1845. The trees on the right conceal the substantial additions that were built later.

Horses at Gogo station in the Kimberleys.

A contract horse breaker fits the first pair of shoes to a horse at Terrick Terrick in central Queensland.

The pub at Conargo in the Riverina district of New South Wales. Founded in 1853, the Conargo pub has been well known to generations of shearers and station hands.

The shearers' quarters at Haddon Rig in western New South Wales. This is a good example of the use of galvanised iron in rural buildings.

Success made tangible—the homestead at Bungaree in South Australia.

Yarding up at the end of a two-week muster at Innesvale in the Northern Territory.

A Furphy water cart with its famous motto: 'Good, Better, Best. Never Let it Rest Till Your Good is Better And Your Better—Best'. These carts, mounted on two wheels, were for many years the only way of moving water.

This old dray at Boonoke in New South Wales is kept as a reminder of the early days.

A bush fire in Victoria. The early squatters had almost no defence against fire because of their lack of mobility and water.

One of the symbols of the Australian bush—a windmill at Brunette Downs in the Northern Territory. Windmills pump sub artesian water from underground lakes and their use brought into production arid land that previously had little value.

Moving a mob of cattle in the Kimberleys. Stockmen were amongst the most highly regarded of rural workers and the source of many legends.

The station buildings at Nappa Merrie, a very remote station on Cooper Creek in the south-west corner of Queensland, established by John Conrick in 1873. The Burke and Wills Dig Tree is a few kilometres to the right.

A group of Aboriginal stockmen at Victoria River Downs in the Northern Territory. Much of the cattle country of northern Australia could not have been developed without the help of men such as these.

Camp drafting at Gogo station in the Kimberleys. Although now a popular rodeo event, camp drafting is still used to select beasts without the use of yards.

A team of shearers in the huge shed at Haddon Rig in western New South Wales. Machine shearing was introduced in the late 1880s and the sound of the engines soon replaced the more muted click of the shears.

Filling a billy with naturally boiling water from a bore in central Queensland. The water comes to the surface under its own pressure.

A stockman rides out at dawn in central Queensland. In many parts of the country the work of the stockman has changed little in the last hundred years.

A group of pure Saxon merinos grazing in the evening light at Winton in Tasmania.

The benefits of petrol-driven vehicles were even slower to come to the bush. By the time cars were common in the major towns they were still rare in the bush even though some motoring pioneers had ventured into the outback on epic trips. Away from the services of a town, cars had to carry all their fuel and oil and they had to be kept supplied with water. In that sense they were far more demanding than a horse and considerably less reliable. The rough tracks cut tyres to shreds and replacing them was time consuming and expensive, and a car could become immovably bogged in a creek that a horse would barely have noticed. Those who did use cars in the bush often had a person behind them with a horse and buggy as a precaution.

Whatever difficulties might be experienced on a journey, the traveller could always rely on the hospitality of the bush. The nature of the hospitality depended on the circumstances of those offering it, but it was rarely withheld. A German traveller, F. Gerstaecker, made a walking tour of the Riverina in 1850 and described how shepherds always allowed strangers to stay with them:

> They will never turn them from their doors, nor ask the least
> remuneration for the shelter and diet they have provided; indeed,
> they seem ashamed to take money from the traveller, and felt
> insulted at the offer. Should he chance to have tobacco with him,
> they will thankfully accept a little.

It was an established custom that almost anybody could call in anywhere and be given food and accommodation for the night. Visitors were not required to answer any questions they did not wish to, nor would they enquire whether a labourer was an assigned convict or a free person. On a big station visitors were given the hospitality of the Big House if that seemed appropriate; if not, they were given room in the men's quarters and had their meals with them. As Trollope said, 'If the house be full, some young man can turn out and go to the barracks, or sleep on the verandah. If all the young men have been turned out the old men can follow them. It is a rule of life on a sheep-run that the station is never so full that another guest need be turned away.'

Bean described how after a ride of about 50 kilometres he arrived at a boundary rider's hut. Two men came out and waited for him as if they had seen him leave every morning and come back each night for the last month. They shared their meal with him and then one of them slept on the floor so that he could have a bed.

There were some rare exceptions to this custom. Mrs Durham, for instance, who had a property on the Hunter River, refused to allow the Duke of Edinburgh to shoot on the property during a visit in 1867 and suggested that if he needed accommodation there were three inns at nearby Warkworth. More typical, though, was the experience of two men who arrived at Undoolya near Alice Springs on a wet and windy night. All the Hayes family, including the women, were out on the stock camp, but an Aboriginal invited them into the house because that was what the family would have wished. They had no sooner settled down for the night than the family returned unexpectedly to enjoy a dry night. When they met the embarrassed visitors the family cheerfully unpacked their gear and camped for the night outside their own house.

If most people travelled only when they had to, there were others who were more or less professional travellers. Shearers, bullockies and drovers travelled as a matter of course, but there were others besides these. At any one time there could be a veritable army of swagmen and sundowners on the roads and tracks between the coast and the dry interior, walking along either singly or in pairs, going somewhere or coming back.

Swagmen were itinerant workers moving from one job to the next, and walking was the only means of getting there even though the distance might be very great. They were recognisable to anyone in the bush, but for those unfamiliar with them a description of a swagman appeared in *Chambers's Journal* in Britain in 1885:

> Picture to yourself a muscular, low-set man walking along at a moderate pace. In one hand he holds a 'billy', black with constant boiling of tea; in the other, a water-bag full of the precious fluid; whilst across the back of his shoulders . . . is strapped a neat but apparently heavy bundle of round, oblong shape, showing only a white calico covering outside. This is the tent; and inside, rolled up in a pair of blankets . . . are his 'gatherings'.

The arrival of the mail at a bush pub in 1865. Mailmen were among the best of bushmen. One stage in South Australia was 550 kilometres long and took four days to ride.

152

People in the bush could often tell which colony a swagman came from by the way he carried the swag. A man from Victoria rolled his swag so that it was about 2 metres long, thin, and tapered at the ends. It was carried over the right shoulder and beneath the left arm. The Queenslander had a short, plump swag which he carried vertically between his shoulder-blades and kept in place with shoulder straps. The man from New South Wales usually carried his swag in a slant from the right shoulder down to the left hip and used a towel as a shoulder strap.

The swagman was essentially, and always, a worker. He preferred to buy his rations from station stores and only resorted to 'traveller's rations' if he was broke. Swagmen might work on a station for a day or two or several months, but in the end they always moved on 'to see a bit of country'.

A man who travelled on horseback while looking for work was called a bagman. He considered himself a cut above a swagman, although in reality they had much in common. He often had two horses, one of which he rode and the other he used to carry his gear. He rarely had a packsaddle and instead used an old riding saddle, across which he threw his swag.

The sundowner, on the other hand, might look like a swagman but he had one essential difference: he was not looking for work. Unlike the others, he was a vagrant who got his name because he would never arrive at a station before sundown, when work was finished for the day. T. Archer, in *History, Resources, and Future Prospects of Queensland*, published in London in 1881, was more restrained than most in his description of a man who did not rate high on the social scale of the bush:

> Next morning he will sometimes apply for work (especially if he has heard that no men are required); or, if he thinks he might be taken at his word, he will be up and away before the manager is about...
> He is, in fact, the product of hospitality run to vice, and a climate that is only too enticing to a man who by nature is inclined to vagrancy and disinclined to work.

Eventually there were so many swagmen, bagmen and sundowners on the road that squatters had to modify the amount of hospitality they offered or risk running out of stores. Instead of providing all meals and accommodation, they gave each man an issue of flour, meat and tea and, if he was not being taken on, he was expected to camp somewhere and look after himself.

The early mailmen were also professional travellers. They were a hardy breed and had to be expert bushmen. The longest route in New South Wales, and possibly the world, ran for 850 kilometres between Wentworth and Bourke. Mailmen left from each end and met halfway at Wilcannia. In South Australia the service between Port Augusta and Yardea was opened in 1864 and ran for 550 kilometres across hot, dry country. It took four days to ride and one section of 70 kilometres was almost waterless, short of feed and cripplingly hot.

The belief that the mail should always get through was perhaps best demonstrated by Henry Peckham, The Fizzer, who was described by Aeneas Gunn in *We of the Never Never*. In 1911 The Fizzer undertook to ride the mail service between Victoria River Downs and Katherine, a distance of about 800 kilometres. On his first journey he was given a letter to a doctor in Darwin asking for advice on how to treat the manager's wife, who had fallen seriously ill.

Thirty kilometres out from the station he found the Victoria River dangerously high and sent his black boy back with a note asking if any of the mail was urgent. If not, he would camp until the river went down. The boy returned with the news that the letter to the doctor was extremely urgent, and so The Fizzer decided to swim the river.

With the black boy in the lead, they urged their horses into the river, but two of the packhorses baulked in midstream and started to turn back. The Fizzer tried to head them off, but fell from his saddle and was swept away in the rushing water. 'Save the mail,' he shouted. 'Save the mail.'

The boy did so. He then searched for The Fizzer before going back to the station to raise the alarm. The body of The Fizzer was found the following day.

14

Staying healthy

T HE death of The Fizzer at Victoria River demonstrated not only the hazards of travelling but also the hazards of falling ill. The urgent letter in his mail bag was being sent to a doctor in Darwin asking for treatment for the wife of the manager of Victoria River Downs. The reply could not have been expected in less than a month, it might not be legible and it might have called for medicines or treatment that were not available on that isolated station. The woman could have been dead before the reply was received, and if she was not the doctor's advice may have been inaccurate or quite wrong. He was, after all, being asked to recommend treatment for a patient he had not seen and whose symptoms were described in writing by someone with no medical knowledge and perhaps not much experience even of writing.

In spite of that, this was the only way, even in 1911, that they could ask for help for this sick woman. There was little chance of her reaching Darwin (The Fizzer himself died on what would have been the first stage of the journey), and there was no better chance of the doctor travelling to Victoria River Downs even if he had been willing to do so. It was medicine by mail order, and it was the best anyone could do.

On many occasions there was not even time for that. Rachel Henning describes what happened to one of their bullock drivers in 1863:

> His dray had capsized in a creek, and, as a storm was threatening which would have spoilt all the cargo, he and the other driver and some men who were travelling up the road with them worked very hard at reloading it. It was a very hot day, and Miller, who was a very excitable man, over-exerted himself, they supposed. Whether it was that or a sunstroke or heart complaint nobody seems to know, but he sat down to drink some water and died in a few minutes.

They buried Miller where he had died. One of them read the burial service over him and when he had finished they built a fence around the grave and moved on.

Falling ill was a hazard in the nineteenth century even in the cities. Medicine was by no means an exact science and many treatments that are taken for granted now were unknown then. But what science could not supply, people could invent. Quackery was widespread and even those with qualifications were happy to use treatments of their own creation. In February 1834 the *Hobart Town Magazine* complained:

> As the law now stands, any druggist's errand boy may bring out his paraphernalia of gallipots and pillboxes, and, fixing half-a-dozen coloured bottles in his window, write himself down as 'surgeon', and kill or cure—as luck will have it—as many patients as may be foolish enough to trust him . . . how are we to discover the incapability of a professional man, till we find he has half killed us with his ignorance, or lamed us for life with his blundering incompetency?

The truth was that there was no way of discovering it. A self-appointed surgeon or doctor, or even a qualified one, might depend far more on a convincing manner and appearance than on knowledge and skill. And if his mistakes were so numerous to become obvious even to those who had trusted him he had little difficulty moving to another part of the colony and starting again.

Many treatments in use then seem outrageous now, but all had their devotees and many were widely used. It was generally accepted by most quacks and qualified doctors that disease could only be cured by purging the bowels. Many medicines were invented that certainly had this effect and they were widely used on young and old alike. One quack in Melbourne said that a double dose of his pills would cure yellow fever, typhus or cholera, and if that did not work he recommended that a sheep's head be boiled until the bones were clean and the liquid given to the patient as a broth. Another Melbourne quack claimed to be able to cure diphtheria by pouring four drops of sulphuric acid down the patient's throat. He was 'called in as seriously as if he were a Fellow of the College of Physicians and a Baronet into the bargain'. Even after a child had died from his treatment, the magistrates of a country town in Victoria found in his favour when he sought to recover his fee.

In some respects those living on the stations were actually safer than those living in the cities. They had to face the hazards of the bush, which included tropical fever, sandy blight and snakes, but the life was healthy in that most of it was spent out of doors, and those who were not fit when they arrived soon were. By contrast,

A bush surgeon's hut in 1871. For many years medical services in the bush were either non-existent or of very dubious quality.

hose in the cities worked in poor conditions, were less fit than those in the country and probably did not eat so well.

The big advantage of life on the station, though, was that it argely escaped the ravages of epidemic diseases. Spread by bad water or sanitation, these diseases often swept through cities with devastating effect. On the stations, though, bad water (in this sense t least) was rarely a problem and although the sanitation might be o better than that of the city it was not used by as many people nd so was not as vulnerable to the spread of infection. Even a arge sheep station might employ no more than 100 people, and a arge cattle station would have only a few dozen, so the risk of nfection was considerably less. In fact, epidemic diseases rarely ppeared on the stations, although when they did there was irtually no defence against them.

The disadvantage was that if doctors were of doubtful ability in he cities, they tended to be even worse in the bush. They fell into ne of two main groups: those who were qualified and those who ere not. Many of those who were qualified came to Australia as hip's doctors, especially during the goldrushes when ships arrived ll of passengers but returned with freight. The more adventurous urned up in the bush and many served their communities well. ower down the scale were those who had studied medicine in urope and had travelled out as assistant to the ship's doctor ithout completing their course. And at the bottom of the scale

157

were those who had never studied medicine and those who ha
but who had since been barred from practising. A. J. Boyd spok
witheringly of one kind and even though this was nearly 50 year
after the article in Hobart the description is remarkably simila
'There then remains a certain class *soi-disant* doctors, who ar
merely quacks. Ignorant, conceited men are these bush quacks
arrogating to themselves the title of an honourable and value
profession, whilst in reality they are a snare and delusion to thos
who employ them.'

As if this were not enough, many doctors were noted drunks
and it was perhaps this weakness that drove them to the bush i
the first place. Some were never known to be sober, others coul
be brought into some degree of sobriety by those who needed the
services, and some were simply not available for weeks on en
even though at other times they were perfectly competent withi
their level of skill.

The other characteristic common among them was greed. The
services were expensive and many were more concerned with the
fee than the recovery of the patient, unless, of course, one began t
jeopardise the other. Boyd describes how a squatter sent for
doctor, who was camped nearby, to tend to one of his shepherds
The doctor arrived but said that he could not possibly see th
shepherd as it was unlikely that he would be paid. The squatte
said that he would pay the fee, and the doctor left to see wh
he could do. He returned saying that he had known all the time h
could do nothing for him. He had been through the pockets of th
shepherd and had found nothing of value. The shepherd died.

On another occasion a doctor was spending a night at a home
stead when the squatter's daughter fell ill. The doctor was asked t
prescribe a medicine, but when he did the child deteriorated s
quickly that it seemed she might die. The family kept watch a
night and by the morning she was showing signs of at least re
turning to the original illness. The doctor, on his departure, aske
for his fee. The astounded squatter said that if the child had died h

A magazine advertisement for
'artificial ear drums', 1881.

would have settled with the doctor by shooting him in the head. The doctor agreed to say no more about it and went on his way.

Doctors of this kind were so common in the bush as to be unremarkable, but there were exceptions even among those who were not qualified. A bullocky heading for a country town broke his leg and sent for the doctor. The man was not qualified but seemed more competent than most and enjoyed a good reputation. He was at a dinner party when the bullocky's mate arrived asking for his help. The doctor immediately changed, mounted his horse and rode 60 kilometres to the bullocky through a violent thunderstorm. He reached the dray at daylight, set the bullocky's leg and had a couple of hours' sleep before starting back.

Qualified doctors were appointed to Aboriginal stations and many supplemented their income by conducting a private practice within the surrounding area. Squatters paid the doctor an agreed sum each year as an early form of medical insurance, while station hands paid for services as they required them. Some squatters paid the doctor on their behalf.

While this provided a competent medical service, the difficulty was that it could be a long time arriving. Alfred Joyce was once thrown from his horse when about a kilometre from his homestead. He crawled all the way home with dislocations to an elbow and both wrists and a sprained ankle and lay in agony for three days until the doctor arrived. At least when he did he was able to reduce the dislocations in minutes, which is more than Joyce could have expected from many doctors.

Distance and isolation were always the most serious factors in the treatment of those on the stations, and this was particularly so in the case of accidents, which were more common than illness. The problem was that treatment was usually needed urgently and if this was not possible a relatively minor matter could become very serious.

In 1899, for instance, William Thompson, the founder of Widden in New South Wales, tore a finger on the hoop of a water cask. He tied it up with a rough bandage but a few days later there were signs of blood poisoning. A doctor was brought on horseback from Merriwa, 80 kilometres away and on his suggestion another was brought from Muswellbrook, which was even further away. It was all to no avail and Thompson died a few days later as a result of an accident that he barely noticed at the time.

Some stations were so isolated that it was impossible to call a doctor at all. In those cases letters had to be sent, as with Victoria River Downs, but a serious injury meant that the patient had to travel to the doctor, no matter how arduous this might be. In 1888

a newspaper reported on the settlement of Innaminka, on Coope
Creek in South Australia:

> Sick men often put in an appearance at this place, and in many cases
> they cannot be taken indoors. Consequently in such cases where the
> assistance of a doctor and hospital accommodation are not to be had
> the poor fellows have to camp out in the creek, perhaps thirteen
> days, awaiting the next coach to Farina. An old man was overheard
> telling a boy that if he were going to break a leg to mind and break it
> a day before the mail left and not the day after. . . Considering we
> are 300 miles from the nearest medical man, and after waiting here a
> fortnight there is still another week of coach travel, the old man's
> advice was good, for the unfortunate with a broken leg would
> assuredly arrive at his destination more dead than alive.

Ten years earlier a stockman on Innaminka station had broken hi
leg. He was taken by buggy to Blinman hospital, 500 kilometre
away and in agony all the way, where the leg was amputated. The
man, 24 years-old and fit, died a few days later.

Some did not even reach Innaminka. At the Nappa Merri
outstation of Baryulah, Queensland, some 100 kilometres from the
homestead, a broken gravestone records the death of a nineteen
year-old stockman who was thrown from his horse.

Sick children were an added worry, and some of the efforts by
parents were little short of heroic. In the 1870s Mrs Crombie rode
150 kilometres up the Barcoo to Tambo hospital leading a pack
horse carrying her son with a broken leg on one side and a stone
on the other for balance. And when one of the Hayes's children
was injured at Undoolya near Alice Springs his parents put him
in the buggy and drove 500 kilometres south to the railhead a
Oodnadatta, where they joined the train for the three-day journey
to Adelaide. The child died there.

For those who were close to it (and not many were) the Overland
Telegraph Line between Adelaide and Darwin provided the mean
for quick assistance after it was completed in 1872. Those lost o
injured could summon help by climbing one of the poles and
cutting the wire. With the line dead, men rode out from the
stations on either side of the break to repair it. As this method cu
the communication between England and Australia, however, i
was eventually discouraged.

Not long after the line was finished it was used to send medica
advice to Barrow Creek in the Northern Territory where the
superintendent had been speared during an attack by Aboriginals
Learning of the attack, Charles Todd brought the man's wife and
a doctor to the telegraph office in Adelaide and transmitted the
doctor's instructions in Morse to Barrow Creek. But it was soo
clear that little could be done and the injured man asked to be
moved to the key. Todd listened as the sound came from thi

An 1872 advertisement for Chlorodyne, a medicine to be found on most stations. Chlorodyne, in common with many patent medicines of the time, contained a significant amount of opium.

remote station in the very heart of Australia and wrote down the message before giving the paper to the man's wife. It read 'God bless you and the children.'

Doris Blackwell described a more successful use of the line after an accident at Alice Springs in 1901 when one of the men broke his thigh. Her father sought advice from Adelaide and received meticulous instructions in Morse from a doctor on how to treat the patient. He was to erect a traction using telegraph wire and fix the injured leg to it with adhesive plaster. He then had to pull the leg until it was straight and as long as the other, and then set it in position. Her father's entry in the station diary recorded the event with the words, 'Oct. 22: Dixon's thigh set.' But at least the man recovered.

Most people in the bush, though, had to manage without doctors and with very little advice. While this was a new experience for most of them, some realised that the Aboriginals had lived that way since time immemorial and they often turned to them for help when no other was available. Kate Parker described how she asked an old Aboriginal woman to look at her husband, who was often lame in one knee. The woman sang for a while then said, 'Too much water there; you steam him, put him on hot rag; you drink plenty cold water...' A few days later an unexpected visit from a travelling doctor produced an identical diagnosis. 'Hot fomentations to the place affected, poultices, a cooling draught. There's a stoppage of fluid at the knee-joint which must be dispersed.'

On most stations the nearest medical centre was the medicine chest. In it was an assortment of bandages, splints, pins and other necessities, together with a selection of drugs and medicines that reflected the preferences of whoever had assembled them. Most of these medicines were commercial products which were

161

either imported or produced in Australia and they were advertised widely and continuously. Indeed, a reader of newspapers and magazines was confronted with such an array of advertisements, each making extravagant claims, that it might seem incredible that anybody should ever fall ill, let alone actually die.

Many of these popular medicines contained opium, and they were so widely used that addiction was fairly common, even though the cause was not always recognised. If a medicine made somebody feel better, then they took it again when they felt the need. But the improvement often came not from the treatment of the problem so much as the presence of opium in the medicine. Until the 1880s about 35 000 kilograms of opium was imported each year into New South Wales and Victoria for use in the preparation of medicines, and in addition to this there was an Australian crop that was used to produce morphine.

Among the drugs in common use, both Chlorodyne and Holloway's pills contained opium, although there were many others as well. Chlorodyne was advertised as the 'most wonderful and valuable remedy ever discovered', and if it had done only half the things claimed it would certainly have been true. Among other things, Chlorodyne was supposed to cure consumption, asthma and bronchitis, cut short attacks of epilepsy and was 'the only specific' in dysentery and cholera. The buyer was urged to avoid imitations, presumably because they were unable to cope with such a wide range of problems. Holloway's pills and the associated ointment were to be found in practically every medicine chest in Australia and were very widely used. Indeed, Thomas Holloway imported so much opium from China that his warehouses there were among the few to be left alone by the Chinese during the opium wars.

Using these drugs was largely a matter of personal choice. Some people swore by one while others staked their life (sometimes literally) on another. Rachel Henning described their 'hit and hope' technique at Exmoor station in Queensland:

> Our stock of medicines is small. I think it consists of quinine, rhubarb, castor oil, laudanum [with a high content of opium] and blue pills. They have taken all the salts; there are Holloway's pills in the store, and when the men have half poisoned themselves with them they come to know what they had better do next. Our treatment is of a highly experimental character. Mr Hedgeland swears by blue pills. Annie believes in castor oil. I generally consider that laudanum will be soothing, and Biddulph recommends quinine as strengthening. Nobody has been poisoned yet, and three men who were really very ill have lately recovered on the station. One shepherd came in to say that he was certain that nothing would cure him but brandy. Biddulph, however, took a different view of the case, and sent him an ounce of salts.

STEDMAN'S

TEETHING POWDERS

TO MOTHERS!

THOUSANDS of persons annually testify to the unfailing efficacy of "STEDMAN'S TEETHING POWDERS" in all those disorders to which fancy is liable during the period of Teeth-Cutting. Unlike most of the so-called SOOTHING medicines, "STEDMAN'S TEETHING POWDERS" are guaranteed by the proprietor and the highest analytical authorities, to contain no **Opium** or other **Dangerously Soothing Ingredient,** and are thereby rendered the **Safest,** as well as the most effective Medicine for children.

Caution.—Ask distinctly for "STEDMAN'S **TEETHING** POWDERS," and be not imposed upon in accepting an inferior or dangerous substitute. Observe carefully that the name "STEDMAN" is spelt with one "E" only.

Each packet should contain **Nine** Powders.   PRICE 1s. 1½d., of all Chemists.

PREPARED BY

JAMES STEDMAN, SURGEON,
East-road, London, N.

Mothers were assured by James Stedman that his teething powder, to be given to children when they were cutting teeth, did not contain opium.

Accidents were, as always, more difficult to handle, but if no assistance was available people had to cope as best they could. During Hamilton's overland trip to Adelaide one of his men was thrown from his horse. He was unconscious for a time and when he recovered he was clearly very ill. The man would not allow them to bleed him with leeches so Hamilton, remembering something he had once read, emptied a cask of its meat, filled it with warm water, and put the man in it as if in a bath. This was successful and the man soon recovered. Unfortunately the rest of the men objected to the meat being returned to the cask because the man had been so filthy when he went in. The cask had to be scrubbed out and inspected by all the men before the meat could be returned and the journey resumed.

Rachel Henning also described an accident that was beyond the capabilities of their medicine chest. A sergeant came to the station with a trooper who had injured two fingers when his carbine had burst. When they examined him they found that the top joint of both fingers had been blown off and the bones were clearly visible. They bathed them in cold water to remove the gunpowder and bound them in a linen rag, telling the man to keep the rag wet, and the sergeant to get the man to a surgeon quickly. He did not do so, but after a few days Rachel Henning said that the man actually seemed to be getting better under the cold water treatment.

If a man was out working by himself and had an accident, his future was very bleak. In 1843 two brothers had a station in the Grampians in Victoria and when one went to visit an outstation the other decided to cut down a large tree that was not far from their hut. Unfortunately the tree fell on him, breaking both thighs in the process, and pinned him to the ground. It was four days before he was found, and it was thought he had died the previous day. He had scraped two large holes in trying to get himself clear.

In isolated parts of the country medical facilities hardly improved during the whole of the nineteenth century—they remained almost non-existent for the whole of that time, and beyond. Elsewhere, country that was isolated when first settled became more closely settled as time went on. Country towns developed and medical help was then closer to hand, but that did not mean that the doctor was either qualified or sober.

People living and working on the stations were aware of the risks they ran, and accepted them because they could not change them. It was not until the introduction of the Royal Flying Doctor Service in the twentieth century that skilled help became available to remote areas.

15

Women and children

NO amount of praise can exaggerate the achievements of those women who ventured into the bush to become wives of squatters or station hands. Indeed, it is surprising that any did as the life could hardly have seemed attractive: living conditions were primitive, attacks by Aboriginals a real possibility and loneliness was inescapable. The fact that many women were prepared to accept all this is remarkable enough— that they went on to make a distinct contribution to station life, to adapt to it and to eventually become an essential part of it is even more remarkable.

It is often said that women were scarce in the bush, but that is not so. It was white women who were scarce. By about 1840 there were, at a guess, probably as many Aboriginal women beyond the settled areas as there were white men. Whatever the figures might have been, Aboriginal women were clearly not scarce.

There is also no doubt that white men had sexual relations with them. Most contemporary writers did not draw attention to this, but there are enough references to show that it was not unusual. Indeed, this is often given as one of the reasons for Aboriginal attacks, although many contemporary accounts indicate that this was not as big a reason as others have suggested.

Many Aboriginal women took part in these affairs willingly and often on the suggestion of her husband. Aboriginal laws certainly restricted intercourse between certain tribes and kin groups, permitting them in some cases and making them taboo in others. But white men were not part of that system. They had no tribe and no kin relationships and relations with them were not prohibited by Aboriginal law because it had never had to recognise that possibility. Provided an Aboriginal woman was well treated and rewarded by the white man, and provided her husband had no objections,

Elegance in the bush,
photographed at Gundagai, New
South Wales, about 1890.

then there was nothing to create conflict. But if a woman was taken
by force against the wishes of herself and her husband that was a
quite different matter. There is no doubt that that happened, and
there is equally no doubt that it often led to concerted attacks
against the white settlers, whether they were responsible or not.

Much of this behaviour arose because there were so few white
women. Men took up land wherever they found it and worked it
with the help of other men. None thought it the place for a white
woman. In any case white women were in short supply throughout
the whole of Australia and even in the towns many men were
destined to remain unmarried. The census of 1841 showed that
in the County of Cumberland, which included Sydney and Par-
ramatta, men represented 58 per cent of the population, but in the
squatting districts beyond the boundaries men represented more
than 83 per cent. Immigration changed this slightly over the next
ten years, but in 1851 men in the squatting districts still accounted
for nearly 70 per cent of the total. In the district of Maranoa, for
example, there were at that time 65 single men above the age
of thirteen and no single women in the same age group. White
women were, as one writer said, 'as scarce as black swans in
Europe'.

The squatter did not usually think of marriage until his station was fairly well-established. This was partly because he had little opportunity or time, and partly because he thought that the place was too rough for a wife. It was only when he was reasonably sure of his success and had the means and the time to provide basic comforts that he turned his thoughts to marriage.

By this time many squatters were no longer young men. William Pitt Faithfull was 38 when he brought his bride, Mary Deane, to Springfield and by then he had been running his station for sixteen years. Squatters did, however, have one advantage over men in towns in that getting married involved them, initially at least, in no great expense. A bachelor in town had to find somewhere to live as a married man, whereas a squatter already had a house and furnishings, even though they might require some improvement to make them suitable for a woman. As Trollope said: 'The thing is so easy that the young squatter simply goes out in his buggy and brings home the daughter of some other squatter,—after a little ceremony performed in the nearest church.' But that was only true when squatters had been married long enough to have daughters.

Women brought with them the need for extra comfort, or their husbands thought they did. The squatter was probably still living in the slab hut he had built when he first took up his land. He might have added to it, and brought in more furniture, but it was still a slab hut with few comforts. Marriage made him realise that it was no longer good enough. Most set about to build a better house, and his slab hut was often turned into a kitchen. He also improved the dairy and perhaps planted more wheat for his own use.

The result was a considerable improvement in the squatter's life. His wife kept poultry and grew vegetables and at last he could look forward to meals that were more varied than the diet of damper, mutton and tea that had kept him alive for so long. He also had somebody to do his washing and mending, or to supervise it with more attention than he had given to such things, and slowly the roughness of station life began to disappear. Samuel Mossman found this very noticeable on a station he visited in the early 1850s:

> Upon our expressing surprise at the comforts and elegancies which surrounded our host, he said his was but a humble mansion compared to many others in the bush . . . and whatever merit it possessed on the score of comfort and elegance was attributed to his amiable partner, who was the presiding genius over the homestead; for his duties took him away to the rougher occupations of the station. 'A sorry place indeed would it have been but for her,' was his warm ejaculation as she left the room. 'When we first settled down upon this spot it was a rough life for the hardiest man to encounter, yet she was not deterred from facing it . . . To us bushmen these are the ministering angels to all our comforts; and you will agree with me when you visit a station where they are not.'

167

A fashion plate from the *Sydney Mail* of 1890 showing a 'gown for country wear'.

The life of the squatter's wife depended on where she was and how established the station was. By the time William Pitt Faithfull married, Springfield was well-established and although it had been remote when he first settled there, the town of Goulburn was now quite large and the district was fairly closely settled. The Springfield that Mary Deane saw in 1844 was more like a country estate than an outback station.

In the outback itself life was much tougher. Ernestine Hill described what a new bride might expect to find there: 'After two thousand miles of hard and hopeful travel, relieved with dreams of "the station", her heart goes down when she sees the old earth-floored lean-to with all its shacks, a patch of grey in a big yellow world.' Her husband goes off to his cattle, telling her he will be back by the seventeenth, leaving her in the care of the lubras and piccaninnies. The day for his return comes and goes. Then she sees dust in the distance and prepares for his return. But it is an Aboriginal carrying paper-yabber from the boss. She reads the letter:

> *Dearest Kit,*
> *There's a mob of bullocks at Bluebush Ted James cut out. I'm going over to get them. Will try to be back by the thirtieth. Give Dandy a batch of bread and a fortnight's tucker. Any chance of a cake? Love, Bill*

Loneliness was inescapable, even in those districts that later became well settled, and contact with other women was almost non-existent. The wife of a squatter who had a station a few kilometres inland from Geelong wrote in *Chambers' Edinburgh Journal* in 1842:

> At this time I had a pleasant visit from Mrs Gibson and her brother; they were on their way to a new station about fifteen miles beyond us. I was delighted to have the privilege of talking to a lady again; it was more than a year since I had seen one; and my little girl had not words to express her delight and astonishment. The sight of a 'white lubra', as she called her, seemed for a time to take away her speech; but she soon began to question her very closely as to where she came from, and whether there were any more like her in her country. I am sure Agnes dreamed of her all night, for she often spoke of the beautiful lady in her sleep; and the moment she was dressed in the morning, she went to look again at her.

In the outback this loneliness was even greater and went on longer—indeed, it still exists. When Bob Watson brought his wife to Victoria River Downs in 1896 she was the first white woman to live there. Her nearest neighbours were at Wave Hill, 160 kilometres to the south, and at Auvergne, 190 kilometres to the north-west.

In settled areas this loneliness was relieved to some extent when squatters started to allow their station hands to marry. At first they were reluctant to do this because wives were simply unproductive mouths to feed. Eventually though, and perhaps in the light of their own experience of marriage, they recognised the settling effect that a wife could have. Boundary riders lived more comfortably, and were less likely to go on a mammoth binge, if they had a wife with them. Soon squatters preferred to employ married men for such work, although itinerant workers usually remained single.

Lonely or not, the squatter's wife had to make a life for herself. She usually became the station nurse, she supervised the running of the homestead (and sometimes ran it herself), and she struggled to raise a garden in a continuous battle against insects, drought, flood and heat that would turn anything decorative into a bare, brown twig. And while doing that she struggled to keep herself presentable. Dresses were made and remade from material sent up from town or occasionally bought from a travelling peddler. There was little chance of being fashionable. Rachel Henning said that Sydney fashion was three months behind London, and the bush a

A life of ease for some—the Cunningham family photographed in 1911 at Tuggeranong in what is now the ACT.

year behind that. 'We get hold of a fashion when we go to Sydney, and wear it till we go down there again.'

Much of the daily routine was boring and repetitive. It was probably so for women in the city as well, but at least they had company when they needed it. Mary Braidwood Mowle, who lived on a property near what is now Canberra, wrote in her diary on 7 January 1851:

> The same old story, get up, dress the children, feed the poultry, breakfast, go to work, put Kate to sleep, hear Florence her lesson, dine, read, feed the chickens, work till sunset, feed chickens, stroll about till dusk, put Kate to bed, have tea, undress the others—play for an hour (my chief solace) work till eleven, go to bed & rise next morning to recommence the same routine.

But they were always part of the station, so that if necessary they had to do things that city women knew little of. Kate Parker described how she was told one day that three sheep were bogged in a waterhole:

> The educated veneer cracked under stress of my one luxury gone. Those bogged sheep make the waterhole impossible for bathing. I had forgotten for a moment how piteous it is to see gaunt phantom-looking, famine-stricken beasts dragging their bones into water, there perhaps to bog and be too weak to get out, a prey to crows. No one who has not lived through a drought can realise the horrors of it.

Some women, perhaps the most remarkable of all, had to take over the running of the property when their husband died. When John

Three bush children at Amosfield, New South Wales, photographed about 1910.

Abbott died on his property in New South Wales in the 1840s he left a young widow and five small children. The property consisted of 6500 hectares and, with the help of an ex-convict, Frances Abbott ran it until her sons were old enough to take over. Also in the 1840s Mrs McMaugh took over Pee Dee station near Kempsey in New South Wales after her busband died and helped to fight off Aboriginals on more than one occasion. And Charlotte May Wright took over the properties in New England after the death of her husband in spite of all the advice to sell. She rode out the depression of the nineties and continued to build a fine herd of Herefords and even bought additional properties. Her son Phillip, who left school at the age of fourteen, later became chancellor of the University of New England.

While that situation was relatively uncommon (for most widows did sell) practically every woman on a station had to face childbirth, and there was nothing routine about that. Often alone and far from medical help, childbirth was either simple or fatal for both mother and child. If complications arose there was not much anybody could do. Even if doctors were available they were not always much use. In 1839 Stephen Henty brought a doctor from Tasmania to look after his wife when she was about to give birth at Portland in Victoria. But when he arrived he was so disreputable that she would have nothing to do with him.

It is not surprising that there are few accounts of childbirth, but those that do exist show some of the problems and traumas that women faced. Katie Hume, living on the Darling Downs and pregnant for the first time, wrote in 1868:

> I have had a very nice book lent to me, called 'Dr. Bull's Hints to Mothers' of which I intend to procure a copy for reference. It is really very valuable for anyone who has not their friends at hand to consult & who, like me, are so ignorant of all that pertains to their new situation. I shall also get 'Dr. Graham on the management of children' which has been much recommended. I hope with these helps to get on in spite of my inexperience.

Of the birth itself, she later said that she had had pains for six hours and had had a severe time: 'The bitterness endured for the night. *Joy* did indeed come with the morning for I cannot tell you my delight when I heard the little one cry & knew she was safe and well.' She had been attended by a doctor and nurse and so, she said, she had 'no prodigious feats to boast of'.

If having children was difficult, watching them die was far worse. Kate Hume's second child died of thrush eighteen days after he was born. In her anguish during the last few hours she suddenly realised that the child had not been baptised and hurriedly sent for a vicar 'who came just in time to administer that sacrament before the little spark of life was quenched & my baby became an Angel in Heaven'.

In Western Australia, Georgina Molloy wrote in a letter: 'Language refuses to utter what I experienced when mine died in my arms in this dreary land, and no one but Molloy near me... I thought I might have had one little bright object left to solace all the hardships and privations I had endured, and had still to go through.'

Kate Parker in New South Wales looked after a small graveyard she found on the station and on All Souls' Day decorated it with flowers 'thinking that possibly a woman somewhere still mourned for them'. One day a woman asked to see her. She was travelling with her husband to his next job and her little girl had died at the last town. She had not wished to bury her in the waste ground next to the pub and in passing the property had seen the graveyard:

> So little Janie was buried in the station burial ground, and round her grave, as round the others, were planted the drought-defying aloes. When the woman, whose tears had seemed frozen in her, came to say goodbye, her calm left her. She thawed; her tears fell, as she gulped out, 'Maybe you'll give 'er a thought now and agen'.

Children might provide a woman with company and pleasure in the bush, but they also created a good deal more work. There were more mouths to feed, more washing to do and more clothes to make and mend. If the family increased each year, this work went on for years before it was finally done. Few women complained about it, however, and many did it for twenty years or more without a break.

The life enjoyed by children depended, as it did with women, on where they were and, increasingly, on who they were. Children of station hands were allowed to run free until they were old enough to work, but even the squatter's children might be required to do quite arduous work while they were still young, especially if the station was not yet fully developed. James Hamilton was set to work as a cattle drover when he was only ten. In 1846, with his elder brother of twelve, he drove the cattle from their run at Kilmore in Victoria to a new run west of the Goulburn River. When he was twelve, James Hamilton helped his father to drive their wool to Portland. When they became bogged, James had to walk 50 kilometres back to the station and single-handedly bring up another team of bullocks. Two years later his father was killed in an accident and the two brothers, then fourteen and sixteen, ran the station while their mother looked after her latest child.

Girls were not expected to work as hard as that, but in a family of similar circumstances they were certainly expected to carry out domestic chores, such as working in the dairy or looking after the

The fourth birthday party of William Pitt Faithfull's granddaughter, Florence (centre), in 1903. All the boys in this photograph were killed in World War 1.

poultry. Later, when squatters were more prosperous, girls were allowed to do very little. Painting, needlework, playing the piano or riding were suitable occupations for girls, and they were not allowed to mix with children of station hands except during formal functions. Indeed, who they mixed with was a matter of considerable concern until they married. At Yulgilbar station near Grafton in the 1870s the would-be aristocrat Edward Ogilvie had all his girls' bedrooms in one corridor and this part of the house was out of bounds to young men. They called it Paradise Lane.

Ogilvie's daughters were not even allowed to saddle their own horse. Instead they had to wait, suitably dressed, on the front steps until a groom brought the horse from the stables. Most girls, even those less favoured, were taught to ride side-saddle. Some were taught that way almost from the start, while others were allowed to ride as they liked until they were twelve or so. Those who enjoyed riding and did it well usually preferred to ride astride in the bush because of the better control it gave them.

Unless they turned into snobs, however, most girls became skilled in bush ways and, until they were older, scorned the refinements they were supposed to adopt. Edward Sorenson in *Life in the Australian Backblocks* described one girl who left a lasting impression on him:

> I was one morning waiting at a station store with some stockmen when a slip of a girl in a tweed cap and satin shoes, and some diaphanous material between, came out of the house with a double-

barrelled breach-loader in her hands. A hundred hawks were
circling overhead. Standing in the garden, she put the gun to her
shoulder and brought down two in quick succession. I had seen
many a smart girl behind a gun . . . but the vision in satin shoes
surprised me.

Children were, of course, faced with dangers that were not known
in the city. There was sure to be a creek or dam not far from the
homestead that would entice young children, especially in hot
weather. Horses might bolt, or snakes suddenly strike at unprotected legs in long grass or at arms trying to retrieve something
from under a log. But the danger most feared by parents was children getting lost.

Surrounded by a vast area of open country this danger was
always present. Children could not be watched all the time and
although the danger of wandering off was impressed on them it was
not always heeded. The trouble then was to find them. Mary
Durack described an incident that occurred in 1877:

> It was during one of Father Dunham's visits, when the family at
> Wathagurra was assembled at Mass, that the three-year-old Annie
> Tully disappeared. Nobody, not even one of the blacks, had seen her
> go and when they found her little pannikin beside the creek they at
> once began dragging the waterhole. Helpers, black and white, came
> over from Thylungra and Kyabra and for three days the search went
> on. Even Pumpkin, Willie and Scrammy Jimmie, notorious trackers
> though they were, could find no trace of footprints on that stony,
> windswept plain where the child had wandered in hopeless circles
> among the breakaways. Young Michael, my father, riding with
> Pumpkin, found the little body at last lying in a gully with some bush
> flowers clutched in her hand as though she had died in her sleep.
> They brought her to Thylungra and buried her with her baby
> brother Francis.

Events such as these were among the most bitter experiences in
the bush. In some cases, however, lost children were eventually
found safe and well, although they had often covered huge
distances before they were found. In the 1880s two young children
got lost when returning from school in Bourke. The policeman and
a black tracker rode out in a circle 20 kilometres from town and cut
the track of the children. The tracker followed the track at a canter,
although the policeman could not see it. Four days after they had
wandered off, and 60 kilometres out, the children were found alive
about a kilometre from the Bogan River. And in 1904 a boy of
two-and-a-half wandered off from a property between Broken Hill
and Milparinka one Thursday afternoon. When they found him the
following Sunday he was still walking.

The social segregation of children on the station also applied to
their education. Children of station hands were educated by their

A group of country girls with their governess (centre), photographed about 1898.

mother, but if she was not well educated herself, which was frequently the case, they might receive very little education and grow up illiterate, or nearly so. If they were on a remote outstation they might also be very shy and run away at the first approach of a stranger. Children of this kind were known as bush rats and although many grew up to become highly skilled hands most parents tried to produce children who were not quite so wild.

The squatter's children were educated by a governess, or more likely several governesses because it was rare for one to stay long. Even when a squatter started a school on the station for the children who lived there, as William Pitt Faithfull did at Springfield, they rarely sent their own children to it.

Governesses, or tutors if they were male, often had few qualifications and might be not much older than the children they taught. An exception was the tutor at Thylungra, an elderly Irishman whose only qualification was that he claimed to have once studied for the priesthood. Nevertheless, he taught the Durack children to read and write and do mathematics, as well as giving them a religious instruction that was so thorough that years later Michael Durack surprised a travelling priest by serving Mass for him without needing a prayer book.

In the second half of the nineteenth century a number of British governesses came to Australia under the sponsorship of the Female Middle Class Emigration Society. As they were not classed as servants (and indeed would have been horrified at such a description) these women were not eligible for government migration schemes. Many were taken on by squatters, although few stayed long as most

175

A mother and her four sons on a sheep station in the west of New South Wales.

found they were too old. Women in their twenties were preferred, and the ability to teach music was essential. Nevertheless, one of them reported that there were advantages in being in the bush: 'Pretty, lady-like girls who go on distant stations, especially in Queensland—are certain to marry well. The Australian men seemed to have quite a fancy for marrying governesses, and it is not at all usual to look for money with a wife.'

Another, Gertrude Gooch, gave a good account of station life, as well as describing some of her problems, in a letter to the Society in 1862:

> Children are very much indulged and have no energy or application, do not like the least trouble. All Australians ride like Arabs, love luxury and money. They live very much out of doors and eat great quantities of fruit. Beef and mutton are very cheap here, rice is eaten as a vegetable and tea is very much taken... Australian children are just like the vegetation here for neither appear to submit to much control... they will not acquire English manners for they do not like them and you can soon see the difference between an English and Australian Lady, but it is very natural. Mothers prefer you to fall into their ways in preference to introducing your own and they do not like to be made to feel inferior.

Interesting though the letter is, Gertrude Gooch missed the point. Squatters had no intention of bringing up their children to be well-bred and English. They probably had at least one example of that working for them on the station, and their opinion of them was not such as to encourage imitation. But, more importantly, Gertrude Gooch missed the qualities that were generally to be found in bush children. These qualities were a product of the bush environment and they were recognised and encouraged in preference to those Gertrude Gooch brought.

For example, Sorenson tells how one day he was trying to catch up a man who was riding a day in front of him. He stopped at a hut and asked a boy if he had seen him pass. The boy could not recognise him from the description:

> But he had seen a person go by wearing a straw hat and riding a brown horse branded H.P., with a star on its forehead, off fetlock white, and carrying its tail a little aside as though it had been broken, and it had cast its near fore-shoe. This was correct in every particular; yet that boy had never seen the horse before in his life, and had just leaned lazily on a rail as it was ridden past him.

The qualities of grit and determination, of being at one with the bush, of being self-sufficient and able to look after oneself and be at ease with oneself—these were the qualities that the second generation of squatters and station hands needed. And, in varying degrees, that is what they had.

They all come together in the case of a widow who had two daughters and a young son. The boy was asked to go into town the following day to do some errands. One of his sisters needed some ribbon, there was butter to be sold and harness to be mended. The following morning the boy harnessed the buggy and left for town. At the end of the day they heard him return but he did not join them at dinner. His mother found him lying on his bed crying. He had done all the errands perfectly and even the ribbon he had brought was exactly right. But he had been suffering from toothache for several days, although he had not mentioned it, so after doing the errands he had found the dentist and had his tooth out without, of course, any anaesthetic. And now it hurt.

He was seven.

16

Technology and change

TECHNOLOGY did not change as quickly in the nineteenth century as it does now, but it changed quickly enough for a world that had seen little technical change in the past. The discovery of electricity, for example, eventually opened up all kinds of possibilities that the previous generation could hardly have imagined. One of these was the telegraph system. It is difficult now to appreciate how revolutionary this was. Until then letters had to be physically carried to the receiver and in the case of a letter from Australia to London that took about three months. The telegraph could now send that message almost instantaneously, and when connection was established with Europe what had taken three months now took about eight hours. We are casual about such things now, but at the time it was little short of miraculous.

Most changes brought about by developing technology were of more significance in towns than in the bush. The supply of mains gas, for instance, transformed the way people cooked their food and lit their homes, just as electricity did later, but the benefits were not felt beyond the cities for a considerable time. And if the telegraph brought information from London to Sydney much more quickly, it still took as long as it ever did to get the information from Sydney to the bush.

But there were some technical developments that had an enormous effect on the pastoral stations, and through them on the economy of the whole of the country. Machine shearing was one, but there were others of equal importance. Few of these brought any benefits to the cities, and consequently their significance has been overshadowed or almost forgotten. But the four described in this chapter—fence wire, corrugated iron, artesian water and commercial refrigeration—changed Australia more dramatically than is sometimes thought, and certainly brought great changes in the way squatters ran their stations.

We have seen how, when shepherds deserted their flocks for the goldfields, squatters found that their sheep were capable of looking after themselves provided they were restricted within the run by fences. The immediate benefit was a saving in cost. A thousand sheep had needed two shepherds and a hutkeeper to look after them, but now several thousand sheep needed no more than one boundary rider to check the fences. The sheep improved too. Putting each flock into hurdles each night might have protected the sheep from dingoes, but the price was paid in a high incidence of disease. Hurdles were moved frequently to guard against this, but that did not protect the flock against an outbreak of infectious disease which may have come from a travelling mob passing through the run.

The need for fencing, and the benefits it could bring, could hardly have been met by traditional methods. Building fences with timber or even felled logs was a lengthy business and, because of that, expensive. When the need for fences was not very great this could be accepted, indeed it had to be, but when the need increased dramatically, as it did with the desertion of the shepherds, such methods cost more than could be saved by having fewer men. It would, in any case, have taken years to fence a station in this way.

What made fencing possible on a large scale was the use of wire, and it was a lucky accident that it became available just as the shepherds were leaving their flocks. Fencing wire was imported into Victoria in the early 1850s and its advantages were immediately obvious. It was relatively cheap, it could be erected quickly and breaks could be seen readily and quickly repaired.

One writer in the 1860s described how a run of 311 square kilometres which had employed thirteen shepherds and seven hutkeepers could be managed by six boundary riders after it had been fenced into paddocks. By 1870 there was more than 32 000 kilometres of fencing in New South Wales alone and by 1880 this had increased to more than 300 000 kilometres. When wire reached the runs in western Queensland in the 1870s the labour force there fell by 80 per cent. Trollope, writing in the early 1870s, said:

> Nothing, I think, gives a surer proof of the wealth of the Australian colonies generally, than the immense amount of fencing that has been put up in the last ten years. A run of twenty miles square, or containing 400 square miles, equal to 256 000 acres, is by no means

179

excessive in size, though it is about as big as a small English county. The squatter who intends to paddock his sheep instead of hiring shepherds to go about with them, has to divide his area into perhaps twenty different paddocks. Should he do this, with the smallest amount of distance of partitions, he would have to make 240 miles of fencing.

In many cases this was the first major improvement that squatters made to their run, and it was made possible by good wool prices and a more secure tenure over the land they occupied. But the cost of fencing on a large scale was considerable. A five-wire fence cost about £40 a mile, so the squatter described by Trollope would have had to find about £10 000 for his 240 miles of fencing.

Few doubted that it was worth it. When James Richmond bought Haddon Rig in New South Wales in 1873 he spent the next two years erecting about 345 kilometres of boundary and paddock fencing and in the process used almost the entire stock of fencing materials held in Sydney and Melbourne.

Wire fences not only reduced wage costs, they also increased the level of stocking. Between 1861 and 1894 the sheep flock of New South Wales increased from 6 million to 57 million, while the total number of cattle barely changed. It was this increase that made sheep graziers important and influential. It had been brought about by a considerable investment on their part and they were conscious of the importance it gave them in the national economy. At the same time, overstocking became a problem and many lessons had to be learnt for the first time.

Wire fencing was, of course, of little value to the squatter who ran cattle. Even the placid beasts of settled country could not be restrained by a few strands of wire and the wild mobs of the north would barely have noticed them. That changed, however, with the later development of a variation of wire fencing that used barbed wire.

In the USA in 1873 Joe Glidden and a couple of friends went to the De Kalb county fair in Illinois and saw a salesman demonstrate a new fence. It consisted of a wooden board with spikes sticking from it which was hung along the top wire of a conventional fence. Cattle would not go near the spikes even when pushed by dogs.

Glidden could see the advantages of the fence but thought there must be a better way than using wooden boards. He tried fixing spikes straight on to the wire, but could not get them to stay in place. Then one day the wires tangled as he was picking them up. He examined the mess, then twisted two strands of wire together and bent a short piece of wire between the twists. Suddenly he was looking at a thorn hedge made of wire.

Machines were developed that could produce this wire at the

rate of 70 barbs a minute and by 1883 one factory alone was producing nearly 1000 kilometres of barbed wire every ten hours. Barbed wire was imported into Australia almost as soon as it became available, and the squatter who ran cattle could at last enjoy the benefits of cheaper fencing.

While the economic benefits of fencing were very important, there was another benefit that was less obvious. Fencing meant that breeding could be carried out with more sophistication. The squatters could now select their best stock and keep them separate from the rest. By breeding from this selected stock they could expect to improve the rest more certainly than they had when it was left to nature. Some squatters had tried to improve their stock by selective breeding since the 1830s and some had become famous as stud breeders, but fencing not only made this easier but also meant that even those who did not want to be stud breeders could still improve their own stock as a result of the better control that fences provided.

At the same time, the introduction of corrugated iron provided a cheap building material in what was another major advance in the bush.

Flat sheets of iron had been available for many years and were used to make buckets and other tools and utensils in factories. But iron was not very rigid when flat and its use was therefore limited. People had known for centuries that metal could be made stiffer by corrugating it, but it was not until the middle of the nineteenth century that this could be done by machine. This also coincided with another essential development—the prevention of rust.

A French chemist called Sorel invented a process in 1836 in which he galvanised iron by dipping it in a bath of molten zinc. Even then he did not entirely understand how it worked, but the

An early artesian bore at Weilmoringle in New South Wales. The discovery of vast areas of underground water in the 1870s meant that many landowners were no longer dependent on seasonal rains, and land that previously had little use was now brought into production.

process produced an alloy of iron and zinc which was able to resist corrosion. When John Spencer invented a machine in England in 1844 that made corrugations quickly by passing the sheets between specially designed rollers, production of galvanised corrugated iron became possible on a large scale.

The product met with resistance elsewhere but found immediate acceptance in Australia. It was an ideal material for roofing, which until then had been made from shingles or sheets of bark, but it could also be used to clad walls as well. Galvanised corrugated iron was cheap, light and easily worked. It was imported into Australia in vast quantities and most of it was used in buildings on the goldfields and on the stations.

Valuable though these inventions were, squatters needed one thing more than any other, and that was water. Indeed, as they fenced their land into paddocks they needed it more than ever, because it was unlikely that each new paddock would have its own source of natural water. Much of the benefit of fencing was lost if stock had to be moved to water.

Squatters still depended entirely on natural water. If there was plenty of it, then their station was in good order and their stock did well. If there was not enough the stock died and there was little they could do to keep them alive.

All they could do to protect themselves from drought was store water when it was plentiful. They did this by putting a dam across the creek or river that had attracted them to the land in the first place. But in doing this they reduced the water supply downstream, which might deprive neighbouring squatters of this most valuable resource, or even make parts of their own run more difficult to manage.

They could also store water in an earth tank that was built to catch the rainwater and, given the right site, run-off from surrounding country, but this was a major undertaking. The first requirement was a supply of water nearby that could be enlarged if necessary to provide enough water for the men and bullocks while the tank was being constructed. The teams of bullocks were then used to pull scoops through the ground to remove the earth, and this earth was used to build up the sides of the tank.

Even after the tank was finished, and at considerable cost, it was often many months and sometimes years before there was enough rain to fill it. And when it was full the earth walls might prove incapable of retaining the water, or might be washed away in a sudden deluge. The squatter might also find, as one man certainly did, that when his property was eventually surveyed the tank he had so laboriously constructed was on the wrong side of his boundary.

Whatever the squatters did and whatever it cost, the fact remained that they depended entirely on rain. What changed that was the discovery of underground water in a quantity that seemed limitless and which covered an area of about 1.7 million square kilometres.

It is strange there should be confusion over the first person to make such an important discovery, but the first flowing bore was probably that at Kallara station near Bourke in New South Wales in 1878, and the first in Queensland was at Barcaldine in 1888. This water came from the Great Artesian Basin and was true artesian water in that when a hole was drilled the water came to the surface under its own pressure, and in many cases at or near boiling point.

Drilling the hole to tap this water was a skilled job and the costs were considerable as it could take anything up to two years to drill a deep hole. Most holes were drilled by raising and lowering a heavy bit, a method known as percussion drilling. The bit was suspended from a tower on a steel cable and was raised and released by a steam engine. At the bottom of the hole the bit produced an accumulation of wet soil which was removed by lowering a sand pump into the hole. The pump collected this loose soil and was then lifted to the surface and emptied. As the hole became deeper, steel casing was lowered to retain the walls. If the soil was unstable the casing might be almost on the bit, but in firmer ground it could be 30 metres above the drilling point. Dropping tools down the casing was not popular as they had to be fished out before drilling could start again. When the bit had to drill through rock the progress might be only a metre a day, and if a layer of granite bedrock was encountered the hole was usually abandoned.

Artesian bores could be a considerable depth—what was then the deepest bore in the world was drilled at Bimerah station in Queensland in 1895 and went to a depth of 1600 metres. Sub-artesian bores were, in spite of their name, not as deep as artesian bores and varied from only 2 metres to about 100 metres. Sub-artesian water did not flow to the surface under its own pressure and instead had to be pumped out. This was done by the familiar windmill mounted on a tall frame above the bore.

Bore water varied in quality. At best it could be used domestically, but the presence of salts and minerals often made it suitable only for stock. The water could be collected at the bore head in an earth tank and supplied to troughs, or it could be fed into open drains which then followed the contours of the ground to distant paddocks. This was particularly suitable with true artesian bores as the water cooled down as it ran along the open drains.

Those lucky enough to have access to underground water no longer had to depend on rainfall for their stock, although they still needed it for paddock growth. Even in the harshest drought the

183

bores continued to supply water. Land which had been marginal, such as that in western Queensland for example, now became usable and could be brought into full production. Previously, settlement had advanced in the good seasons and had been driven back when the droughts came. Now, the land could be used with confidence all the time.

Bores also took the uncertainty and much of the danger out of cattle droving. Previously the drover had relied on natural water, but in a dry period there was often not enough to keep his mob alive and on a long trip he could become stranded as the waters ahead of him failed. Now, governments installed bores at suitable points along the major stock routes and droving became much more certain.

The discovery of artesian water coincided with another major technical development: commercial (and especially marine) refrigeration. Refrigeration meant that Australian growers had a market beyond Australia, and artesian water brought new land into production on which the herds could be raised. This combination turned cattle-raising into a major Australian industry.

Techniques of preserving meat in tins had been known for some time. Indeed, a 2 kilogram tin of roast veal accompanied Sir William Parry's expedition on a journey to the Arctic Circle in 1824 in an attempt to discover a north-west passage around the top of the American continent. This tin survived another trip two years later without being eaten, perhaps because the instructions on the can read: 'Roasted Veal, cut round on the top near to the outer edge with a chisel and hammer'.

A canning factory was started in Australia in 1847 and by the 1860s large amounts of tinned mutton were being exported to England. But while it found a steady market it was not an overwhelming success. The meat remained in good condition but unfortunately lost so much flavour as to be practically tasteless. It cost about half the price of good English meat and was welcome for that reason alone, but most people still preferred to eat English meat even if they had to settle for half as much.

In one sense the solution to preserving meat was well known. Food that was surrounded by ice kept for a long time, and meat was no exception. But the practical application was another matter. Meat being sent to England from Australia faced a long sea voyage and crossed the equator on the way. Keeping meat frozen long enough on a ship was a technical problem that remained unsolved for many years.

The first breakthrough came in the early 1870s when Professor Linde of Munich invented a machine that used compression to lower the temperature of an insulated room. Meanwhile, in Australia James Harrison, the editor of the *Geelong Advertiser*, was experimenting with a machine of his own. He recognised that ice alone was not sufficient to preserve meat on the long voyage to England—the meat itself would have to be frozen first. The method he developed froze the carcasses right through, yet the flavour remained when they were thawed. In 1873 Harris staged a banquet in Melbourne at which the guests were served poultry, fish and meat that had been frozen for the past six months and which was the equal of any that had been freshly killed. Later that year Harrison shipped 20 tonnes of frozen lamb to England on board the *Norfolk*. Unfortunately the machinery broke down during the voyage, the meat was ruined, and so was Harrison.

The next person to try was Thomas Mort, who devised a system that depended on ice to keep the holds of a ship at a temperature below freezing. The ice was made during the voyage and this was a major engineering achievement at that time. Or it would have been had it worked. In 1877 his first shipment went bad because the machinery failed before the ship had left Sydney Harbour, and Mort was £80 000 the poorer.

In the end it was two young Scottish shipowners, McIlwraith and McEacharn, who succeeded where Harrison and Mort had failed. In 1879 they chartered the *Strathleven*, an emigrant steamer, and fitted it with a compact refrigeration plant. About 80 tonnes of butter and 30 tonnes of meat were loaded in Australia and when the ship reached England the following year the cargo was still

Part of the cargo of frozen meat and butter on the *Strathleven* in 1879. This was the first successful shipment of refrigerated produce and it opened the first export markets for Australian meat producers.

185

in perfect condition. On 26 March 1880 *The Times* in London, reporting the success, said: 'It is accordingly established that meat can be frozen in Australia and delivered to all appearance in prime condition in London... Before long it may be no uncommon thing for an English family to dine on fresh meat which was fed and killed at the Antipodes.'

At last the Australian cattle industry had a market beyond its shores. It had always been able to supply more meat than the domestic market needed, but here was a market that could take all it could produce.

The immediate effect was a large pastoral development in western Queensland and, later, the Northern Territory. Further south, in settled areas, there was not much room for expansion and much of the country was given over to running merinos for wool. But in the north there was land on a vast scale which had not been taken up, and most of it was quite unsuitable for sheep. Indeed, without the use of artesian water it was unsuitable for almost anything. It was this fortuitous combination of market and water that allowed Australia to become one of the world's leading producers of beef.

There were other consequences too. The development of refrigeration meant that meatworks could be established near the cattle stations instead of near the cities. Meat frozen there could be shipped to the domestic market or to the ports for export. So the station owner no longer needed the drover to overland mobs of cattle to the coast. There remained the need to overland cattle to other properties for fattening, and to take cattle to the new meatworks, but these journeys were not as long as they once were.

Although the benefits of these technical developments, especially artesian water and refrigeration, had a considerable effect on the Australian economy, none of them involved governments directly or the use of public money except for the bores that were sunk along the stock routes. Squatters paid for their fencing and their bores, shipping companies installed refrigeration in their ships, and the benefits to the whole of Australia were enormous.

17

Enjoying success

SUCCESS was very selective. Indeed, there were so many factors seeming to conspire against the squatters that it is remarkable that any survived at all. They selected their land simply on what they could see and without knowing whether they were seeing it at its best or its worst. Or they bought it when the original owner could continue no longer, and often paid a price that reflected boom conditions that did not last. They faced open hostility from Aboriginals, they saw their stock die from drought or diseases for which they had no cure, and they coped with the vagaries of market prices and the shocks to the national economy.

A great number did not survive. Almost any one of these factors could bring about the downfall of a squatter. It was not that the squatter was always incompetent (although some were) but that things simply went wrong. Some circumstances made failure almost inevitable, such as insufficient capital or land that was incapable of supporting enough stock. But it was the unpredictable that did the most sorting out. Some squatters had to fight the Aboriginals longer, some had droughts that went on longer than most, some had stock disease longer and on a larger scale than others, some happened to be weak financially (and sometimes uncharacteristically) when the economy tumbled. The strong-willed and competent had more chance of surviving than the rest, but only a little.

Those who did survive were nearly always strong in every sense of the word. Perhaps they had a little more determination, perhaps they also had a little more luck, but the squatters who did survive, among the first generation at least, all seem to have had qualities that would probably have made them successful in other ventures. They were tested as much as the others, but they survived where others failed. But even that success could be ephemeral, as many children of pioneers found during the 1890s.

High wool prices in the 1860s and the next twenty years allowed many squatters to build huge mansions in the bush. This picture is of Rupertswood near Sunbury in Victoria. The house had its own railway platform for the convenience of visiting guests.

The successful squatters eventually reached a position that was quite different from the circumstances of their earlier days. Their success became visible, and inevitably it was envied. Those who resented these signs of success, then and later, often overlooked that success had been a long time in coming. And real success, measured in the ability to ride out bad times with confidence, took even longer.

The effort that produced success of this kind was counted in generations. The appearance of wealth came at a late stage, but because it was visible it seemed to others as if it was instant. It rarely, if ever, was. Macarthur's property at Camden Park is a case in point. When John Macarthur died in 1834 the property was still being developed and he had never lived on it. By the time his sons had raised it to a degree of success and security the family had been running Camden Park for 65 years, John Macarthur had been dead twenty years and his sons were in middle age.

This was true of nearly all successful properties. A man who started a property, perhaps in the thirties or forties, had to work 30 years before he could claim to be successful, and his family had to continue that work when the old man died.

By the 1870s, though, many of the original squatters could claim to be successful and were enjoying an affluence that they had barely dreamed of when they first walked their stock on to their land. But in spite of this affluence, the original pioneers did not change very much. Their children might be very different, and those who had bought successful properties might also be different, but the pioneers remained true to what they had set out to do.

Men who became successful and wealthy in other occupations often measured their success by how far they could distance themselves from its source. Industrialists might not see their factory from one week to the next, professional men might cease to practice and enjoy the life of a gentleman instead, so that in time the source of their wealth might become so distant as to be almost invisible.

This was never so with the pioneer squatters. They remained actively involved with their land and stock all their life. They might not work each day, as they once had, but they knew which of their stock was doing well, which experiments were succeeding and which were not, what needed to be repaired around the place and how much wool or meat they had produced last year and what prices they had brought. In 1888 William Pitt Faithfull was 82 years old when he wrote to his daughter complaining: 'I have not a horse to ride or a bullock to drive, you may just think what an old man has to go through.' It is difficult to believe that many bankers of that age yearned for the touch of blotting paper, or lawyers their wigs.

If the squatter had not changed much, the property had. The land was now settled and much of the ruggedness had gone. Henry Cornish, a visitor from India, described the property of Langford, near Hamilton in Victoria, in his book *Under the Southern Cross* in 1880:

> I was not a little surprised, when we arrived at the end of our journey, to find myself before a large, well-built country-house surrounded by a tastefully laid-out garden; a fine sheet of water in an adjoining field, with rowing boat thereon; a well-stocked orchard, of three or four acres in extent on one side, a carriage drive lined with avenues of trees on the other . . . It might have been a country-house in England so far as all the immediate surroundings were concerned.

In the 1860s even the political attempt to reduce the size of the landholdings was successfully resisted by most squatters. Those who had come to Australia in search of gold objected to the fact that much of the land was securely held and there were few

A Riverina homestead in 1874.

opportunities for people to own land of their own. The popular cry
went up to 'unlock the land' and governments obliged by passing a
series of Selection Acts under which anybody could select up to
260 hectares of a squatter's land and establish themselves on it as
cropping farmers.

Squatters resisted this, sometimes with little effort, sometimes
at considerable expense. They were allowed to buy their homestead block for £1 an acre and the rest at valuation. But they were
also allowed to select land like anybody else. So they selected land
with water frontages (called peacocking), thus denying access to
those selecting other blocks, and if that was not enough they
arranged for members of their family, and even 'dummies', to
make other selections. The land had to be occupied, but that could
be done by erecting a portable hut so that it stood at the inter-
section of four selections and so occupied them all.

In the end, selection failed. Some people selected in order to
sell the land back to the squatter for a profit, others sold when they
found that 260 hectares of grazing land was incapable of supporting
them as farmers. The result was that most squatters not only
retained their land, but were often able to increase their holding
by buying more.

By the 1890s many squatters had holdings of enormous size.
Tyson, then reputed to be the wealthiest man in Australia, ran
70 000 head of cattle on one of his many properties; the adjoining
stations of Mergular and Canonbar in New South Wales were
bigger than the whole of Belgium, and Brookong station, owned by

William Halliday, covered 81 000 hectares and ran a quarter of a million sheep. Cordillo Downs covered 2214 square kilometres and it was said that there were always 150 men employed—50 on the property, 50 on their way there and 50 on their way back.

With bigger properties, the squatter had to employ more people to run them. It was not simply a matter of employing more boundary riders or stockmen, it was also a matter of employing people for jobs that had not existed until now.

One of these new jobs was that of manager. On properties owned by companies, such as many of the northern cattle properties, managers were employed from the start, but they now came to be employed on sheep stations when the squatter started to take a less active role, and especially if he had no sons, or they were too young, to take over from him.

The manager was a most important and respected person. On company-owned properties his role was the same as if he owned the place, but even when the owner was still living and working on the property the role of the manager was very important. Outside the Big House his control was usually absolute, although some squatters had difficulty recognising this. The manager hired and fired the men, sold and bought stock, saw to the shearing and generally kept the whole place in working order.

Some managers were legendary. One was Billy Young, who managed Lansdowne in central Queensland from 1889 to 1898. He is said to have marked 9000 lambs in one day and a working day that started at daylight and finished at dusk was known as a 'Billy Young day'. But his most notable characteristic was his thoroughness. He refused to pay for fence posts that were not absolutely true and well planted, or a yard rail that was not exactly to specification. Even nuts and bolts had to be perfectly square. When a later manager watched one of Young's yards being dismantled he found that the posts that held the drafting gates were sunk in the ground to a depth of nearly 2 metres even though there was little more than a metre above ground.

Some managers, especially on company-owned cattle properties, did little stock work themselves and instead left it to the overseer. The overseer was usually a young, single man who, like the manager, was socially far removed from the people they employed. Many overseers went on to become managers, others remained with one station and became indelibly associated with it.

Another new job that came into existence at this time was that of bookkeeper. On a small property the accounts were kept by the owner or the manager, but on a large place this became a specialised job. Most bookkeepers were young men who lived in a cottage if they were married, or in the men's quarters if not. Many

The house at Belltrees, near Scone
in New South Wales,
photographed about 1910.

were well qualified and took the work in order to save money,
others were notorious drunks who were not capable of holding
down a professional job in the city. Those who stayed were
generally unambitious, and needed to be because there was little
hope of promotion.

By this time the centre of the station looked like a small town.
There could be 60 or 70 men employed there, and with their
families this might mean that the population of the station was
more than 100 people. They all had to be accommodated. Large
barracks housed the single men, while married men lived in
cottages that were often built in rows to form complete streets.
There was the men's dining room and kitchen, run by the station
cook, and there were tradesmen's workshops arranged all around
this central area. Nearby was the woolshed and shearers' quarters
with a kitchen of its own. There were stables for horses, sheds for
wagons, barns for feed and, most important, the station store
where the married men drew their rations and which could supply
anybody with most of the comforts they could buy in town. On a
big and isolated station the profit made by the store was an important part of the total income. To cater for other needs there
might be a church, a school and a graveyard.

Many men spent their entire working life on one property, and
expected their sons to be employed there when they became old
enough. It was not unusual, as time went on, for a property to have
employed three generations of the same family, and sometimes all
at once. Men and their families associated themselves totally with
the property. It was their home. Some had been born and brought
up there and most continued to live there when they retired.
These people had little in common with itinerant workers. They
had roots and loyalties and moving to another property was a major
trauma.

And at the top of this structure were the squatters, who ruled a self-contained empire with benevolence or autocracy depending on their nature. The autocracy and arrogance are the best re-membered and the benevolence has been largely forgotten. But many squatters were benevolent even though it was not always apparent. A man might seek financial help when in difficulties and be given it, but not publicly; another might be kept on long after illness had made him unable to work. Most squatters realised that the welfare of their staff and their families was in their hands, and they accepted this responsibility without hesitation. This letter, sent to William Pitt Faithfull's eldest daughter by a former employee, provides tangible evidence:

> The reason I write is to thank dear Miss Deane and you all for your kindness in teaching me when I was young. I think it is more than ten years since I left Springfield and ever since I have thought the very least I could do was to let you know your labour was not in vain. I have always thought it very ungrateful on my part not to thank Miss Faithfull and Miss Deane for the lessons they used to teach me for my good. I am married and got four dear little children to care for and a comfortable and happy home. I wish I had the opportunity of thanking you in words—it seems as if I cannot express my thankfulness in writing.

It is hardly surprising if the lifestyle of the wealthy and successful squatter changed considerably from what he had known as a young man. Here, once again, is the man in the photograph—secure, affluent and master of all he usually sees. Many saw no need to

A wedding party at William Pitt Faithfull's Springfield station in the 1890s. Most of the people in this photograph are station hands and their families.

193

change anything, but their family did. After spending years with the most basic comforts, there seemed little point in not changing them when success provided the opportunity. Indeed, the squatters often realised, perhaps with a little help, that they had neglected their family in favour of the property; that their land was now watered with tanks or bores, that their yards were more substantial and more numerous, that their hands were well fed and housed and the quality of their stock was vastly improved.

Some acted out of guilt, some out of personal needs, and many overreacted and spent so lavishly and adopted such airs that they drew ridicule upon themselves. Trollope described wryly how some became carried away:

> A hundred thousand sheep and upwards require a professional man-cook and a butler to look after them; fifty thousand sheep cannot be shorn without a piano; twenty thousand is the lowest number that renders napkins at dinner imperative. Ten thousand require absolute plenty, meat in plenty, tea in plenty, brandy and water and colonial wine in plenty; but do not expect champagne, sherry or made dishes...

Some, conscious of their importance in the colony and especially in their own locality, dreamed of an Australian aristocracy of which, of course, they would be leading members. It was a hopeless dream. Wentworth's proposal for a system of hereditary peerages in Australia had been met with derision when it came up

Oil lamps and ornaments in the dining room at Rossiville, near Goulburn in New South Wales.

for debate in the House of Commons in the early 1850s. The idea was revived in the 1860s, especially in Queensland, but this time it had even less effect.

Apart from the natural hostility most Australians had to such an idea, there was another difficulty that the squatters could not overcome. The British gentry exercised their influence through their control and command of the civil service and the armed forces, but in Australia these were firmly controlled by the British government and did not lend themselves to infiltration and patronage in the same way. So the children of successful squatters went into the professions, often with success, instead of exercising control through public positions.

Some carried their dream to extremes. Edward Ogilvie became obsessed with his belief that he was heir to a British peerage. He received an encouraging response from London in 1886, was later allowed to use the motto of the family on which he based his claim and in 1892 he was allowed to patent his own coat of arms. But that was all he did get after trying for six years and incurring considerable expense. Ironically, his real claim came earlier, in 1889, when he married his second wife, who was the granddaughter of Lord Tottenham, but as his son William said realistically, 'Having a title does not mean that a man breeds better sheep'.

Those who were disappointed at not being a lord could at least live like one if they wished. And even those who had no thought of being an aristocrat were encouraged to live like one whether they wanted to or not. The symbol of rural wealth was the Big House, a homestead that expressed the substance and security of the station and which allowed, or even demanded, a lifestyle that seemed to have little in common with its source.

Wool prices remained high throughout most of the sixties, seventies and eighties and seasons were good. The result was that no squatter could plead to his family that he could not afford to build a bigger house than his neighbour. His family knew damned well he could afford it, and the sooner he started it the better.

This is not being overgenerous to the squatter. Although some embarked on such projects willingly and enthusiastically, many did not. In 1875 Niel Black of Mount Noorat in Victoria wrote to his partner: 'I even dread that the prevailing mania may infect myself and induce me to erect a more expensive building than will be suitable for the estate under more adverse circumstances which I fancy I can see looming in the distance.'

Black originally intended to spend no more than £3000 on his house and hoped it might be similar to the mansions of his native Scotland. But by the time the architect had finished it had cost nearly £20 000 and it had nothing in common with Scotland. Black

195

later described it as 'the crowning folly of my life. I was swept into building it as the strong man is drawn into the stream he cannot resist. I regard it as a burden that may encumber my son's life.' In spite of his melancholy, however, it hardly burdened his. When Black died in 1880 he left an estate of £179 208.

Even more impressive was the house at Werribee Park built by Thomas Chirnside. The house had 60 rooms contained in two wings but was occupied by the Chirnsides for only fifteen years before being taken over as a seminary. Rivalling that was the house built by Sir William and Lady Clarke at Sunbury on the land acquired by the old pioneer, Big Clarke. It is perhaps not surprising that the house was started in 1874, the year he died. It took two years to build and when it was finished there was a private railway platform for the convenience of guests. Hundreds might arrive by special train from Melbourne, but even on more modest occasions it was not unusual to have 50 guests for dinner.

Perhaps the most incredible of all was the house built by Edward Ogilvie at Yulgilbar near Grafton in New South Wales. In 1858 Ogilvie married Theodosia de Burgh in Ireland and immediately told her that he intended to build a fine house for her on a site he had picked many years earlier. He may, indeed, have been trying to impress the Irish landed gentry by proving that an Australian could rival them when it came to building a mansion. If not, he certainly impressed everybody else.

Ogilvie started by importing ten Germans to start the work in

The entrance hall at Duckenfield Park, near Morpeth in New South Wales.

1859, and these were followed by more Germans and several English stonemasons. The house was 28 by 26 metres and was largely designed by Ogilvie himself after a Florentine palace. By the time it was finished in 1865 it had needed 3500 tonnes of rubble and 110 000 bricks, all of them made by hand. The staircase was of carved cedar and there was even a huge chandelier of crystal which Ogilvie had somehow imported from Florence. The whole structure, which had about 40 rooms, was estimated to have cost about £40 000. It was known to everybody except Ogilvie as the castle, for that is what it looked like.

Guests were expected to behave in a manner appropriate to the house. Pre-dinner drinks were served in the drawing room or library, and then everybody left to change for dinner. This was not always what might have been expected, however. One grazier's wife said after a visit: 'A manservant would appear at your elbow with a great silver dish. When he took the silver cover off, you would find only a single mutton chop.' Edward Ogilvie died in 1896 after being thrown from his horse and his will caused much bitterness within the family and led to the ruin of Yulgilbar. After being sold in 1926, the house fell into decay during the Second World War and is now only a shadow of the folly that Ogilvie built.

Nor was lavish spending confined to the station homestead. Soon, no squatter worthy of the name could be expected to exist without a house in town. They bought vast mansions in smart suburbs, or built new ones as close as they could, and many were so huge that they have long since ceased to function as houses. John Simson of Trawalla station in Victoria built Studley Hall in the suburb of Kew in Melbourne. The house contained a ballroom which has seated 600 people in comfort, but the house later became a preparatory school. Another splendid house, Como, which was built by C. H. Armytage on 22 hectares in South Yarra, is now the headquarters of the National Trust of Victoria.

In country towns the squatter was even more impressive, although the impression was not always as they imagined it to be. H. P. Tritton, in his book *Time Means Tucker*, describes how he went to Gunnedah for the 1905 show:

> I saw very little of the Gunnedah show. But I saw the entry of the Willsallen family into town. This was a show of its own and one of the main events of Gunnedah. An old-fashioned coach imported from London, four high-stepping bay horses, coachman and footman on the box seat, another footman on the back step, all in silver braided livery complete with top hats and cockades, it was an imposing sight. But this being a weekly feature, the locals did not spare it a second glance. Many visitors were greatly impressed but the lower classes,

197

to which group I belong, were not very respectful; in fact, most of
their comments were rather coarse. . .

By then, coaches were already being replaced by motor cars, and
graziers welcomed these enthusiastically even though they were
not always reliable. Most acquired chauffeurs as well and the whole
turnout was no less impressive than the Willsallen's coach. In
1907, for example, Kimberley pioneer Isadore Emanuel, now
living in Perth, paid £830 for a 30 horsepower Beeston Humber
'complete with Cape Court Hood and Screen; 2 headlights, 2
sidelights (kerosene), 1 tail lamp, 1 check cover, speedometer, 2
tubes, 2 sleeves, 2 levers, jack, pump, horn, and extension'.

Cars even came to Springfield, although William Pitt Faithfull
was dead by the time they did. But his granddaughter Bobbie was
taught to drive by her father when she was fifteen. He sat alongside
her and shot rabbits in the paddocks as they passed.

For a while it seemed as if there was no limit to the way graziers
could indulge themselves. In 1902 Henry Dutton in South
Australia imported a steam yacht from Scotland. It was over 40
metres long and had three boats and cabins for eight as well as the
crew's quarters. Called the *Adèle*, it was anchored at Port Adelaide
and was the only Royal Yacht Squadron steam yacht in Australia.

Most of this conspicuous spending was done by the second
generation, not the first. They enjoyed the wealth the station
produced, and some even helped to produce it, but few had the
dedication that their parents had. Daughters had grown up in a
social life that was far removed from the working world, and
married squatter's sons who had been educated overseas knew
little about crutching sheep or treating them for footrot.

In many cases their wealth was shortlived. The station was
jeopardised when children wanted to draw out their share of the
inheritance, or the place was ruined when the crash of the 1890s
made it impossible to support the debts that had been raised to
finance this new way of life. Those that survived did so by largely
ignoring the excesses which made the rest so noticeable, and by
working the station along the prudent lines that had been set by
their father. And if they could not remember what those were, all
they had to do was look at the photograph.

One of the best tributes to these men came, surprisingly
perhaps, in an article published in *Scribner's Magazine* in New
York in 1892:

> The station owners, who have had the courage, foresight, and
> endurance to develop the enormous domain of pastoral Australia,
> form a distinct and characteristic class in the population of the
> Colonies. They are, almost without exception, men of strong

physique and enormous vitality, as befits pioneers in a land which, while it has offered encouragement to enterprise, has set the price of success very high in drafts on pluck and energy... This generation of pioneers is passing away in ripeness of years and the glow of great success.

18

Running the big house

NOT all station homesteads were opulent mansions built in the frenzied splurge of wealth in the '70s and '80s. Many squatters were content to retain the house they already had, or build on a relatively modest scale. In Queensland the mania for mansions had very little effect. Away from the coastal fringe, most stations were still at an early stage in their development at that time and there was little money or inclination for show. Even in well-settled areas homesteads were more restrained. And where properties were owned by companies there was even less incentive to improve the homestead, for it was simply the manager's quarters and while it should be comfortable it was not expected to be lavish.

The homestead, big or small, lavish or modest, was the centre of the station. It usually included the station office, especially where the squatter still ran the station, which had its own entry door so that station hands could reach the office without using the front door. Indeed, the front door of the homestead had great social significance. Tradesmen and employees never used it and even clients of the station might be expected to use a slightly less important entrance. Only guests or others of similar social standing were entitled to use the front entrance, and those who were not sure did not need to ask. One descendent of a squatter once said of a famous Australian prime minister that he would not have been allowed to use the front door in her grandfather's time, and it was probably true.

Homesteads of this kind were organised in the same way as English country houses, or at least that was the aim. The family of a successful Australian squatter measured success by how closely

AMERICAN COOKING STOVES.
THE LATEST APPROVED PATTERNS,
DESIGNED AND MANUFACTURED EXPRESSLY FOR THE COLONIES,
FOR SALE, AT REDUCED PRICES.
Delivered and set up in Melbourne, Collingwood, St. Kilda, Prahran,
Flemington and Emerald Hill.
JNO. C. M'NULTY, 129 Russell Street.

An 1863 advertisement for an American stove. This was the first major improvement to homestead kitchens as it removed the discomfort, work and risk associated with a large open fire.

they could imitate the lifestyle of wealthy landowners 'back home'. In the USA and South Africa wealth that came from the land was expressed in a more independent style, but in Australia the aspiration was to imitate Britain as closely as possible.

A big homestead was run by its own army of domestic staff under the control of the squatter's wife. This staff was organised around its own very formal structure. Below the wife was the house-keeper, if the place ran to one, and then came the cook, the parlour maids, the upstairs maids and the servants who worked in service areas associated with the house, such as the laundry, and who were not visible from the inside. If there was no housekeeper the cook was the senior of the domestic staff.

In a smaller homestead the squatter's wife virtually ran the place with the help of one or two servants. Meals might be supplied by the station kitchen and in some later homesteads the station kitchen, and the men's dining room, was an extension of the homestead so that the same kitchen could supply both.

The kitchen was the centre of most domestic work in the home-stead. Until the mansions came this was always separate from the house and indeed was often the slab hut that the squatter had built when he first arrived. Because of this it could be some distance from the homestead and much time and labour was spent ferrying meals and debris backwards and forwards. Alfred Joyce was unusual in that his kitchen was inside the house, but that was because his wife had no servants and he was anxious to save her as much trouble as he could. He even had water piped in and intended to install a covered drain to carry away dirty water which, in 1855, was very novel indeed.

201

Most kitchens consisted of the original slab walls and bark roof, with a large gap in one wall to take a fireplace about 2 metres square. The chimney was made of stone or galvanised iron and the fireplace contained metal beams from which pots could be suspended. Camp ovens were used directly on the fire.

A special oven for baking bread was built outside, often as much as 20 metres away from the kitchen, but sometimes it was built against an outside wall. This oven was a dome of clay with a door at the front and a chimney at the back. The floor of the oven was made with bricks and the whole structure was supported on logs so that the base was about 50 centimetres off the ground. A wood fire was lit inside the oven and when the oven was hot enough, about two hours later, the ashes were raked out and the loaves pushed inside on a flat piece of wood with a long handle, called a peel.

The first major improvement to the kitchen was the American stove, which came into use about 1855. This stove was made of cast iron and contained an oven and hotplates which were heated by a wood fire inside. It stood on its own three legs, was easily transported, and did not need any brickwork around it. It could be stood anywhere provided the smoke could escape, and was ready for use as soon as the fire was hot enough. The big advantage was that the huge fireplace was no longer needed for cooking and life in the kitchen, especially in the summer, became a little more bearable.

The popularity of the American stove prompted Australian manufacturers to produce designs of their own, and these were known as colonial ovens. In its most basic form this consisted of an iron box with shelves inside and a hinged door. Others were double-walled and were set in brickwork under a chimney. When a fire was lit underneath the heat and smoke passed between the double walls and then escaped up the chimney. Another type had a fire on top of the stove as well as underneath. The top fire was covered with a grill to support pans and kettles and the other fire, at the side or the bottom, was lit only when it was needed.

These ovens were produced in huge quantities and were almost universal in homestead kitchens. A basic colonial oven cost no more than £1 and a double range about 5 metres long and containing five ovens and two boilers for hot water cost about £90. One firm alone was making 2000 colonial ovens a year by the 1860s and by the 1890s Simpson & Son of South Australia, who claimed to be the first to manufacture ovens of any kind in Australia, had sold over 15 000 of its original Simpson's oven.

There was, however, a real skill in using these ovens, and most of it was in knowing how hot it was. Experienced cooks could judge this by holding their hand close to the open door but those with less experience relied on some simple tests. One was to sprinkle a spoonful of flour on a baking dish and to leave it inside the oven for five minutes. The heat of the oven could then be determined by the colour of the flour: if it was pale brown the oven was cool, a golden colour indicated a moderate heat, and if the flour was dark brown the oven was hot. Another method was to put a sheet of white paper in the oven for a few minutes. Again, the colour of the paper indicated the heat. If the oven was too hot to be used it was cooled by standing a basin of cold water inside.

Kate Parker discovered some of the intricacies when she used one of these stoves for the first time:

> It had seemed as simple as a penny-in-the-slot when glibly explained by a smug-faced young man with affable manners in mutton-chop whiskers; an in-with-the-wood and out-with-the-pudding sort of thing. However I found it not so simple when the smug-faced young man's theories came to a bush cook's practice.

She made a custard pudding with a meringue top and enlisted the the station cook to help her with the cooking, although he had no faith in the new stove. While the pudding was cooking he called her from the veranda, saying that he thought it needed attention: 'What a smell of burning! I opened the stove door, burnt my fingers in my haste, and saw such a wreck; pudding everywhere and the dish in pieces. That pudding had to be taken out with the kitchen stove!'

The cook had put another handful of wood on the fire, and that had been the undoing. She asked him to make a rice pudding for dinner and his triumph was complete when he told her she had used the last of the eggs.

Large ranges such as this were soon commonplace in homestead kitchens and many remained in use for generations. The tap on the right supplied hot water. From an advertisement of 1888.

203

As we have seen in an earlier chapter, keeping food usable was a perpetual problem. Food had to be protected from the climate and from insects, and neither was easy. The simplest method was to use a small cask as a meat safe. The ends of the cask were knocked out and the end hoops carefully removed. A piece of cheesecloth was fitted over one end and the hoop replaced to hold it in place. Another piece of cloth was used at the other end, but the hoop when replaced held only part of it. The loose end was knotted or tied after the meat had been put inside. The cask was slung from the roof of the veranda.

More sophisticated and more efficient was the Coolgardie safe, because this kept food cool as well. It consisted of a four-sided stand with shelves inside and a water tank on top. The frame was enclosed with a hessian curtain which was kept clear of the frame by wires. Wicks were placed with one end in the water tank and the remainder draped over the top of the hessian. The water soaked into the hessian and was collected in another tray at the bottom. The evaporation of the water from the cloth reduced the temperature inside the safe. The legs were stood in individual jars of water to stop insects from climbing up them.

Butter was kept cool by putting it in a dish in an earthenware bowl that had been soaked in water. The lid, which was also soaked, was put on and the bowl hung in a shady place that caught the breeze. Again, it was the evaporation of the water that cooled the inside. To preserve butter for a longer time it was covered with a layer of brine and stored in a cool place. Milk was preserved for a short time by scalding it, that is, heating it over a pan of boiling water until the top of the milk became thick but not boiling. Some people then cooled it and stored it, others kept it hot for an hour before doing so.

Killing day meant a lot of work because the meat had to be taken care of immediately. Rachel Henning described some of this activity:

> About once in ten days a beast is hunted in and slain. The best joints are reserved for the house, an immense roasting and spluttering takes place all over the station, and the rest is salted down into casks and kept in the meat store, a small room behind the other store. We have a smoking-house now, made of zinc, where the beef kept for the house is hung up and smoked with damp wood. An immense improvement in the case of beef.

One of the side products of killing days was the stockpot. This was kept over a slow heat for days and bones and small pieces of meat were thrown in as they became available until it was eventually replenished after the next killing day. If there was no meat available before then almost anything would do, as Mrs Rawson explained in the *Antipodean Cookery Book and Companion*:

> When the meat and bones are exhausted, a fowl can be added; no
> matter how old, it will make soup; the heads, legs, giblets of
> chickens, that have been killed for the table, the hindquarters of a
> wallaby, a kangaroo tail, and any wild fowl or small birds, so long as
> they are properly cleaned and chopped up, will make stock.

Cookbooks themselves were a rarity. Mrs Beeton's famous work
was not published until 1861 and was therefore late on the scene.
Nor were they always much help and Rachel Henning complained
that they never told you exactly how to do things. When she
wanted to know how many peas to use in a tureen of soup the
recipe simply told her to 'take peas'.

Insects, and especially flies, mosquitoes and ants, were a
common nuisance against which there was little defence. Louisa
Meredith found ants the worst:

> Not an atom of anything sweet can be hidden from their attacks;
> sideboard, pantry, storeroom, cellar and kitchen, are all alike
> besieged by the industrious little torments. They bury themselves in
> sugar, and drown in jam, cream, custards, or tarts; and their odour
> and taste are so immediately nauseous that their repeated visitations
> become rather expensive.

Insects were as much a pest inside the house as they were in the
kitchen. There were no fly screens and the only real protection was
to keep windows and doors closed. There were a number of recipes

Wash day at Marengo, near Tilba
Tilba in New South Wales,
photographed about the turn of
the century. Washing for a large
house was a laborious and constant
job.

that were supposed to trap insects. One was to mix finely ground black pepper and raw sugar with cream and to place saucers full of the mixture around the room. Another was to coat sheets of brown paper with a hot glue made from castor oil and resin as an early form of fly catcher, but in this form they were as dangerous to humans as they were to flies.

One of the most laborious and constant jobs done by the staff of the homestead was the laundry. In a large homestead with a big family there was an enormous amount of washing to do, and even a modest house still generated enough for it to be a major job. There were clothes, bed linen, towels, tablecloths, kitchen cloths and much besides. None of these things were easy to wash. Clothes and tablecloths might contain lengths of lace that had to be handled with great care, many items had to be starched, and ladies dresses could be a nightmare to iron. All this had to be done by hand, and often.

The simplest way was to wash the laundry in the nearest creek, using a kerosene tin over a wood fire as a copper, but this was suitable for only the smallest and least pretentious households. Most homesteads had a separate laundry in one of the outbuildings that made up the service area at the back of the house.

The first job was to sort the clothes and linen into bundles of the same fabric, as different fabrics had to be washed separately to make sure they did not shrink or lose their colour. The clothes were then rubbed with soap against a board and left to soak overnight in cold water.

The next morning the clothes were soaped again and placed in warm water. Meanwhile a wood fire had been lit under the washing copper, which stood outside the laundry. When the water boiled, the clothes were dropped in with some soap and boiled for about an hour. The clothes were then taken out and rinsed in warm water.

The next job was to remove as much water from them as possible. This could be done by hand wringing, but that was difficult with large items such as bed sheets. A better method was to pass them through a mangle. This was a huge machine made of cast iron which had two large wooden rollers turned by a handle at the side. Even though the handle worked through gears it needed considerable effort to turn the rollers, especially if the clothes were thick. Care had also to be taken to avoid breaking buttons and other fastenings. The mangle had little in common with the modern wringer—it looked like an industrial machine that might produce sheets of galvanised iron.

The clothes were then hung out to dry in the sun. Or they were on the good days. If it was raining they had to be dried in front of the kitchen fire, to the annoyance of those trying to work there. When they were dry, collars, lace and frills were dipped in starch and patted dry between two towels.

The clothes were now ready for ironing, and this process required much care. The first irons were flat irons that were heated on the stove. The temperature was a matter of judgment and was tested either by holding the iron near the face, or spitting on it if nobody important was looking. Two irons were usually in use at a time: one being heated on the stove while the other was in use on the clothes. When the iron was removed from the stove the bottom was rubbed with a cloth containing beeswax. Much care had to be taken with frills and ruffs, and very small irons were used on these. Scorching was a constant fear. Marks were difficult to remove, but people tried with a mixture of vinegar and Fuller's Earth.

It was a long time before this work was made easier by labour-saving machines. The earliest washing machines simply tumbled the clothes in a tub of hot water, but the water still had to be heated over a fire and the machine had to be turned by hand. A weekly magazine described the Hutton's Patent Australian Washing Machine in 1878: 'This machine accomplishes the work of washing clothes or anything of a like nature by a combination of four things, viz., hot air, dash of water, rubbing over fluted services and by continual presentation of fresh surfaces to be operated on.'

The manufacturer claimed that a load of 8 kilograms could be washed by a child of ten in five minutes. A similar claim was made for the Lowe Patent Washing Machine, which had a container for a fire. There is no doubt that these machines took much of the hard work out of this part of the process, but it is doubtful if they were ever as easy to use as their makers claimed.

Another improvement came with the introduction of self-heating irons. These had a container which held hot ash or charcoal and a chimney at the rear for the smoke. When the heat started to diminish it was revived by briskly swinging the iron.

Apart from these improvements, doing the laundry hardly changed until well into the twentieth century when electric machines and irons became available.

While the inconveniences of the kitchen and laundry concerned only those who had to work in them, the rest of the house was often a curious mixture of comfort and hardship. The hardship came about either because there was no alternative or because the squatter did not think the cost of removing it was justified.

There might, for example, be hardly any piped water. A pump near the kitchen might supply not only the service parts of the house, but the bathroom as well. Hot and cold water had to be

An 1887 advertisement for a mangle (left) and an early washing machine.

carried in buckets to wherever it was needed. Most houses, though, had piped cold water as this was a simple installation using either a pump or gravity from a high tank. With this supply of cold water it was also fairly simple to have a supply of hot water. This could be produced in the bathroom by a chip heater, which was a wood-fired boiler which was remarkably efficient.

Most early houses, though, did not have a bathroom. Anyone wanting a bath (and it was not a widespread social habit then) used a hip bath in the bedroom. This was an uncomfortable affair as it was almost impossible to sit, stand or lie in it. Hot water was brought from the kitchen in buckets and the used water taken away by the same method.

A bathroom was often one of the reasons for building a better house, as the benefits were enjoyed by those living in the house rather than working in it. If a new house could not be built, or the existing one converted, an outbuilding near the house might be fitted out with a zinc bath and heater, and perhaps water troughs as well.

In any case, the use of water depended either on the supply from the creek or rainwater collected in tanks, and sometimes both. During a drought there was little of either and water then had to be used very sparingly, even in the most opulent homestead.

Slush lights were used in early homesteads but by the time the house had any pretension candles were used instead. These were not bought, as most of the material needed to make them was already on the station.

The simplest candles were made of clarified fat and beeswax, but these were rather soft. Harder candles were made from lard, alum and saltpetre, but the most common ingredient was tallow, which

A washing machine of 1907—
Marshall's 'Lily White Washer'.
Many manufacturers claimed that
their machines could be used by
children.

was also used in candles that were produced commercially. Candles were made in moulds, and the first step was to insert the cotton wicks after they had been dipped in a mixture of water, lime and saltpetre. Tallow was then poured into the mould and the wicks held clear by pushing a stick through them and resting this on the top of the mould. After the tallow had set hard, which could take up to 24 hours, the candles were released from the mould and were ready for use.

It was a constant job. Sarah Midgley in her diary of 1858 wrote: 'Been busy making candles today. Killed two snakes. Father commenced plucking the grapes this afternoon and Mother has been busy bottling grape wine and making tomato jam. Mother finished making candles tonight and there was in all 48 dozen.'

Candlesticks varied in design from elegant ones of brass or silver to severely practical ones of tin. When used outside, candles were mounted in lanterns that had a reflector inside and a lens on the front. Scissors were used to cut the burnt length of wick from the top of the candle, otherwise the light became very dim, and the best way to extinguish them was with a snuffer, an inverted cone which was held over the flame until it went out. Blowing a candle out produced a column of acrid smoke. Even lighting them was not as easy as one might think. Matches did not become available in Australia until the 1840s. At first they were wooden sticks coated with sulphur and were lit by drawing them through folded sandpaper. If they could be persuaded to burn at all they did so with an acrid blue smoke. These were replaced by wax matches which were almost as difficult to light and which at first were very expensive.

The discovery of kerosene in 1850 by Dr James Wood, a Scottish inventor, made lighting much easier and considerably better. The first kerosene lamps were imported by T. W. Stanford, who had a business in Melbourne, and they were soon available in a wide range of models. Later models used pressure and an incandescent mantle instead of a wick. The glass covers were a recurring expense as they were easily broken. They were cleaned by boiling in water and rubbing with salt when they were dry.

A less common method of lighting was acetylene gas. This used a combination of carbide and water and was used on early bicycles and other outdoor uses. It could also be used for lighting a house, but it needed a substantial plant outside the house and the gas had to be piped inside. For those who could afford it, however, it had all the convenience of lighting by mains gas.

Whichever method of lighting was used, darkness had to be prepared for. Candles and kerosene lamps had to be placed near the door of a room so that they could be found in the dark, and

A selection of bathroom fittings available in 1888. Note the 'artistic' closet, bottom left.

lamps had to be filled with kerosene and have their wicks trimmed. Even the gas plant needed attention, as the supply of gas stopped when the carbide was exhausted.

The first electricity in the homestead was produced by a generator which was driven either by a petrol engine or by a windmill. They produced only enough power for lighting, however, and further uses of electricity had to wait for mains electricity or more powerful generators. It was often a long wait. The elegant 40-roomed homestead at Springfield, for example, continued to use kerosene lamps and carbide gas for lighting and wood fires for cooking and heating water until the arrival of mains electricity in 1951.

Of the few labour-saving machines that did become available in the bush in the nineteenth century, perhaps the most important was the sewing machine. The first sewing machine that really worked was invented in America by Isaac Singer, who gave the world a memorable quote when he said, 'I don't care a damn for the invention, the dimes are what I'm after.'

The Singer Manufacturing Company established an agency in Sydney in 1865 which made machines from imported parts. Although the real value of this invention was in the mass production of clothing, housewives took to it with enthusiasm as an alternative to the laborious business of hand-sewing. It was, indeed, one of the few inventions that could be used in the bush as well as it could anywhere else, and as women there had less chance of buying ready-made clothing the labour it saved was considerable. Katie Hume, who had a machine in 1866, wrote

> The machine is always occupied. I have made 5 large Verandah curtains—3 yds square, which were absolutely essential to keep the sun off the dining room. I have made Baby sundry frocks & a set of petticoats (for she is shortcoated) & am now making white alpaca coats for Walter, which is rather troublesome work.

A machine that was frequently not as reliable as the sewing machine was the clock. Timekeeping was not an essential part of life on a station, but if the clock stopped there was almost no way of knowing the time before the days of broadcast time signals. Rachel Henning described what might happen then:

> Our clock has stopped, a great misfortune where it cannot be repaired. An unearthly sound proceeded from its inside the other evening at twenty minutes past seven, and there the hands stand. Annie's watch is the only timepiece in the house—Biddulph's does not go; Mr Hedgeland's is gone home to be repaired; Julian took his into the wash-pool one day when he was washing sheep, and it immediately struck work; and Beckford does not possess one. When the shadow of the lambs' pen reaches a certain point, it is time to

give them milk; and when the sun is within a yard or so of the blue
mountains, it is time to go out walking.

If the only clock stopped, perhaps by being allowed to run down,
starting it again was largely a matter of guesswork. The only
accurate way was to look up the time of sunrise in an almanac or
diary and set it from that.

There is no doubt that servants in the Big House worked very
hard, although this depended to a large extent on how many there
were and how hard they were driven. The day usually started
before 6 a.m., when the maids dressed in their uniform of a long
black dress, white starched collar and cuffs, a cap and a large white
apron which came over the shoulders and was tied at the back.

The first work was to clean and polish the lamps and refill them,
and to lay fires if they were needed. Breakfast might be an extended meal depending on how many people there were to be
served and their ages. This meal, like all others, had to be carried
into the dining room from the distant kitchen and the remains
carried back for washing up. With that out of the way, the rest of
the day was spent in cleaning out rooms, making beds, carrying
water, cleaning silver, laying the table and serving other meals.
The day might finish after dinner had been served, although kindly
wives often allowed their maids to be free during the afternoon.

All the rooms, including the bedrooms, were swept out every
day, and each room was 'turned out' once a week. This was a big
job, especially in a cluttered Victorian parlour. The maid had to
climb a step ladder to remove ornaments and vases from the
shelves and the clutter from the mantlepiece and place them on a
sofa and cover them with a dust sheet. She then sprinkled damp
rose petals on the floor if she had them, or small pieces of damp
paper if she had not, and swept them with a straw broom into a
dustpan. The dust sheet was then removed and all the ornaments
dusted and glass washed before being carried back up the steps and
returned to their original position. There was no way any of this
could be done quickly.

Much of the well-being of the homestead, indeed of the whole
station, depended on the prompt arrival of stores. These might have
to be freighted over many hundreds of kilometres and not only was
their arrival uncertain, but it was a costly exercise that could not be
repeated too often. Because of this, stores might be ordered only
twice a year and on a large station this involved huge quantities.
The inventory of Bangate station, New South Wales, in 1886, for
example, showed that the stock included 3 tonnes of flour, 20 bags
of sugar each weighing 30 kilograms, 53 kilograms of pepper, 10
kilograms of mustard and more than a tonne of fencing wire.

Each order had to be prepared with great care as anything

Imported household goods, 1888.

overlooked had to wait for the next order. The house also had to rely on the integrity, and taste, of the supplier. The order might include items such as crockery and dress material which had to be described as best they could. White dinner plates with blue edging might produce the correct article or it might not, and an order for a length of red galatea could produce almost anything and still fall within that description.

The arrival of the stores, perhaps after weeks of travelling, was always a time of great excitement. Doris Blackwell described what it was like when the annual supplies arrived at Alice Springs by camel train from Adelaide:

> Everyone stopped work. We deserted the schoolroom and our governess, who was just as excited; Aborigines came running from the creek; the staff stood around while my father ceremoniously took delivery of the station's goods. Slowly, silently, the great packing cases creaking as they swayed, the long string of camels came padding into the station compound, looking haughty and slightly disdainful... The great packs, weighing as much as five hundred pounds, were unlashed—and then these marvellous beasts of burden could rest for a few days... All hands got to work at once, opening cases and carrying goods to storerooms. We'd topple into cases head first in our eagerness. Even such mundane things as groceries were a thrill when they came only once a year.

Many homesteads were extremely comfortable for those who lived in them, and those with a taste for entertaining often indulged it on a grand scale. Candles and lamps were lit in profusion, silverware shone on the cedar dining table and pictures of ancestors, sometimes of unknown origin, looked down from the walls. Guests in evening dress talked as they were served by a team of uniformed maids and a manservant flitted around the table pouring wine into long-stemmed glasses.

But even the most elegant household had to accept the reality of life in the bush. Edward Ogilvie at Yulgilbar, magnificent though his house was, still received stores only once a year, and his bullock drays were as likely to become bogged as anybody else's.

Some comforts could be bought for a price, some could be provided by an army of staff and some could not be had at all. It was this combination that made life in a station homestead, or anywhere else on the place, so distinctive.

19

How people passed the time

THE way people spent their time in the bush depended, as so many other things did, on who they were and where they were. The view that Australian society was egalitarian simply does not stand up to scrutiny. Most country towns, such as Bathurst and Goulburn, had a rigid class structure that was little different from that in England. There was 'society' and the rest, and upward mobility had to wait for a later generation.

Even on the stations there was a structure of sorts. Most obvious was the dominance of the squatter and his family, but there were other differences of status that were no less important. Even that most egalitarian group, the shearers, had a pecking order. It was based on ability, to be sure, but all pecking orders are based on something.

Pastimes were a reflection of this class structure. The way the squatters spent their spare time, at least when they had become established, had little in common with the way the station hands spent theirs. And even if it did, they certainly would not have spent it together.

For the station hand or itinerant worker there was no pastime more highly regarded than that of getting gloriously and comprehensively drunk and staying that way for as long as possible.

There were several reasons for this. The most important was that drink was not allowed on the stations. Even shearers remained dry while they were on a station, and that included the time when they were not actually in the shed. Station hands and other workers accepted this without question. Indeed, the fact that nobody was allowed to drink was the reason some of them were there. It was much easier for a man to keep off the drink when it was not

For station hands and itinerant workers there was no better way of passing the time than getting gloriously drunk. Knocking down cheques, 1888.

available and on a station there was no risk of being tempted by others. But it was a different matter when he was off the station. Having been dry for however long it had been, he saw no harm in getting drunk when he had the chance. He would, in most cases, soon return to the station and sobriety.

Another reason was that his departure from the station was also the time he was paid. A station hand needed little cash while he was working. He was fed each day and the extras he drew from the stores were debited to his wage account by the squatter, together with any advances he might request, perhaps to order goods from town or to send money to a distant family. Settling day was when he left, either permanently or for a holiday. The balance standing to his credit was then given to him by the squatter in the form of a cheque.

This was also true of shearers, who were paid by the number of sheep they shore. Tallies were kept each day and the amount credited to their account. From this was deducted the cost of their rations and the amount they paid to their cook. The balance was paid, again by cheque, when the shed cut out.

These cheques could be for large amounts. The station hand might have a full year's pay, and the shearers, especially good ones, could earn a considerable sum in one shed. But the cheques were of limited use until they were turned into money. And the best place to do that was the nearest pub. 'Knocking down the cheque' is usually seen in the context of shearers, but it applied to station hands as well. The difference was that there were considerably more shearers, they received cheques far more often and many of them received them at the same time. A station hand might make his way to the pub alone, but shearers were likely to

215

swarm on it as a mob. Alone or in company, their intention was the same.

It was hardly surprising. They had worked hard, many had no dependants and owning land or stock seemed too remote to be considered. Saving money had little purpose unless there was something to be achieved by it, and most thought there was not. As Trollope said:

> This sobriety...during the period of employment has become so much a thing of course, that it is expected and is a matter of no complaint. They smoke much tobacco, drink much tea, eat much mutton,—and work very hard. Then comes the short holiday, in which they knock down their cheques and live like brutes.

Those running the pubs were only too willing to help them. Indeed, their sole purpose was to help them do it as quickly as possible. The man passed his cheque across the bar into the safe keeping of the publican and told him to inform him when it had been cut out. The publican needed no urging on this matter. He supplied as much drink as the man demanded and kept his own He supplied as much drink as the man demanded and kept his own tally of the cost. Eventually he told the man that the money was finished and sometimes gave him a bottle of rum to help him get back to the station or to his next job, in which case he was thought to be very fair. If the man complained that he had not been there very long, the publican reminded him of the many times the man had shouted for the whole of the bar. The man may have done so or he may not, but it was unlikely he would remember.

Nat Gould claimed that a rabbiter with a cheque for £970 was thrown out of the pub a fortnight later without a penny to his name, even though £100 would have bought all the grog in the house.

Many publicans hastened the process by doctoring the drink. Bad rum could be 'improved' by adding tobacco, sulphuric acid and laudanum. The mixture was shaken up and then allowed to stand a while. As this concoction left a dark stain on a glass it was usually served in tin pannikins. Customers had no objection to this treatment as it meant they wasted very little time in getting drunk.

Another method was that used by a German called Charles Carl—German Charlie—who opened a pub at Poolamacca in the Barrier country, New South Wales, about 1867 and where Sidney Kidman worked as a youth. German Charlie improved his brandy by adding nicotine which he obtained by boiling a quantity of old clay pipes. Flat beer was brought back to life by putting a bar of soap in the keg and shaking it. It was even said that he was so concerned about the health of his customers that in hot weather he had a grave ready nearby in case one of them should need it.

A group of men in a pub had several ways of determining who should pay for the next round. One was the game of Tambaroora. Each man threw in a sum of money that was twice that needed to buy one drink. The game was then played with dice. Each man threw them three times and whoever threw the highest took the money and bought the next round. He was left with an equivalent sum as his winnings. Another game for the same purpose was Odd Man Out, which was usually played by three men. Each put a coin in a hat, which was then shaken vigorously and the coins tipped out onto the bar. If a coin came up tails its owner retired from the game knowing that his next drink was paid for. The other two threw again until one of the coins came up tails. The owner of the other coin, heads, bought the round.

Although this drunkenness, and the behaviour that was associated with it, was almost universally condemned by those who did not take part, it was for a long time part of the fraternal behaviour of the bush. It was about being with mates and having a good time in contrast to the often boring, and always dry, life on the station. There was a human side, even though it might not have been obvious to observers. Particularly appealing is the story of the man who rode into a town with the intention of enjoying Christmas. He was

Knocking down a cheque could take days or even weeks and was often done in company. Here a group of station hands play billiards, although the glasses are never far away.

drunk for nearly a fortnight and when he recovered slightly he asked the publican how many days there were to Christmas. 'About three hundred and fifty seven , he was told. 'Yesterday was New Year's Day.' The man asked if he had spent a good Christmas and was told he had had a roaring time. 'That's all right, then. Got to keep up Christmas. Let's have a drink. Happy New Year to you, and many of them.'

In the end it was the arrival of women that made men more sensible. When station hands were able to marry their life became less solitary and the splurge less necessary. And the responsibility of a wife and family meant that there was a good reason to keep the money instead of spending it. By the time Bean toured the bush in the early years of the twentieth century he found that the practice of knocking down the cheque had almost died out.

One pastime that was enjoyed by most men, squatter to itinerant worker, was smoking. As Mossman said in 1853:

> Every man and boy in the bush smokes. Morning, noon, and night, you are sure to find the bushman with his pipe in his cheek after meals. He says, at breakfast it helps him to swallow his damper; at dinner it assists the digestion of the mutton; and at supper it acts as a soporific against the astringent properties of the tea; besides sundry pipefuls he smokes during the intervals, for which he has no other excuse than that it fills up the time.

Smoking always meant using a pipe, as cigars were rare and cigarettes unknown. And the pipe was made of clay, not wood. Moulds for clay pipes were brought to Australia in 1808 by William Cluer, who started work with a pottery maker in Sydney. Each half of the

Drink was not allowed on the stations and spare time was passed differently: in this case with a knock-up game of table tennis.

mould was filled with finely ground clay—pipeclay—and the halves carefully joined. They were then fired in a kiln and the moulds removed to reveal a new clay pipe.

Bushmen preferred their pipe to be as short as possible and cut the stems until they were barely 2 or 3 centimetres long. In this form they were known as dudeens. They also liked them to be richly coloured, even black if possible. Men competed to see who owned the darkest and shortest pipe, and the best were very highly regarded. Sherer said:

> Pipes such as these, of extraordinary merit, are too precious to be carelessly handled and are usually enshrined in cases of silver, by which they are protected from all accidents of field and flood; but the ordinary practice is to wear them in the hatband, after the graceful fashion adopted by the Irish peasantry.

The tobacco was either Barrett's twist, which came in long square twisted sticks each weighing an ounce, or Negrohead, which came in twisted rolls about 20 centimetres long and which were known as figs. Both had to be cut and rolled by hand before they could be smoked.

Before matches became available (and long after they did) pipes were lit with a burning stick taken from the fire. If that was not available the smoker used a form of tinder box. This was a small cylindrical brass box with a tight fitting lid which was attached by a

The squatter's family passed their time more sedately than the station hands. This is the front veranda of Yandilla in Queensland in 1885.

short length of chain. Inside the box was a tightly rolled piece of rag, about 8 centimetres long and 3 centimetres in diameter, which was charred on the top. When needed, the lid was removed and a piece of quartz held over the rag. The quartz was struck with a knife until a spark dropped onto the rag, which was then blown gently until the rag glowed. The box was then held close to the pipe and the tobacco lit from the glowing rag. When this had been done, the box was closed so that the tinder went out and was ready for the next time.

On cattle stations men amused themselves with competitions that were related to the skills they used when working. One game consisted of throwing a tomahawk at a small mark on a tree while riding past on a galloping horse. The tomahawk was thrown from about 10 metres and the aim was to bury the blade in the mark, which was about 8 centimetres in diameter. Or two men might face each other a few metres apart in a duel with tomahawks. One man threw a tomahawk at the other and the receiver had to catch it by the handle and return it. Games with stockwhips were also popular and took many forms. One consisted of whipping a small coin off the ground and catching it while riding past, or the men stood in a large circle and tried to flip a small coin over, once only, with their whip. Another was to stand in front of a tree and cut their name or the station brand in the trunk with the whip. While there is no doubt that some stockmen were expert at these games, some of the expertise grew in the telling. Sorenson said, 'I have heard of the man, too, who could cut the eye out of a flying mosquito without touching his eyelash, but I never met him.'

Making things was also a popular pastime, especially among those, like shepherds or boundary riders, who were often alone. One favourite was to make a cabbage tree hat, which remained a symbol of the bushman until the end of the nineteenth century. The cabbage tree palm grew only in the rainforests between the coast and the Great Dividing Range and although cabbage tree hats were made commercially and worn throughout the bush, making them as a pastime depended on having a supply of this material. The leaves were split into ribbons about a centimetre wide with a home-made tool which had triangular metal teeth. The strips were then plaited into braids about 2 centimetres wide and the edges turned over as the work progressed so that they were firm and serrated. The braids were then sewn together to make a hat with a flat crown and a broad brim.

Men also made possum rugs, using techniques they learnt from the Aboriginals. The skins were pegged out with the fur side down on a piece of bark or timber and were dampened and scraped to remove any flesh from the inside. The skins were removed when they had dried and were sewn together to form a rug or cloak, one doubling as the other. Between 30 and 60 skins were needed for one cloak.

Stockmen also made equipment such as whips, harness and belts from leather. Some of this work showed an extremely high skill and much of it was produced as craft to be admired rather than to be used.

Reading was an almost universal pastime and it was said that lending a book to another man was nearly as great a favour as buying him a drink. Trollope said that it was generally recognised that anybody who settled in the bush without taking a supply of books was certain to have a miserable future. Of the 30 or so stations he visited, not one failed to have a collection of books, and he guaranteed that they all contained a copy of Macaulay's *Essays* and a complete Shakespeare. Curr also described how important his books were:

> At that period reading became our chief resource at Tongala. In the matter of books I believe we were better off than most of our neighbours, though those in our possession had been got together in a haphazard sort of way, at various times and without any idea of making a collection for the bush . . . These volumes, our great resource for years against *ennui*, for want of something new, were read, re-read, and discussed I cannot say how often.

Even those who could not read, and there were many, were not cut off from the pleasure of books so long as they could find somebody to read aloud. James Demarr, in his *Adventures in Australia Fifty Years Ago*, described how a man started to read *Nicholas Nickleby* aloud in an outstation hut one night. He was asked to stop until the others could round up men from the nearby stations so that they could enjoy it too. He read aloud for several nights by the light of a slush lamp and his audience would have stayed until dawn had he been able to read that long.

When mail services were introduced they brought with them a refreshing supply of newspapers and magazines to add variety to a collection of well-read books. Curr says that he was then 25 and had probably not read more than a dozen newspapers in his life. He was intrigued by the medley of advertisements and articles, but soon became disenchanted because, he said, the leading articles on bush matters were written by people with a very scant knowledge of the subject.

Inside the homestead, writing letters was not only a pastime but also a social necessity. Although the family might be isolated there were relations elsewhere who were keen to hear all their news. Those who had come from overseas felt it a duty to supply an almost constant stream of letters to those 'back home'. Writing a

221

TIRRANNA RACES.

TO START AT ELEVEN O'CLOCK SHARP.

FIRST RACE.—TIRRANA CUP.

One mile and a distance, heats; weight 10 stone.

Edwin G. Atkinson's c.h. PROTECTOR .. { Pink jacket, white sash, and pink and white cap.
S. F. Gibson's blk.m. BRUNETTE.........Scarlet jacket and black cap.
R. H. Blomfield's c.g. ORLANDO.........Scarlet jacket and black cap.
F. F. Gibson's b.g. BANJO ..Lavender jacket with scarlet sash and cap.
H. G. Stuckey's br.g. METEOR ....Green and white jacket and cap.
Reginald Faithfull's c.g. LUCIFER ....Plaid jacket and cap.
A. G. Finlay's b.g. GLENFRUIN (late COMET) ....Mauve jacket and cap.
F. R. L. Rossi's br.h. ORVILLE ..Blue jacket and cap with yellow band.

SECOND RACE.—LADIES' PURSE.

One mile and a distance, heats; weight 10 stone.

F. F. Gibson's b.g. BANJO ......Lavender jacket, scarlet sash and cap.
H. G. Stuckey's br.g. METEOR........Green and white jacket and cap.
J. Chisholm jun.'s c.g. VOLUNTEER ....Black and white jacket and cap.
E. R. Deane's br.g. ANYTHING ....Plaid jacket and cap.
C. W. Church's b.g. GANEM.................Black jacket and cap.
A. G. Finlay's b.g. DON QUIXOTE (late CHARNWOOD) Mauve jacket and cap.
R. E. Zouch's c.h. WRESTLER ....Yellow jacket and black cap.

THIRD RACE.—BACHELORS' PURSE.

One mile and a distance, heats; weight 10 stone.

Edwin G. Atkinson's c.h. PROTECTOR .. { Pink jacket, white sash, and pink and white cap.
S. F. Gibson's blk.m. BRUNETTE.........Scarlet jacket and black cap.
R. H. Blomfield's c.g. ORLANDO.........Scarlet jacket and black cap.
F. F. Gibson's b.g. BANJO ..Lavender jacket with scarlet sash and cap.
H. G. Stuckey's br.g. METEOR........Green and white jacket and cap.
J. Chisholm jun.'s c.g. VOLUNTEER ....Black and white jacket and cap.
Reg. Faithfull's c.g. LUCIFER ....Plaid jacket and cap.
A. G. Finlay's b.g. GLENFRUIN.................Mauve jacket and cap.
A. G. Finlay's b.g. DON QUIXOTE.................Mauve jacket and cap.
F. R. L. Rossi's br.h. ORVILLE ..Blue jacket and cap with yellow band.
R. E. Zouch's c.h. WRESTLER............Yellow jacket and black cap.

FOURTH RACE.—ARGYLE PLATE.

Heats, once round; weight 10 stone.

S. F. Gibson's blk.m. BRUNETTE.........Scarlet jacket and black cap.
F. F. Gibson's b.g. BANJO ..Lavender jacket with scarlet sash and cap.
H. G. Stuckey's br.g. METEOR ....Green and white jacket and cap.
J. Chisholm jun.'s c.g. VOLUNTEER ....Black and white jacket and cap.
E. R. Deane's br.g. ANYTHING ....Plaid jacket and cap.
C. W. Church's b.g. GANEM ....Black jacket and cap.
C. W. Church's g.m. FETNAH ....Black jacket and cap.
A. G. Finlay's b.g. DON QUIXOTE ....Mauve jacket and cap.
F. R. L. Rossi's br.h. ORVILLE ..Blue jacket and cap with yellow band.

FIFTH RACE.—WELTER RACE.

Twice round the course, one event; weight 12 stone.

Edwin G. Atkinson's c.h. PROTECTOR .. { Pink jacket, white sash, and pink and white cap.
S. F. Gibson's blk.m. BRUNETTE.........Scarlet jacket and black cap.
R. H. Blomfield's c.g. ORLANDO.........Scarlet jacket and black cap.
J. Chisholm jun.'s c.g. VOLUNTEER ....Black and white jacket and cap.
E. R. Deane's c.g. QUIZ ....Plaid jacket and cap.
A. G. Finlay's b.g. GLENFRUIN ....Mauve jacket and cap.

SIXTH RACE.—GALLOWAY RACE.

Mile heats; catch weights.
Entrances will be received for this Race up to within an hour of starting.

SEVENTH RACE.—HACK RACE.

Mile heats; post entrance; 10 stone.

The winner of any previous race in this card, if entered for another, to be handicapped by the gentlemen appointed.
Twenty minutes before starting a bell will be rung and a white flag hoisted Ten minutes before starting a second bell will be rung and a red flag hoisted in place of the white; and after the red flag has been up ten minutes a third bell will be rung and the red flag hauled down. The horses will be then started, and those not at the starting-post at that time will be disqualified.

Picnic races were popular throughout the bush although in more settled districts there was much regard to class distinction. The exclusive Tirrana Picnic Race Club was formed near Goulburn in New South Wales in 1855 and held a two-day meeting each year until it disbanded in the 1930s.

letter was the only way of conveying this news and it was usually done with diligence and often with considerable style.

There was one mail ship to England each month for much of the nineteenth century and its sailing date was well advertised. Prior to its departure, therefore, people hurried to write all the letters they might have done more comfortably had they started sooner. This was mostly done by the women. They had the information that relations most wanted to hear, and they had the time to spend on the slow task of committing it all to paper. Rachel Henning, herself a prodigious letter writer (much to our benefit now), described what she saw around her while writing a letter one Sunday afternoon in 1862 at Exmoor station in Queensland:

> Biddulph arrayed in white trousers, white coat and regatta shirt (nobody ever sits in the parlour without a coat) is lazily reading in an armchair in the pleasant recess where the books are. Mr Hedgeland in a similar airy costume is writing to his aunts, the Miss Hedgelands at Exeter, at the table. Annie, in a very pretty black and green mohair dress trimmed with green silk lozenges, is also writing—to Amy. Mr Taylor and Beckford, who came in last night, one from Seven Mile, and the other from a station forty miles off, are sitting on the veranda discoursing.

This also captures the flavour of life in the homestead. People passing the time here were not likely to indulge in riotous drinking or noisy gambling games or demonstrate their skill with a stockwhip while standing on the well-kept lawn. Beyond the homestead fence was a hard-working world and the squatter was part of it, but inside the house the emphasis was on more gentle things such as the womanly skills of needlework, painting and music. Good taste and an air of discrete refinement were likely to pervade the homestead rather than the smell of sheep and leather.

Music was a popular pastime for those with ability. For much of this time the only music available came from a live performance. A person played or sang while others listened. In order to listen to a Beethoven sonata one either had to be able to play it, or find somebody who could.

Once a piano had been obtained, at considerable cost and effort, it was put to frequent use. People enjoyed making music together, and those who could play or sing well were highly regarded. Out in the middle of nowhere people gathered around the piano and, lit by the candles in their elaborate holders, sang the ballads of the day or listened appreciatively while somebody played a particularly popular or difficult piece.

Keeping the piano in good order was not always easy, however, as Katie Hume discovered:

Picnics were a popular way of entertaining visitors to the Big House. They were often carried out with much style and in clothes that were hardly appropriate for the Australian climate.

> I am very tired, as I have just had a 'bout' of piano-tuning. This is the first time I have tried to tune it *throughout*, altering the pitch & I find it dreadfully perplexing and tiring, but I think I shall manage it, with the help of my tuning forks, which give a whole octave . . . I hope I shall succeed in making it *passable* for Xmas, but those buzzing base notes are very puzzling!

The invention of the phonograph eventually made music more widely available, and in a form that could not be performed on a piano. The machine was invented by Thomas Edison about 1877 and was first demonstrated in Australia, unsuccessfully, at the Royal Society of Victoria the following year. Another demonstration two months later produced a version of *For He's a Jolly Good Fellow* in 'a wonderfully distinct manner'. Phonographs were imported in the late 1880s and by the 1890s they were in wide use in homesteads. They had a harsh tone that was more suitable for brass bands and gutsy solo singers, but few minded those limitations.

It would be wrong to imply that the love of music was restricted to the homestead. Accordions and Jew's harps were popular among shepherds and for many years the shearers and station hands at Cordillo Downs put on an annual concert in aid of the Shearers' Ward at the Adelaide Children's Hospital. But while music was a matter of communal enjoyment, in the homestead it was a sign of civilisation and refinement.

Indeed, these features came together in another ritual that was widely practised in homesteads that were not far from town: the tea party known as being 'at home'. This called for much ceremony, and any breaches were closely observed and widely discussed. Women and their daughters arrived dressed in their finest and were ushered into the drawing room. There, the wife of the house poured tea from a huge silver pot while a maid in uniform handed around freshly baked scones and cakes. The guests, still wearing gloves and with the veil of their hat lifted slightly above their nose, drank, ate, and talked at the same time. The ceremony lasted about twenty minutes.

Part of the ritual involved the leaving of visiting cards, and this was done at other times as well. A women had cards separate to, and slightly smaller than, those of her husband, and grown up daughters were shown on her card beneath her name. When a woman called on another and found she was out or unavailable, she left one of her own cards and two of her husband's in the tray in the hall. If she was received, then she left two of her husband's cards only.

Even in the bush women took pride in observing these customs, perhaps to show that they had not left good manners behind and that whatever their surroundings they were still capable of observing the social niceties of the day.

House parties were also much enjoyed, although not all that common. Guests were entertained by outside activities during the day and spent the evening around the piano or playing games. Trollope once tried to start a game of whist but remarked sadly that men who could quote the price of wool to a fraction of a penny seemed incapable of remembering the highest card of a suit.

Outside, polo and hunting were popular. Coursing is said to have started with wallabies in South Australia in 1867 and the first genuine meeting (with hares) was held in Victoria in 1873. Shooting was also popular, as game abounded and birds could nearly always be found around the waters. They were easy to approach and just as easy to shoot. Others who wanted to shoot more productively used a punt gun. This was about 2 metres long and was mounted on the bow of a punt. The shooter (clearly not a gentleman) paddled as close to the birds as he could and then fired his artillery. He could get up to twenty birds with one shot.

Horse racing was another popular pastime and was enjoyed by almost everybody in the bush. In the backblocks races were informal picnics where men rode their own horses around a temporary course. Nat Gould knew these meetings well:

> Some of these picnic race-meetings are most enjoyable, but others are anything but socially conducted. After the picnic and the races, a ball generally follows in the best public room available in the town. The expenses of the ball are defrayed out of the club funds, and consequently it is a rare opportunity for some members to take it out in champagne—which they do with a vengeance.

In the settled areas these picnic race clubs stood at the very pinnacle of the social scene. The Terranna Club near Goulburn was one of the oldest in the country and held one meeting a year. The meeting lasted two days and finished with a magnificent ball during which the eighteen-year-old girls 'came out'. Membership of the club was restricted to 'gentlemen', mostly local landowners, and even the most successful and wealthy shopkeeper knew there was no point in seeking membership. This club survived until the 1930s.

Katie Hume reflected the atmosphere in a description of a race meeting held between Drayton and Toowoomba in Queensland in 1866:

> It was my first introduction to a Colonial crowd & I must say I was very much amused. A great part of the equestrians seemed as if they had never been 'outside a horse' before, & behaved accordingly, riding about amongst the trees in the most reckless manner and tearing around the course between races like madpeople. What struck me particularly was the number of *women* on horseback for at home one sees none but *ladies* riding & never very many of them—here there were as many women almost as men, but hardly any *ladies*.

Balls of any kind were popular because it was one of the few ways that young people could meet each other. Families travelled long distances to them, and often stayed a few days in town as well. Rachel Henning, more tolerant than Katie Hume, described a subscription ball at Bathurst in 1861:

> Some of the colonial girls are excessively pretty, while they are very young—such complexions as you hardly ever see. There certainly is a curious state of society here. The richest man in the district, who was chief steward of the ball, and who was so good as to escort Amy

Agricultural shows, which became popular in the 1860s, gave the squatter and his family an excuse to go to town, but most squatters were glad to return to their station after a few days.

into the room, met with a 'misfortune' many years ago, and was transported for life for horse-stealing. That was in the palmy days of the colony, and he soon made a fortune, got first a conditional pardon, then a free one and now is a great man here!

Agricultural shows also provided a welcome chance for a trip to town and for the socialising that went with it. Shows were started in the 1850s but it was not until the 1860s that they became successful. But while the squatters might look forward to the shows, they were usually happy to return to their station. By this time they had little need of the city and the novelty of it soon passed.

Epilogue

MOST of the stations founded by the pioneer squatters are still doing what they set out to do: running sheep and cattle. Some have been submerged under later developments, such as the building of Canberra and the Ord River irrigation scheme. Others have become part of larger stations, so that what was once a station in its own right is now an outstation of a larger property. But many stations are little different in size and activity and the pioneers who started them would not have much difficulty finding their way around them.

Some aspects of station life and work are dramatically different while others have hardly changed at all. Location has much to do with this. Stations that are in districts that are now well settled enjoy the facilities that settlement brought. Mains electricity, good roads, public transport, high schools and medical services make life a good deal less arduous than it once was. Indeed, it is sometimes difficult to realise now that when such land was first taken up it was on the very edge of settlement and as remote, measured in travelling time, as the outback is today.

In areas that are still isolated, such as much of the Top End and the Kimberleys, the changes are less dramatic. Life is certainly more comfortable and safer than it was, but many of the problems of isolation remain.

It can be seen, then, that some aspects of station life have changed and some have not, and that the changes are different in different parts of the country. Perhaps the most significant changes, especially in the outback, are those which have improved the quality of life or simply made it safer.

What has not changed are the people who live and work on the stations. They still have much in common with the pioneer squatters, and indeed in many cases are descended from them. They prefer the ways of the bush to those of the city, the simple values to the more sophisticated that can be changed beyond recognition by mere fashion.

The people on the stations today are the custodians of an industry that was founded on hope and which prospered, when it did, on hard work and determination. In spite of the great diversity of rural Australia, they are its most enduring theme.

Sources of Illustrations

Note: Numbers refer to the page numbers on which the illustrations appear.

5: Faithfull/Maple-Brown Collection, Springfield.
15: *Illustrated London News*, 20 April 1850. National Library.
20: National Library.
23: National Library.
26: Nationl Library.
29: National Library.
31: *Illustrated Sydney News*, 28 March 1874. National Library.
35: *The Three Colonies of Australia*, Samuel Sidney, 1852. National Library.
37: *Illustrated Australian News*, 28 May 1864. National Library.
40: Wood engraving published in Victoria, 1873. National Library.
42: *Illustrated Sydney News*, 15 October 1864. National Library.
43: *Australian*, Fr Christman, Leipzig, 1870. National Library.
47: *The Three Colonies of Australia*, Samuel Sidney, 1852. National Library.
53: National Library.
55: *Australasian Sketcher*, 29 September 1882. National Library.
57: *Illustrated Australian News*, 7 November 1885. National Library.
59: National Library.
62: *Town and Country Journals*, 29 April 1871. National Library.
66: *Aboriginal Life in Australia*, Alfred Scott Broad. National Library.
67: Ibid.
70: Greenwood Station, New South Wales, *c.* 1872. National Library.
74: *Cassell's Picturesque Australia*, ed. E. E. Morris, London 1889, Vol 3. Mitchell Library.
75: National Library.

78: F. H. Broomhill Collection. National Library.
79: Harry Reynolds at Burracoppin Depot, Western Australia, 1926. Ibid.
83: Faithfull/Maple-Brown Collection, Springfield.
86: National Library.
89: National Library.
92: National Library.
97: *Australasian Sketcher*, 3 October 1874. National Library.
98: National Library.
102: National Library.
104: National Library.
109: *Illustrated Sydney News*, 16 October 1865. National Library.
111: *Illustrated Sydney News*, 16 August 1865. National Library.
112: National Library.
113: National Library.
115: *Illustrated Australian News*, 1 September 1890. National Library.
117: National Library.
118: *The Fifth Continent*, E. O. Hoppe. National Library.
122: National Library.
123: *Among Cannibals*, Carl Lumboll, London 1890. National Library.
126: *Illustrated Sydney News*, 16 December 1865. National Library.
127: National Library.
128: *Illustrated Sydney News*, 30 September 1871. National Library.
133: *Australasian Sketcher*, 22 April 1882. National Library.
136: *Australasian Sketcher*, Supplement, 4 November 1883. National Library.
139: Keast Burk Collection. National Library.
144: National Library.
146: *Victoria & its Metropolis: Past & Present*, Alexander Sutherland, Melbourne, 1888. National Library.
149: *Illustrated Sydney News*, 23 February 1878. National Library.
150: National Library.
152: *Illustrated Sydney News*, 16 August 1865. National Library.
157: *Illustrated Sydney News*, 12 June 1871. National Library.
158: *Illustrated Sydney News*, 6 August 1881. National Library.
161: *Illustrated Sydney News*, 11 May 1872. National Library.
163: *Illustrated Sydney News*, 11 May 1872. National Library.
166: A. C. Butcher Collection. National Library.
168: *Sydney Mail*, 1 February 1890. National Library.
169: National Library.
170: Greenwood/Gillstrom Collection. National Library.
173: Faithfull/Maple-Brown Collection, Springfield.
175: Tilba Tilba Collection. National Library.

231

176: National Library.
181: National Library.
185: *Illustrated Australian News*, 24 December 1879.
    Mitchell Library.
188: *Illustrated Australian News*, 7 October 1874.
    National Library.
190: *Australasian Sketcher*, 31 October 1874. National
    Library.
192: National Library.
193: Faithfull/Maple-Brown Collection, Springfield.
194: National Library.
196: National Library.
201: *Illustrated Melbourne Post*, 24 December 1863.
    National Library.
203: *Australasian Ironmonger*, 1 October 1888. National
    Library.
205: Tilba Tilba Collection. National Library.
207: *Australasian Ironmonger*, 1 July 1887. National
    Library.
208: National Library.
210: *Australasian Ironmonger*, 1 February 1888. National
    Library.
212: *Australasian Ironmonger*, 1 April 1888. National
    Library.
215: *Victoria & its Metropolis: Past & Present*, Alexander
    Sutherland, Melbourne 1888. National Library.
217: *Australasian Sketcher*, 1881–82. National Library.
218: National Library.
219: National Library.
222: Faithfull/Maple-Brown Collection, Springfield.
223: National Library.
225: *Illustrated Sydney News*. National Library.
226: *Australasian Sketcher*, 23 September 1882. National
    Library.

Bibliography

Adam-Smith, Patsy *The Shearers* Melbourne: Nelson, 1982

Archer, T. *History, Resources, and Future Prospects of Queensland* London: S. W. Silver & Co., 1881

Atkinson, J. *An Account of the State of Agriculture and Grazing in New South Wales* London: J. Cross, 1826

Barnard, A. (ed.) *The Simple Fleece* Melbourne: Melbourne University Press, 1962

Barrie, Douglas M. *Valley of Champions* Melbourne: Cheshire, 1967

Bartley, Nehemiah *Australian Pioneers and Reminiscences 1849–1894* Brisbane: Gordon & Gotch, 1896

Bean, C. E. W. *On The Wool Track* Sydney: Angus & Robertson, 1910

Beckett, Richard *Convicted Tastes* Sydney: Allen & Unwin, 1984

Besnard, T. P. *A Voice From the Bush in Australia* Dublin: William Curry, Jun. and Company, 1839

Black, Niel. Unpublished papers and letters in the State Library of Victoria

Blackwell, Doris and Lockwood, Douglas *Alice on the Line* Adelaide: Rigby, 1965

Bolton, G. C. and Pederson, H. 'The Emanuels of Noonkanbah and Gogo' *Journal of the Royal Western Australian Historical Society* Vol. 8, Pt 4, 1980

Bonnin, Nancy (ed.) *Katie Hume on the Darling Downs* Toowoomba: Darling Downs Institute Press, 1985

Bourke and District Historical Society *The History of Bourke* Bourke, 1968

Boyd, A. J. *Old Colonials* London: Gordon & Gotch, 1882

Bride, Thomas F. *Letters from Victorian Pioneers* First published 1898 and reprinted Melbourne: Lloyd O'Neil, 1983

Brodribb, W. A. *Recollections of an Australian Squatter* Sydney: John Woods & Co., 1883

Brown, Ruby, and McCarthy, Marion *The Explorer's Country Kitchen* Yass: the authors, 1986

Bull, J. W. *Early Experiences of Colonial Life in South Australia* Adelaide: Advertiser, Chronicle and Express, 1878

Campbell, John F. 'The First Decade of the Australian Agricultural

Company, 1824 to 1834' *Royal Australian Historical Society Journal* Vol. 9, Pt 3, 1923

Cannon, Arthur *The Bullock Driver's Handbook* Shepparton: Night Owl Publishers, 1985

Cannon, Michael *Who's Master? Who's Man?* Melbourne: Nelson, 1971

——*Life in the Country* Melbourne: Nelson, 1973

——*Life in the Cities* Melbourne: Nelson, 1975

Carrington, G. *Colonial Adventures and Experiences* London: Bell and Daldy, 1871

Casey, Lord *Australian Father and Son* London: Collins, 1966

Clarke, Patricia *The Governesses* Melbourne: Hutchinson, 1985

——*A Colonial Woman, the Life and Times of Mary Braidwood Mowle 1827–1857* Sydney: Allen & Unwin, 1986

Cornish, Henry *Under the Southern Cross* Madras: Higginbotham, 1880

Crowley, Frank *A Documentary History of Australia* Melbourne: Nelson, 1980

Curr, Edward M. *Recollections of Squatting in Victoria* Melbourne: George Robertson, 1883

——*The Australian Race* Melbourne: Government Printer, 1886

Demarr James *Adventures in Australia Fifty Years Ago* London: Swan Sonnenschein & Co., 1893

Denholm, David *The Colonial Australians* Melbourne: Penguin, 1979

Derrincourt, William *Old Convict Days* London: Fisher Unwin, 1899

De Satge, O. *Pages From the Journal of a Queensland Squatter* London: Hurst and Blackett, 1901

Dunderdale, George *The Book of the Bush* London: Ward Lock, c. 1870

Durack, Mary *Kings in Grass Castles* London: Constable, 1959

Dutton, Geoffrey *The Squatters* Melbourne: Currey O'Neil, 1985

Faithfull family papers, unpublished, in the National Library, Canberra

Falkiner, Suzanne *Haddon Rig—The First Hundred Years* Sydney: Valadon, 1981

Farwell, George *Squatter's Castle* Melbourne: Lansdowne, 1973

Gerstaecker, F. *Narrative of a Journey Round the World* London: Hurst and Blackett, 1853

Gillison, Joan *Colonial Doctor and his Town* Melbourne: Cypress Books, 1974

Gollan, Anne *The Tradition of Australian Cooking* Canberra: Australian National University Press, 1978

Gould, Nat *Town and Bush* London: Routledge, 1896

Gunn, Mrs Aeneas *We of the Never-Never* London: Hutchinson, 1908

Hamilton, George *Experiences of a Colonist Forty Years Ago* Adelaide: Williams, 1880

Hardy, Bobbie *West of the Darling* Brisbane: Jacaranda, 1969

Harris, Alexander *Settlers and Convicts* London: C. Cox, 1847

Henning, Rachel *Letters* Sydney: Angus & Robertson, 1963

Hewat, Tim *Golden Fleeces* Sydney: Bay Books, 1980

Hill, Ernestine *The Territory* Sydney: Angus & Robertson, 1951

Hodgson, C. P. *Reminiscences of Australia* London: Simpkin and Marshall, 1846

Hooper, Meredith *Everyday Inventions* Sydney: Angus & Robertson, 1972

Horne, Donald *The Story of the Australian People* Sydney: Reader's Digest, 1985

Idriess, I. L. *The Cattle King* Sydney: Angus & Robertson, 1936

Joyce, Alfred *A Homestead History* Melbourne: Oxford University Press, 1942

Kelly, William *Life in Victoria* London: Chapman and Hall, 1859

Kerr, J. H. *Glimpses of Life in Victoria* Edinburgh: Edmonston & Douglas, 1872

Lang, J. D. *An Historical and Statistical Account of New South Wales* London: Cochrane and M'Crone, 1834

Lilley, G. W. *Story of Lansdowne* Melbourne: Lansdowne Pastoral Co, 1973

McKey, Rev. J. *The Warwick Story* Warwick: The Warwick Newspaper, 1972

Macqueen, T. P. *Australia As She Is and As She May Be* London: Simpkin Marshall, 1840

Makin, Jock *The Big Run* Adelaide: Rigby, 1970

Meredith, Mrs. Charles *Notes and Sketches of New South Wales* London: John Murray, 1844

Mossman, Samuel, and Banister, Thomas *Australia, Visited and Revisited* London: Addey & Co, 1853

Murray, R. D. *A Summer at Port Phillip* Edinburgh: William Tait, 1843

Ollif, Lorna, and Crosthwaite, Walter *Early Australian Crafts and Tools* Adelaide: Rigby, 1977

Parker, Kate Langloh (Muir, Marcie, ed.) *My Bush Book* Adelaide: Rigby, 1982

Pownall, E. *Mary of Maranoa* Melbourne: Melbourne University Press, 1959

Reynolds, Henry *Frontier* Sydney: Allen & Unwin, 1987

Roberts, Stephen H. *The Squatting Age in Australia 1835–1847* Melbourne: Melbourne University Press, 1935

Sawry, Hugh et al. *The Stockman* Sydney: Lansdowne, 1984

Serle, G. *The Rush to be Rich* Melbourne: Melbourne University Press, 1971

Sherer, John *The Gold-finder of Australia* London: Clarke, Beeton, 1853

Sidney, S. *The Three Colonies of Australia* London: Ingram, Cooke, & Co., 1852

Sorenson, Edward S. *Life in the Australian Backblocks* Melbourne: Whitcombe and Tombs, 1911

Spence, W. G. *Australia's Awakening* Sydney: The Worker Trustees, 1909

Stone, Derrick I. and Garden, Donald S. *Squatters and Settlers* Sydney: Reed, 1978

Taylor, Peter *A Taste of Australia in Food and in Pictures* Sydney: Pan, 1980

——*Pastoral Properties of Australia* Sydney: Allen & Unwin, 1984

——*Thoroughbred Studs of Australia and New Zealand* Sydney: Allen & Unwin, 1986

——*Springfield: The Story of a Sheep Station* Sydney: Allen & Unwin, 1987

Taylor, Vera C. *Winton Merino Stud 1835–1985* Melbourne: Neptune Press, 1985

Thomas, Athol *Bulls and Boabs* Adelaide: Rigby, 1977

Tolcher, H. M. *Drought or Deluge* Melbourne: Melbourne University Press, 1986

Tritton, H. P. *Time Means Tucker* Sydney: The Bulletin, 1959

Trollope, Anthony *Australia and New Zealand* London: Chapman and Hall, 1873

Unstead, R. J. and Henderson, W. F. *Pioneer Home Life in Australia* London: A. & C. Black, 1971

Wadham, Samuel *Australian Farming 1788–1965* Melbourne: Cheshire, 1967

Ward, Russel *The Australian Legend* Melbourne: Oxford University Press, 1978

——*Australia Since the Coming of Man* Sydney: Lansdowne, 1982

Weelhouse, F. *Digging Stick to Rotary Hoe* Melbourne: Cassell, 1966

Willey, Keith *The Drovers* Melbourne: Macmillan, 1982

Winter-Irving, W. A. *Beyond the Bitumen* Adelaide: Rigby, 1971

Index

237